Exposition of

ISAIAH
Volume II
Chapters 40—66

Exposition of

ISAIAH
Volume II
Chapters 40 – 66

13317

By H. C. LEUPOLD

BAKER BOOK HOUSE
Grand Rapids, Michigan

Library of Congress Catalog Card Number: 68-29787
Standard Book Number: 8010-5506-7

PRINTED IN THE UNITED STATES OF AMERICA

INTRODUCTION

Introduction

No one questions that the second half of this book commonly designated "Isaiah" begins at this point. Questions of authorship and composition have been sufficiently discussed in the Introduction in the first volume, so that we may address ourselves to the exposition of the chapters as such. We merely recall in passing that we still consider the possibility of unit-authorship of the entire book by the prophet Isaiah himself to be a reasonable and therefore tenable position.

Many are the outlines that have been proposed for these chapters. Almost each one of those proposed has its merits. We have found those of the character of *von Orelli's* as helpful as any. This writer suggests that Chaps. 40-48 deal with the Lord's measures for the Deliverance of his people; Chaps. 49-57 center attention of the Lord's Agent for the achieving of this work; and Chaps. 58-66 treat of the Consummation of the Lord's salvation.

We are not claiming that a close-knit sequence of thought is to be traced through each chapter. The logical sequence is not always expressed, but there is so obvious a measure of coherence that, though the case may be worded differently at times, the basic progression of thought is not hard to discover.

The material of the second part of Isaiah obviously implies that the Exile of the children of Judah has taken place: it has run on for decades. In fact its termination is about to take place. This fact is most clearly to be observed in Chap. 1.

Just about every author presents his own outline for the contents of these chapters. We offer ours as just one more attempt to confine the rich material of the chapters within the confines of a more or less logical outline.

7

DETAILED OUTLINE

I. THE SECOND PART OF ISAIAH (chaps. 40-55)

A. Judah's Impending Deliverance from Captivity and the Great God Who Brings It About (chap. 40)

   1. Judah's Impending Deliverance from Captivity (vv. 1-11)

     a. The Theme: Comfort for God's Afflicted People — the Restoration from Babylonian Captivity (vv. 1-2)

     b. A Call to Make Ready the Way for the Lord (vv. 3-5)

     c. The Frailty of Man and the Enduring Character of God's Word (vv. 6-8)

     d. Zion's Proclamation: God Has Come to Her (vv. 9-11)

   2. The Great God Who Brings This About (the incomparable greatness of the Lord) (vv. 12-31)

     a. Over Against the World He Has Created (vv. 12-14)

     b. Over Against the Nations of the Earth (vv. 15-17)

     c. In Contrast to the Vain Idols (vv. 18-20)

     d. In Contrast to the Mighty of the Earth (vv. 21-24)

     e. God's Masterful Control of the Stars (vv. 25-27)

     f. The Lord, the Source of All Power (vv. 28-31)

B. A Court-trial of the Nations and Their Gods (chap. 41)

   1. A Summons to the Coastlands to Test the Power of Their Gods: Can Their Gods Bring up a Cyrus on the Scene as Yahweh Did? (vv. 1-4)

   2. The Consternation of the Coastlands at the Rise of Cyrus, Manifested by the Manufacture of New Idols (vv. 5-7)

   3. God's Reassurance to Israel That She Has Not Been Cast Off (vv. 8-10)

4. His Further Assurance That Israel's Opponents Will Not Prevail against Her (vv. 11-13)
5. Rather, Israel Will Prevail against Her Foes (vv. 14-16)
6. Israel, Suffering in Captivity, Will Dwell in a Paradise Rather Than in a Wilderness (vv. 17-20)
7. The Gods of the Nations Are Challenged to Give Proof of Their Divine Powers by Divulging the Future (vv. 21-24)
8. On This Score the Gods of the Nations Fail Utterly (vv. 25-29)

C. The Work of the Servant of the Lord (chap. 42)

1. The Servant of the Lord, Meek and Unassuming, Yet Successful (vv. 1-4)
2. The Lord's Relation to His Servant Defined (vv. 5-9)
3. A Summons to Praise the Lord for the Work of His Servant (vv. 10-12)
4. How the Lord Himself Will Participate of the Achievement of His Servant's Tasks (vv. 13-17)
5. The Blind and Deaf Servant, Who Failed God and Suffered the Consequences (vv. 18-22)
6. An Indictment of the Deaf Servant for His Failure (vv. 23-25)

D. Restoration by Divine Grace (chap. 43)

1. Restoration of Israel Impending (vv. 1-7)
2. A Court Trial of the Idols (vv. 8-13)
3. The Captivity of the Chaldeans (vv. 14-15)
4. The Remarkable Exodus (vv. 16-21)
5. Israel's Guilt — Yahweh's Grace (vv. 22-28)

E. The God of Grace vs. the Impotent Idols (chap. 44:1-23)

1. The Blessing of the Spirit to Be Poured Out on the Unworthy (v. 1-5)

H. The Overthrow of Babylon Triumphantly Predicted (chap. 47)

1. It Is Impending and Inevitable (vv. 1-5)
2. It Is Largely Due to Her Misunderstanding Israel's Overthrow (vv. 6-7)
3. But It Is Also Due to Her Own Unseemly Pride (vv. 8-11)
4. Sorcery Is of No Avail in This Calamity (vv. 12-15)

I. A Sharp Rebuke and a Gracious Challenge (chap. 48)

1. A Solemn Introduction of a Sharp Rebuke (vv. 1-2)
2. The Beginning of the Pronouncement (vv. 3-5)
3. The Same Control of History Displayed by God's Foretelling of a New Set of Events (vv. 6-8)
4. Sparing of Sinners Due to God's Grace (vv. 9-11)
5. All Things Take Their Beginning from the Lord (vv. 12-13)
6. The Sending of Cyrus, Further Proof of God's Control (vv. 14-16)
7. If Israel Had Hearkened in the Past . . . (vv. 17-19)
8. Israel Invited to Go Forth from Babylon (vv. 20-22)

J. The Servant's Assignment Redefined and Israel Reassured of Recovery (chap. 49)

1. The Servant Disappointed but Recommissioned (vv. 1-6)
2. The Servant's Reassignment in Terms of a Glorious Restoration of Israel (vv. 7-13)
3. Misgivings of Zion Alleviated (vv. 14-26)
   a. The Lord Has Abandoned Us (vv. 14-18)
   b. The Land Is Waste and Its Inhabitants Few (vv. 19-23)
   c. Captives Cannot Be Liberated (vv. 24-26)

K. Israel Self-rejected, the Servant Steadfast (chap. 50)

1. Another Misgiving Alleviated: Is the Covenant Ab-

2. This Promise Reinforced (vv. 4-10)
3. The Future Glory of Zion (vv. 11-17)
   a. Costly Building Materials (vv. 11-12)
   b. Fear Vanquished (vv. 13-14)
   c. The Futility of Enemy Attacks (vv. 15-17)

O. Zion Called to Appropriation of Salvation (chap. 55)

1. An Invitation to Accept God's Free Blessings (vv. 1-3)
2. If She Accepts, Zion Will Become a Blessing to the Nations (vv. 4-5)
3. But These Blessings Must Be Eagerly Sought with a Penitent Heart (vv. 6-7)
4. God Is Magnificent in Forgiveness (vv. 8-9)
5. This Forgiveness Comes by Way of the Word of God (vv. 10-11)
6. The Great Joy Resulting from the Deliverance from Captivity (vv. 12-13)

II. THE THIRD PART OF ISAIAH (chaps. 56–66)

A. A Supplement to Chapter 55 (chap. 56)

1. The Importance of the Observance of the Law (vv. 1-2)
2. Admission of Strangers and Eunuchs to the Congregation of Israel (vv. 3-8)
3. Israel's Degenerate Leaders (vv. 9-12)

B. The Triumph of Divine Grace over Israel's Infidelity (chap. 57)

1. The Perishing of the Righteous — an Unheeded Warning (vv. 1-2)
2. Rebuke of Sorcery and Idolatry (vv. 3-10)
3. A Threat of Judgment (vv. 11-13)
4. A Promise of Salvation (vv. 14-21)

C. Abuses That Retarded the Recovery of Post-exilic Israel (chap. 58)

    1. The Wrong Kind of Fast (vv. 1-5)
    2. The Right Kind of Fast (vv. 6-7)
    3. Blessings That Will Result from a Proper Fast (vv. 8-9a)
    4. The Abuses That Are to Be Put Aside (vv. 9b-10a)
    5. A Further Group of Resultant Blessings (vv. 10b-12)
    6. A Kindred Reform in the Matter of the Sabbath (vv. 13-14)

D. The Hand of the Lord Is Not Too Short to Save (chap. 59)

    1. The Nation's Ungrounded Complaint (vv. 1-2)
    2. The Unrighteousness Prevailing in Israel (vv. 3-8)
    3. The Resultant Moral Confusion (vv. 9-11)
    4. A Frank Confession (vv. 12-15a)
    5. The Lord's Intervention (vv. 15b-21)

E. Zion's Future Glory (chap. 60)

    1. A Summons to Zion to Greet the LLight That Is Dawning up Her (vv. 1-2)
    2. What Men Are Bringing to Zion from the West and from the East (vv. 3-9)
    3. The Attitude of Those Who Are Coming to Zion (vv. 10-12)
    4. The Attitude toward Worship Displayed by Those Who Are Coming to Zion (vv. 13-17)
    5. The Higher Level of Life in Evidence in the New Jerusalem (vv. 18-22)

F. Good News for Zion (chap. 61)

    1. The Messenger Who Brings the Good News (vv. 1-3)
    2. A Nation Fulfilling Its Destiny by Accepting This Good News (vv. 4-7)

THE SECOND PART
OF ISAIAH

Chapter XL

A. JUDAH'S IMPENDING DELIVERANCE FROM CAPTIVITY AND THE GREAT GOD WHO BRINGS IT ABOUT (Chap. 40)

Many very suggestive titles for this chapter have been offered. Delitzsch gives the caption: "The Word of Comfort and the God of Comfort." von Orelli sets forth in the form of a statement: "Let Zion take comfort for her Mighty Lord draws near." We have chosen to capture what we deem the essence of the chapter in the heading: Judah's Impending Deliverance from Captivity and the Great God Who Brings It About.

As to form, this section is commonly rated as a modified "herald's-message" (*Botenspruch*). Before this type of terminology was in vogue, *G. A. Smith* had already labelled the piece as "The Four Herald Voices." There is a certain vagueness and indefiniteness about these beautiful words as far as the possible speaker of them and as far as the recipient of them is concerned. Four significant voices of messages sound sweetly and meaningfully on the ear. Present-day exegesis has tried to relieve this vagueness first by discovering a location from which the speaker proclaims his message. It is now quite commonly accepted that the setting for these words must be that heavenly council from which messages or courses of action are known to have emanated in times past, namely, the heavenly council of none less than Yahweh himself. Instances where this council may be referred to are Isa. 6:1 f.; Jer. 23:22; and I Kings 22:19. Some would add passages like Gen. 1:26 ff. We regard these passages for the most part as figures of speech by which, in a colorful way, the thought is brought home that certain decisions are the result of the careful planning of the Almighty. But already in Gen 1:26 ff. it may very reasonably be doubted

19

whether the Scriptural statement aims to convey the impression that any one may serve as counsellor for the Great Lord in any of the works that he does. In Chap. 40 of Isaiah in particular, vv. 13 and 14 clash very directly with the very possibility of the Lord's ever seeking any counsel for the great tasks that he undertakes. It must be admitted that the material for construing a complete heavenly council as a session is hardly available in this chapter.

Another attempt to make what is intentionally left indefinite more precise and concrete: it is in our day commonly being suggested that the opening verses of Chap. 40 are a record of the call and commissioning of II Isaiah. This approach seems to grow out of the uneasiness felt over the fact that the so-called Deutero-Isaiah is an entirely anonymous figure and this anonymity is disturbing. But no one person stands out as recipient of the message to be spoken and so the whole of this approach rests on very fragile foundations.

A far more suggestive and unimpeachable approach in our day merits very serious consideration, and that is the observation that the whole chapter directs its glance to the Lord himself as the only one who can restore Israel and give her help. The material of this chapter is God-centered, not man-centered or problem-centered, as v. 9 puts it: "Behold your God."

It should also be noted that the tone of this chapter is rather at variance with the note so commonly sounded by the prophets of old. Very often these prophets were heralds of doom. If they did offer a brighter outlook for the future that outlook was directed to the good things that lay far in the future, in the final consummation of all things, in the perfection that God would bring as the climax of the Messianic Age. But this prophet offers the sweetest words of comfort for the time immediately impending.

1. Judah's Impending Deliverance from Captivity (vv. 1-11)

a. The Theme: Comfort for God's Afflicted Peo-

ple — the Restoration from Babylonian Captivity (vv. 1-2)

40:1-2 1. Comfort, O comfort my people, says your God.
2. Speak kindly to Jerusalem and proclaim to her
that her term of service is finished,
that her guilt is pardoned,
that she has received from the Lord's hand ample punishment for
all her sins.

Verse 1. This verse presents the theme of the book from Chaps. 40-66; at the same time it presents the theme of this particular chapter. Its abruptness is startling, and in a sense annoying by its vagueness. Who is to be thus addressed appears clearly from v. 2. But there is no explicit indication as to who is to administer this comfort. Apparently this vagueness is intentional. Prophets were not usually commissioned in such vague terms. If priests were to be the speakers, nothing in the text points in this direction. Being so general a statement it is best left in as general a form as possible. Anyone who catches the message that God would have comfort spoken to his people should spread the good news. The time has come to pass on the good word that comfort is at hand. That something very specific is after all involved develops as the reader moves on from step to step. It becomes increasingly apparent that the comfort to be offered is the good news that restoration from Babylonian Captivity is about to take place. This is exactly what the next verse conveys. For the present let only this be added: The verb-form at this point indicates that the Lord would have this comfort reiterated over and over again till finally the unbelieving and doubting heart begins to accept it as fully determined in the counsels of God. The repetition of the verb here, as often, spells urgency. The help stands ready at the door.

Verse 2. The comfort involved is so rich that it takes a number of statements to unfold the fullness of what is implied. It may be paraphrased: "Speak kindly to Jerusalem." The expression involved is almost untranslatable. It means to lay something tenderly close to the heart of another (cf.

Hos. 2:14). From this point on, more and more, terms like "Zion" and "Jerusalem" stand as synonymns for the holy people of God, the true believers in Israel. Like a gentle balm this message cools and soothes the troubled heart.

Or the message to be spoken may be paraphrased: "Proclaim to her that her service is finished." Literally the statement really runs as *KJ* has it, "that her warfare is accomplished." That means, however, that the harsh rigors of service on the field of battle are at an end. Nothing other than the hardships of the Captivity is meant by these words. The term of conscription is over; let her relax.

Or the message may be paraphrased: "her guilt is pardoned." Not every affliction is immediately to be traced back to sin as its source but, more commonly by far than not, this is the case. When Captivity struck Jerusalem it was for the obvious sins of the nation as the prophets had abundantly told. In sin lies the deepest and most virulent root of the evils that befall men. An obvious prerequisite is implied in all this. God does not pardon the impenitent. Therefore a preceding repentance must have been shaping up. In fact this matter of forgiveness is of such moment that another statement deals with it at greater length from another point of view: "she has received from the Lord's hands ample punishment for all her sins." "Punishment" from God is in the forefront of this statement. It had to be bestowed in full measure for the sin had gone deep and had been of long standing. But in so far as a correspondence exists between guilt and punishment, in this instance at least all the needs of the case had been fully met; "ample" punishment has been visited upon the heads of the guilty. Who other than the Almighty can determine whether all the needs of a given case have been adequately met? As one commentator puts it: her guilt has been "sufficiently expiated." — "Ample" is better than "double" (*KJ* and *RSV*).

b. A Call to Make Ready the Way for the Lord (vv. 3-5)

40:3-5 3. A voice is heard making a proclamation:
"Make ready a way for the Lord in the wilderness;
make a straight highway in the desert for our God;
4. Every valley should be filled in,
and every mountain and hill should be levelled off;
and the steep ground should be made level country,
and rugged heights a plain.
5. Then shall the glory of the Lord be revealed,
and all flesh shall see it together.
For the mouth of the Lord has so said."

Verse 3. Who is making the proclamation here referred
to? Answer: It does not matter, and therefore the speaker
is not identified. To say, it is to be done by hermits, introduces an utterly extraneous thought, which is not suggested
by anything in the text. To claim it is angels, is an equally
unsupported guess. The message as such claims attention,
not the one who speaks it. Preparations are to be made; a
way is to be gotten ready. Everything depends on the basic
approach here used. Who is to use the way that is to be prepared? Answer: the Lord himself. In that sense it is "the
way of the Lord." At this point nothing is more helpful than
to recall some thoughts that Ezekiel presented rather strongly
in his day. Comparing the following passages from this
prophet — 10:18, 19; 11:23; and 43:1-3 — it becomes apparent that where once the Holy City and the Temple had
been the dwelling place of the Lord, finally there came a
time, before the Captivity of the city, when the Lord with-
drew from the holy place; he abandoned the city that he had
so highly honored. Ezekiel sees the glory of the Lord depart
and vanish out into the desert lands of the east. That state of
affairs prevailed during the entire period of the Captivity
(587-538 B.C.). Now says the prophet, a new day is dawn-
ing; God will again take up his habitation among his people.
If that be so, his people should give tokens of their appreciation and put things in readiness. In typical Oriental
fashion they are even to smooth the way for their king. Since
he went into the wilderness, from the wilderness he will
again come. Therefore even a highway should be made

ready for him. We must therefore abandon suggestions such as: This highway is for the children of Israel to travel on as they emerge from Captivity. But we must hold fast, as has now been abundantly shown by many writers, that the terminology of the Exodus pervades these chapters, especially the thought that the Lord is on the march through the wilderness, guiding the destinies of his people.

Verse 4. Of course, the language is a bit exuberant. With road-building in the state that it was among Oriental nations of those days, even the picture involved does not really think in terms of having all these preparations done according to letter of this pronouncement. But surely this much is meant: Make preparations for this monarch that are in keeping with the honor that he confers upon you by coming as he does: fill in valleys; level off mountains; make steep ground level; make rugged spots smooth. This is what you "should" do. In this sense the "shall" of our versions is meant (e.g., "shall be lifted up," etc.). This is an obligation that grows out of the dignity that God would bestow upon his people by coming to dwell among them again. In a general way all this is to be interpreted spiritually. The nation is to remove every spiritual barrier that might hinder the coming of their God. But that does not mean that each term ("valley," "mountain" etc.) is to be explicitly related to some form of spiritual block that lies in the way. The picture as a whole describes a situation as a whole.

Verse 5. If Israel properly prepares to receive its Lord, he will come. But this coming is here again spoken of in the terminology of the Exodus days. Then, when God appeared among his people it was often said: "And the glory of the Lord was revealed," as Exod. 16:7, 10; 24:15, etc. indicates. So here: "Then shall the glory of the Lord be displayed," means: The Lord will appear to you as in days of old. This need not mean an appearing which is physically visible. God's glory may be seen by the eyes of faith as well as by the physical eye. But the fact that the Lord has again taken an active part in the affairs of his people will be obvious to all who give any thought to what is happening to Israel. In other words, "all flesh together shall see it." Even the eyes of the unenlightened could not help but see that what happened to Israel in her Return from Captivity had to be a divine accomplishment. The heathen were made to marvel over the unique power of the Lord of Israel. With solemn assurance this fact is underscored by the concluding remark, "for the mouth of the Lord has so said." God is predicting Israel's deliverance. This deliverance must surely come to pass.

c. The Frailty of Man and the Enduring Character of God's Word (vv. 6-8)

40:6-8 6. A voice is heard saying: "Call out!"
Then some one said: "What shall I call out?"
"All flesh is grass,
and all its beauty like the flower of the field.
7. The grass withers, the flower fades,
when the breath of the Lord blows upon it.
Surely the people is grass.
8. The grass withers, the flower fades;
but the Word of our God shall stand forever."

Verse 6. Another voice! No connection between this one and the one preceding is indicated. But a deep underlying logic is nevertheless easily discernible. With the emphasis on how frail man really is and how enduring the Word of God, by contrast, must we not conclude that some connection like the following is being indicated? God's great work of Restoration of Israel has just been revealed. It is now being indicated that much as Israel might want to rebuild herself in her own strength — and who would not want a share in the achievement of great things? — human strength is too utterly inadequate a thing to achieve results like these. Only the powerful, creative Word of the Lord can suffice for such an achievement. This double truth is what this verse wants to have "called out." This verb is one that is frequently used for strong, emphatic prophetic proclamation. The brief dialogue indicates also how man may be at a loss as to what proclamation to stress particularly in these stirring times. "All flesh" after the analogy of Gen. 6:13, must refer to all forms of existence, to all creatures that live. But they are insufficient for an emergency like the present, for the word "flesh" already by itself connotes weakness in the Old Testament. This thought is further underscored by the assertion that "all flesh is grass." Grass came out beautifully in spring in the Holy Land and after a few weeks withered and shrivelled. So is man with his human strength. It demands greater resources than these to build in a lasting way in the kingdom of God. Passages like 37:27; Ps. 90:5; 103:15; and I Peter 1:24 f. convey the same thought of the inadequacy of man.

Verse 7. It takes nothing more than "the breath of the Lord" — we might say "any passing wind" — to bring about the quick withering of the grass and the fading of the flower. Now we have the measure of "the people," i.e., of mankind as a whole (cf. "people" used in the same sense in 42:5).

Verse 8. In solemn reiteration this thought is repeated. It falls on the ear with a certain mournful cadence. But the writer does not end on this note of weakness. He knows a power by the use of which eternal results can be achieved. That power is the Word of the Lord. Heaven and earth may pass away; not that Word. Trusting in that Word and using that Word, God's people can confidently face the future, which will bring for Israel results that are otherwise humanly impossible. We may aptly compare 55:8-11 at this point.

Summing up the three emphases that have thus far been set forth by this chapter, we learn first that comfort, hope of the nation's restoration, lies ready for Israel. But secondly she must remove all obstacles that sin has put into God's way, that is to say: She must repent. Then, thirdly, she must build not in, or on, her own strength but on the clear prophetic Word of the Lord. All of these are abiding truths that, for that matter, apply to every age and generation in the life of the church of God.

d. Zion's Proclamation: God Has Come to Her (vv. 9-11)

40:9-11 9. Get up on a high mountain, O Zion, heraldess;
raise your voice mightily, O Jerusalem, heraldess;
raise it, be not afraid;
say to the cities of Judah: "See, there is your God!"
10. Lo, the Lord comes as a mighty one,
and his arm rules for him.
Lo, his reward is with him,
and his recompense before him.
11. Like a shepherd he tends his flock,
and gathers the lambs in his arms,
and carries them in his bosom,
and gently leads those that are with young.

Verse 9. This is a sort of climax of the initial voices that have been heard. Put more abstractly, here is the last major emphasis for the day of Restoration.

The true believers among the people of God ("Zion") are to make known what their faith has grasped, the fact namely that God is graciously returning to his people, in fact, has returned. They are to publish these glad tidings throughout the whole land, i.e., "to the cities of Judah." If perhaps in the preceding verses, the setting was still the land of Captivity, now the scene is the Holy Land itself. That is a more satisfactory way of putting it than to say that it has shifted from heaven to earth. The message to be published is so momentous that Zion is bidden to go up into a high mountain in order that her voice may carry far and wide (cf. Judg. 9:7). The same behest is given to Jerusalem, which here apparently is used as substitute for Judah, since the term Jerusalem is used more than thirty times in these chapters for Judah. In fact, all the members of the nation are mutually to reassure one another of the good news that is breaking. All timidity about the future is to be banished — "be not afraid." This again is one of the key-notes of the message for a dispirited people, for it keeps recurring (cf. 41:10, 13, 14; 43:5; 44:2; 51:7; 54:4). When the title "heraldess" is used with Zion and Jerusalem, it is a term that could well be translated "bearer of good tidings," and is used in the feminine, for women were commonly regarded as the ones that did most to spread abroad the message of victory (cf. I Sam. 18:7). Or it could be said that the feminine is induced by the fact that personifications of cities usually regard them as female figures. But the message, the message that is to be proclaimed is: "See, there is your God." The proclaimers are, as it were, to point directly to the one who has just appeared on the scene, and to exclaim: He is in your midst.

Verse 10. Two figures are used at this point to convey somewhat of an impression of what manner of God the Lord is under the circumstances here involved. First of all, he is a conquering hero, or a "mighty one." The same thought is expressed by the statement "his arm rules for him." That is to say: His strength prevails and gains the victory. But the statement now following adds a very significant thought. The "reward" or "recompense" that this conquering hero brings with him is nothing other than his people, whom he has regained as his own and delivered from the power of the enemy. Though it may seem that at this point we are after all conceding that the road to be prepared was for the use of the returning captives, that is not the case. The figure of the road to be prepared (vv. 3-4) has by this time been abandoned. The victor and those whom he has redeemed are on the scene.

Verse 11. As so often, the figure swiftly changes. Now it is the Shepherd who is approaching, a figure often used in the Old Testament to describe God's relation to his people (cf. Mic. 2:12; Jer. 31:10; Ezek. 34:11 ff.; Ps. 78:52; 80:1). His most tender care is reflected in the various activities that the Shepherd engages in for his flock: "he leads them" not drives them. He gathers the newly-born lambs in his arms and carries them in his bosom. And where mother-sheep are almost at the point of giving birth to their young, he takes especial care of them. These are the things that Zion is to publish throughout the cities of Judah. But she cannot publish them effectively unless she first appropriates them in faith. On this positive note the initial Four Voices of this book begin.

2. The Great God Who Brings These Things About (the Incomparable Greatness of the Lord) (vv. 12-31)

Israel's initial reaction to the great promises God had just given may well be: These things can never come to pass; no nation has ever returned from a captivity and survived; how could we? More significantly now than even before, the message directs attention to the Lord himself. If he be kept in mind and truly believed, this all can come to pass. It is with this in mind that the incomparable greatness of God is now very emphatically set forth by the prophet.

a. Over Against the World He Has Created (vv. 12-14)

40:12-14 12. Who has measured the waters in the hollow of his hand,
and determined the measure of heaven with a span,
and gathered the dust of the earth in a measure,
and weighed the mountains in scales and the hills in balances?
13. Who has determined the measure of the spirit of the Lord
or given him instruction as his counsellor?
14. With whom did he take counsel and let himself be instructed,
and who gave him instruction in the way of justice
and taught him knowledge and imparted to him deep insight?

Westermann very properly draws attention to a peculiarity of the style of the prophet, the fact namely that at times the prophet resorts to the use of a series of double questions (cf. 40:12, 18, 25, 27) or a series of double imperatives (51:9, 17; 52:1) to introduce new subjects and so ties them together into a unity. *Westermann* rightly regards this as indicative of the fact that the material in this part of the book was intentionally arranged as a major composition and does not consist of a series of detached fragments, which have been casually placed side by side.

Here the remark is in order that the meter is a bit difficult to determine for this section and for the rest of the chapter. The meter keeps changing. As to form, it may be admitted that we have here a sort of "hymnic monologue" (*Muilenburg*). That the language is highly impassioned must also be granted at the outset. Nature is explored repeatedly from different points of view, especially as being under the sovereign control of God. Where this occurs it must be observed that such an approach can be very effective. *Westermann* reminds us that vv. 12-31 constitute a *Disputationsrede*.

A number of questions are asked. Though there is some merit in the suggestion that they could be answered: "God only," the fact of the matter still is that the speaker is looking about on earth, so that the more appropriate answer would be: "No one among the children of men can do these things." But all the activities mentioned could be achieved with comparative ease by the Almighty.

Verse 12. Especially in this verse the idea of God's doing of mighty works with great ease is achieved by employing a number of vessels and containers for measuring, that are of comparatively trivial size: the hollow of the hand, the span, the measure (a few pecks), scales and balances. Yet the things referred to are vast: the waters, the heavens, the dust of the earth, the mountains and the hills.

Verse 13. Perhaps the "spirit of the Lord" is here being thought of as the powerful agent through which he does his creative work. So the question asked amounts to this: Is there anyone who can determine the extent of the creative power of God? Again the answer is: There is no one. Or for that matter, in the use of his divine power, who could have given him instruction or been his advisor? Answer: the same (cf. Rom. 11:34; I Cor. 2:16). God is quite self-sufficient and far above the capacities of mere mortal man.

Verse 14. The questions are still further piled up to show man's utter incapacity and God's illimitable ability. In a word, could God be conceived of as sitting down at any time with one of the children of men to solicit advice! The "way of justice" which he alone administers is the just apportionment of all things that fall under his administration. He always deals with men as they fully deserve. "Knowledge" and "insight" are lastly mentioned as qualities which he also possesses and so never stands in need of having anybody provide him with needed facts. He alone sees through things and is able to judge impartially on the basis of the full knowledge of all facts. So looking abroad at the world that came from the Creator's hands, there is no question about it that he is able to regulate the affairs in it, affairs like the destiny of Israel.

b. Over Against the Nations of the Earth (vv. 15-17)

40:15-17 15. Lo, nations are like a drop of water dripping from a bucket;
they are reckoned like fine dust on scales.
Lo, he lifts up the coastlands like a bit of dust.
16. Lebanon is not sufficient to provide the fuel,
nor the creatures found on it sufficient for a burnt-offering.
17. All the nations are as nothing before him;
they are reckoned as ciphers and a vacuum.

Verse 15. The area of investigation to determine the power of the Almighty shifts from nature to history, the history of the nations. This verse could be misunderstood. But it surely does not mean that God cares nothing for the nations. Rather, if their importance over against him is to be measured, they are of very trivial account. In the forefront of consideration, though not specifically mentioned, is Babylon, the power that could attempt to resist the Lord's efforts to free his people from Captivity. But the figures setting forth the comparative unimportance of the nations over against God are very striking. Nations factually amount to no more in his sight than does a mere drop running down the side of a bucket as a man draws water from a well. Or they could be likened to the light dust that has accumulated on the apothecary's scales, which dust he lightly blows away before he starts weighing. In fact he could, if he were so minded, even lift up "the coastlands" as a man picks up a bit of earth. The coastlands include all the far-distant areas around the Mediterranean Sea, however remote they may be. For there is no geographical limit to the Lord's power.

Verse 16. Thinking in vast terms geographically, the writer brings in an illustration of a different sort to make his point. Suppose one were to think in terms of cultus, especially in terms of a sacrifice actually worthy of a God as great as Yahweh is. Taking all the vast timber values of the famous Lebanon range for fuel, and laying upon it all the creatures that inhabit these forests, one still would not have constructed a sacrifice worthy of him. In an effort to speak in terms of vastness, momentarily the writer passes by the obvious fact that the wild beasts of the forest are not fit for sacrifice in the worship of Yahweh. In its character, this comparison is much in place and need not at all be regarded as intruding into what is purely an issue of history (contra *Volz*).

Verse 17. Coming back to the point already made — how the nations rank in the sight of the majestic Lord of all — the author offers a few more hyperboles. The nations are "as nothing," "as ciphers and a vacuum." Not the value of the human beings that make up the nations is under consideration; but the potential strength and importance of the nations when contrasted with the God of Israel.

c. In Contrast to the Vain Idols (vv. 18-20)

40:18-20 18. To whom then would you liken God,
or what likeness is there that you could array over against him?
19. An idol! The craftsman casts it;
the goldsmith overlays it with gold;
and a metal-worker decorates it with silver chains.
20. A man too poor for such a contribution chooses wood that will not rot;
he selects for himself a skilful craftsman
to prepare an idol that will not totter.

Looking about him for further comparisons of powers that are ranked as great, the author comes to a field where the whole world of that time thought that the greatest powers of all were to be found — the field of idols. As has been suggested, this section is not primarily a polemic against idols; it is a positive setting forth of the omnipotence of God by way of contrast. Similar passages are to be found: 41:6 f.; 44:9-17; 45:16; 46:5-7. We have here a practical exposition of the commandment: "Thou shalt not make unto thee any graven image" (Exod. 2:4). It is as though the author said: There simply is no being that can in any wise even remotely compete with God, or that could be "likened" to him. Since in those days idolatry among the nations was very real and a major factor in their life, Isaiah can very aptly bring the famous images of well-known heathen gods into the picture. Note, he does not admire the beauty, and the skill of the sculptor who produced the image, as art-lovers might be wont to do in viewing such idol-images of old as have been recovered through the years. Biting sarcasm falls from his lips, that is, implied, not expressed, sarcasm. In reality the author merely gives a precise account of the process of manufacture of an idol.

Verse 19. Take any idol — it is the work of the craftsman who cast it. Here is not a case of God making man, but one of man making a god. A product of solid gold would be both too heavy and too expensive. So the quality of the product lies practically entirely in the option of the manufacturer. He constructs a basic structure which then the goldsmith overlays with gold-plating. The silver chains mentioned are very likely only ornamentations. They could be thought of being used to hold the image in place lest it fall. The product in any case is a manufactured god. If it be protested that the heathen well knew the distinction between gods and idols that represented these gods, it has been noted time and again that in practice this distinction fell away and the common worshipper regarded the image as though it were the god.

Verse 20. But then there is the case of a devotee of a god, who desires to make an image of his god but lacks the means for a more expensive production, he chooses a suitable piece of a type of wood that will not rot. He must engage a craftsman to do the job, a "skillful craftsman," lest the image appear unworthy of him whom it represents. Besides, it took some skill to prepare an image that would not totter. The point that is being made has gotten enough attention for the moment; the writer will come back to it later.

In striking contrast to Isaiah's description of the process of the manufacture of idol images stands an Accadian directive which instructs a workman how to prepare certain smaller idol images for a great impending idol festival of the New Year. Materials and procedures are indicated. The workmen took their task very seriously. The document in no wise senses that there might be something trivial and ridiculous about the whole procedure (cf. ANET, pp. 331 f.).

d. In Contrast to the Mighty of This Earth (vv. 21-24)

40:21-24 21. Don't you know? Can't you hear?
Has it not been told you from days of old?
Haven't you understood since the world was founded?
22. It is he that sits enthroned above the circle of the earth
so that its inhabitants are like grasshoppers.
It is he that spreads out the heavens like a veil
and stretches them out like a tent to dwell in.
23. It is he who makes dignitaries of no account
and renders the judges of the earth as nothing.
24. Hardly are they planted; hardly are they sown;
hardly has their stock taken root in the earth;
then he blows upon them and they wither,
and the storm carries them away as stubble.

Though at first it would appear in this section that the Lord as the great Creator is under consideration, this his creative work is only brought into the picture for the purpose of providing the background against which the *mighty of this earth* function. These mighty ones are being evaluated over against the Almighty.

Verse 21. A certain tone of impatience, and even of exasperation, appears to be struck here at first. The prophet is speaking of certain elementary truths concerning which there should really be no need that he instruct the people of God. The facts at stake are too basic, and have really been set forth in one form or another "from days of old." "Since the world was founded" they were common knowledge among the people of God. He means, of course, the frailty of the ones who are esteemed great among men on a purely earthly level. In passing, a few typical works of the Lord are mentioned to remind men of his greatness. He, for example, being as high as he is, "sits enthroned above the circle of the earth" so highly exalted, as it were, that when he looks down upon the children of men they "are like grasshoppers." This "circle of the earth" means the dome of the heavens. Or to use another approach, as a man might with infinite ease spread out a light veil, so it in days of old cost the Lord no more effort when he for the first time created and "spread out the heavens." Or still a third approach, as a man pitches a tent, with ease and in quick order, this being a common occupation among men, with the same ease the Lord spread out the heavens like a tent to dwell in.

Verse 23. This Lord, now, is able to deal with "dignitaries" and has dealt with them in times past in such a way that he makes them of "no account." They just vanish off the scene when he decides that their work is done. Or, for that matter, "the judges of the earth" become as nothing when they have accomplished what he has assigned for them. How often have the mighty fallen in the course of history!

Verse 24. In another powerful figure their vanishing is described. They are likened to plants, which have just scarcely been planted, or sown, or have just begun to take root, when, because he is done with them, the Almighty One blows upon them and before the hot blast of his mouth they first wither and then are carried away by the storm; and, to use another Biblical phrase, "the place thereof shall know them no more." How great must he be who disposes of earth's mightiest men with such consummate ease!

One further bit of groundwork has to be built in before the prophet can bring things to the desired conclusion.

e. God's Masterful Control of the Stars (vv. 25-27)

40:25-27 25. To whom then would you liken me
that I should really resemble him, says the Holy One?
26. Lift up your eyes on high and see:
Who created these?
He who brings forth the host of heaven by number,
and calls them all by name.
As a result of the greatness of his might
and the abundance of his strength
not a one of them is ever missing.
27. Why do you say, O Jacob, and speak, O Israel:
"My lot is hidden from the Lord
and my rights are disregarded by my God"?

Verse 25. The incomparable greatness of the Lord is still under consideration and now in the light of a realm which he alone controls. But this is introduced by a reminder that nothing has in the present investigation been found to be in any sense worthy of comparison with him or is in any sense actually like him.

Verse 26. One of the realms that is under his control is "the host of heaven." What makes this comparison all the more meaningful is the fact that especially in the land of the Babylonians, where the children of Israel had been in bondage, the heavenly bodies were regarded astrologically, as controlling the affairs of men, that transpired down here on earth. Their control of these affairs was absolute, far beyond that of the gods themselves. Not so in the religion of Israel. There they appeared first of all merely as part of the creation of God. "Who created these?" allows for only one answer: the God whom Israel worshipped. And as they once originated with him, so they forever remain under *his* control, his "who brings forth their host by number." The spectacle of the starry skies, night for night, is, figuratively speaking, nothing other than a case where the Almighty Maker of the universe brings them out as a shepherd brings forth his flock. Besides, the count is made, as it were, night for night, and the sum-total remains the same invariably. The figure may be regarded as blending into another one at this point: the Lord of this heavenly host is a shepherd, who calls forth these sheep of his, night for night, as the shepherd calls forth his sheep one by one out of the fold. As it were, in his astronomy he has them all named from the time when they were created and he may be thought of as remembering their name. It is not due to the laws of nature and their normal operation that the stars all appear nightly. It is rather the "result of the greatness of his might and the abundance of his strength" that "not a one of them is ever missing." The utmost simplicity of argument is blended with the greatest of insight in this illustration.

Verse 27. Now comes the point toward which this whole discussion has been moving since v. 12. With such a God as its Lord, how could Israel ever have ventured to *have misgivings* about God, whether he be able to control the destinies of his people. For that was practically what they did when they made complaints such as, "My lot is hidden from the Lord." When they said that they meant: God is not even aware of what is befalling me from day to day. The same was true when they uttered the complaint: "My rights are disregarded by my God." By that they meant: I have certain rights as nation, particularly in view of his election of Israel as his people; but my God disregards them. But with a certain impatience again the prophet challenges these statements, when he exclaims: "Why do you say, O Jacob and speak [thus], O Israel?" Littleness of faith, failure to think things through is the reason for your attitude, charges the prophet.

Much of what is written in the second part of Isaiah is deeply colored by the terminology of the Psalms, as *Westermann* abundantly indicates. "Hidden" (v. 27) is an indication of this fact (see Ps. 13:1; 22:24; 27:9; 30:7; 44:24; 69:17; 88:14; 102:2; 104:29; 143:7). "Rights" — i.e., "vindication" or "justice" — is another such a word (cf. Ps. 26:1; 35:23; 37:6; 140:12; 146:7). In its distress during the Captivity days Israel was finding expression for its distress of soul in the vocabulary of the well-known Psalms.

f. The Lord, the Source of All Power (vv. 28-31)

40:28-31 28. Have you not known, have you not heard?
The eternal God, the Lord, the Creator even of the ends of the earth, does not faint or grow weary;
his insight is unfathomable.
29. He gives power to the faint;
for them that lack might he increases strength.
30. Even youths may faint and grow weary;
young men may utterly totter.
31. But they that wait for the Lord shall renew their strength;
they shall mount up with wings like eagles;
they shall run and not be weary;
they shall walk and not grow faint.

Verse 28. Again a few questions marked by a justifiable, impatience; "Have you not known, have you not heard?" These truths, such as, the Lord is the source of all strength, have been proclaimed as long as Israel has been God's people. The prophet makes his starting point, as he presses home his argument, the concept of God as *Creator.* Should not he that made the world and what is in it, be able to control his creation? Besides, he is "eternal." Besides, he has created the "ends of the earth." There is a vastness about the reach of his power that is downright overwhelming. It is simply unthinkable with reference to him that he should "faint or grow weary," especially in regard to the project that he has in hand. Nor, for that matter, is there lack of insight with regard to the issues that confront him; for "his insight is unfathomable."

Verse 29. The truth of the matter is really the very opposite. He not only does not lack strength. He supplies it, supplies every bit of strength that man may ever need or has needed.

Verse 30. A good comparison is the youth of the nation, these beings that seem so full of energy and so tireless at times. For contrasted with the Lord, they too will "faint and grow weary" from time to time. They may even "utterly totter."

Verse 31. Now comes the practical thought: How may men come to have a share in this boundless power of the Lord? They shall have it if they will learn to "wait for the Lord." This expression is merely a synonym for *faith*, and is one of the "cardinal expressions in the Old Testament" for this highly to be desired attribute (see 49:23; Ps. 25:8; 33: 20). It means to lean heavily on the Lord for strength and to bide his time till it comes. Such persons will have the experience that "they shall mount up with wings like eagles" above the difficulties they encounter. For that matter they shall even be able to go on miraculously, if need be, running and not wearying, walking and not growing faint. Here Israel's course and source of strength is clearly portrayed in an utterance of surpassing faith and insight.

Notes

Verse 1. The verb *yo'mar* is perhaps best taken as the imperfect of continuing action. See *GK* 107 f.

Verse 2. The three *ki* that appear in this verse, standing, as they do in a sort of series, should be translated alike, as "that," introducing the indirect discourse.

The noun *kiphláyim* does mean "double," but in this case it is not to be construed in the sense of careful computation, exactly twice as much as should be, for that would involve a criticism of God and his dealings. It should therefore be taken in a loose sense, perhaps as "ample."

Verse 3. The opening word *qol* has been very properly translated as "hark." See *GK*. 146 b.

The phrase "in the wilderness" can be joined with what precedes or with what follows. Either makes good sense. It may be intentionally ambiguous and be construed both ways.

Verse 6. The verb *we'amar* is usually corrected into *wa'omer* ("and I said" for "and some one — impersonal use — said"). Such a correction is not necessary. The message counts, not the person.

Verse 9. We have not translated the phrase *lakh*, for it is one of those untranslatable ethical datives (*KS* 35).

Verse 10. The *be* before *chazaq* is the so-called "beth of essence" (*GK* 119), telling not only what one is like but what he actually is.

Verse 13. The *yodi'énnu* is one of the many imperfects that is in the imperfect because it is separated from the *waw* consecutive that really controls it. *KS* 368 h.

Verse 15. The phrase *middeli* is an instance of the use of a preposition instead of the construct state. *KS* 278 c.

Verse 18. We have here one of those peculiar constructions where a positive rhetorical question really has the force of a negative claim. *KS* 352 a.

The *mah* before *demuth* does not mean "what" but "what kind of." *KS* 69.

Between vv. 19 and 20 many commentators are persuaded that they should insert 41:6-7. This is a purely subjective opinion. The text makes perfectly good sense as it stands. The correction poses the question: How did the two verses of Chapter 41 slip from their anchorage into another chapter?

Verse 21. The noun *ro'sh* stands without article. This here makes it to be a sort of proper noun, "the absolute beginning." *KS* 294 f.

Verse 22. Gunkel has pointed out that the participles that appear here belong to the hymnic style of prophetic writings. They express that which is essential and abiding.

Verse 25. The "then" that we have inserted appears already in the *Septuagint*, and is at least logically quite in place.

Verse 29. The verb *yarbeh* is an instance of the construction where first the participle is used, then the finite verb. The same construction occurred in v. 26b.

Chapter XLI

B. A COURT-TRIAL OF THE NATIONS AND THEIR GODS (Chap. 41)

In the previous chapter Israel was addressed. In Chap. 41 the prophet addresses himself to the "coastlands," that is to the areas lying around the Mediterranean. In the previous chapter the incomparable greatness of God was strongly outlined; here the emphasis lies on the impotence of the idols. Besides this chapter is marked by a striking note of assurance on the part of a minority group, the children of Israel, who were thought of but lightly by the nations surrounding them, especially since the chapter thinks of this people in terms of a Captivity. A rather polemical note is sounded: the incapacity of the gods of the surrounding nations — they cannot begin to compare with the God of Israel.

The point of time to which the writer has transported himself is that period of history where Cyrus the Great was beginning to make great conquests and many nations were beginning to be alarmed at his success.

The whole chapter assumed more or less the form of a court-trial, as our heading indicates. It could be termed a kind of lawsuit. The Germans call it a *Rechtsstreit*, a literary form which appears rather commonly in the Old Testament. To state it a bit more accurately, it is, as *G. A. Smith* said, "loosely cast in the form of a Trial-at-Law," as Chap. 1 also is to an extent. The trial begins vv. 1-7. Then comes something in the nature of a digression, vv. 8-20. The trial is then resumed and summed up, vv. 21-29.

Some writers have pointed out that this situation takes us into the midst of the time when the Semitic era was coming to an end and the Persian era was taking its beginning.

1. A Summons to the Coastlands to Test the Power of Their Gods (vv. 1-4)

41:1-4 1. Listen to me in silence, O coastlands;
let the peoples pick up fresh strength.
Let them approach; then let them speak;
together let them draw near for a court-trial.
2. Who has stirred up from the east
one whom victory attends at every step?
He gives up nations before him,
so that he tramples kings under foot;
With his sword he makes them like dust;
like scattered chaff with his bow.
3. He pursues them [i.e., the kings], passes on safely,
by paths his feet have not trodden.
4. Who has wrought and done this?
He that calls the generations from the beginning,
I, Yahweh, the first and with the last, I am he.

Verse 1. This piece may be classed as a herald's call (*Heroldsruf*), except that in the first line, the sender of the herald himself speaks. It certainly is a divine pronouncement. It is addressed to the "coastlands." Since this special term refers to the irregular shores of the Mediterranean and beyond, it covers the West as over against the East of that day. But at this particular juncture in history the two outstanding leaders were Croesus of Lydia and Cyrus of Persia. The western nations had cast in their lot with Croesus. Yet in the divine purpose, Cyrus was the figure to which importance was to be attached. His importance is to be demonstrated to the western groups by this challenge. They particularly are being apprised of the fact that Cyrus is Yahweh's man of destiny. So they are being bidden to draw near in reverent silence into Yahweh's presence and listen to his instruction about the course history is taking. They are also encouraged to "pick up fresh strength," that is, as they recover from the shock of having stepped into the presence of the Most High God. Then they are to step still closer — "Let them approach." Already they are being spoken about, not spoken to, as they were in the opening address. The Lord is letting them feel a bit of the tremendous distance existing between them and him. They are then invited to speak, if they should have anything to say in the trial that is about to take place. They will be given a fair hearing. They are allowed to come as one huge group for this court-trial. All this is merely a figurative way of bringing home to them that some great issues have to be settled; a few basic facts have to be cleared up.

Verse 2. Now comes the issue that is at stake. Some one has appeared on the stage of history. For the present his approach is cloaked in a measure of secrecy. He is somewhat vague. The identification is far from clear. He is a person of mystery. All that is indicated for the present is that he has come from the East. As things develop, it becomes apparent that the East refers to Persia. The remarkable thing about him however is that he is one "whom victory attends at every step." Apparently there was but one person of whom this claim could be made at that time. This was Cyrus, the Persian. One after another of the nations fell before him. Yet such a claim is inaccurate since *Yahweh* was giving them up before him (cf. Josh. 10:12). This conqueror was virtually "trampling kings under foot." So little could men stand up against him that it is claimed that "his sword made them like dust;" his bow made them "like scattered chaff."

Verse 3. His career to date is further described as "pursuing" them, i.e., the kings of v. 2. The assumption is that he overtakes these kings whom he pursues, vanquishes them and then "passes on safely." He emerges from each battle unscathed. And as he passes on, it is "by paths his feet have not trodden." This statement is meant in the sense that he is always striking out into new territory; no opposition can stand before him. He does not have to retrace his steps.

These conquests of Cyrus are so important, especially for the children of Israel, that Isaiah comes back to this subject repeatedly. Cf. 44:28 and 45:1, where the conqueror is even mentioned by name; but cf. also 45:13; 46:11; 48:14-16. When it is claimed that Yahweh brought this king on the scene that is a claim analogous to the one of 10:5 and 15, where the Assyrian is described as a tool in Yahweh's hand. Strangely at first glance it appears that in II Chron. 36:22 and Ezra 1:1, this word about Yahweh's bringing Cyrus on the stage of world-history seems to be attributed to Jeremiah. In fact what is ascribed to Jeremiah in these two passages is the fact of the restoration of Israel from captivity (see Jer. 25:11 ff.). The issue is not Cyrus' conquests.

Verse 4. But the main point at issue is not the coming of Cyrus as such, but the question who it was that brought Cyrus on the scene: "Who has wrought and done this?" i.e., who started this enterprise and finished it? That is, finished it as far as it has been finished to this day. The Lord himself gives the answer in terms of other things that may be attributed to him. First he describes himself as One who is wont to do even greater works than raising up one conqueror. For he is the one that "calls the generations from the beginning." It was he who brought generation after generation out upon the face of the earth, ever since generations have been appearing. Here "from the beginning" means from the very time of creation itself. So he further identifies himself and answers his own question by saying: "I, Yahweh, the first and with the last, I am he." Here he adds the claim that he not only brought the first and all other generations out upon the earth, but that he will also still be on the scene when the last generation that ever will appear puts in its appearance. It must be admitted that this last statement has a solemn dignity and serves admirably to close an effective answer. It is at the same time reminiscent of a similar divine utterance spoken with unusual emphasis, namely Exod. 3:13 ff.

2. The Consternation of the Coastlands at the Rise of Cyrus, Manifested by the Manufacture of New Idols (vv. 5-7)

41:5-7 5. The coastlands saw it and were afraid;
the ends of the earth trembled; they drew near and came.
6. One helped the other

and said to his brother: "Have courage!"
7. The craftsman encouraged the goldsmith;
he that smooths with the hammer, him that pounded the anvil,
saying of the soldering: "It is good!"
and they fastened it with nails so that it should not sway.

Verse 5. The writer envisions what reaction the initial successes of Cyrus produced way out in the western world. He describes it all as having already taken place, so sure is it to come to pass. When they noted the phenomenal success of the opponent of King Croesus of Lydia, whom they favored, they "were afraid; the ends of the earth trembled." Panic seized the western world, even its remotest corners. They begin first of all to congregate in order to map out some course of action: "they drew near and came."

Verse 6. They are about to engage in concerted action in one particular field of endeavor. The writer delays as long as he can to identify what this field of activity will be, that when it is named it may appear as the anticlimax that it actually is. Men are shown first of all as encouraging one another before the protective measure is undertaken. One says to the other: "Have courage!" Some have rendered this verb: "Cheer up!"

Verse 7. A momentary perplexity comes upon the reader as he notes that a very particular class of men are being depicted as engaged in defensive projects. There is the "craftsman" — the word could also be translated "the ordinary smith." He is speaking to the "goldsmith"; and besides, the man who "smooths with the hammer" speaks to him "who (pounds) the anvil"; and they are talking about soldering and saying, in effect, You have made a good job of it. They have fastened down something with nails "so that it should not sway." Yet the objects made are not identified precisely. What is this mysterious something on which these craftsmen are working? Isaiah 40:19-20 gives us the needed clue. New and better *idols* are being manufactured; perhaps even larger ones. By such means the conquests of Cyrus are to be stopped. Of course, here as so often, the image and the thing it represents are practically being identified. So we could have said: the manufacture of new and better gods is their surest means of defense, it would seem. There is again a biting sarcasm behind what is here written. Very likely this was the best opposition that the coastlands had to offer at the prospect of the impending conquests of Cyrus.

3. God's Reassurance to Israel That She Has Not Been Cast Off (vv. 8-10)

Vv. 8-13 are a *Heilsorkal,* an oracle of salvation.

41:8-10 8. But you, Israel, my servant, Jacob whom I have chosen,
the descendants of Abraham, my friend,
9. whom I fetched from the ends of the earth,
and called from the remotest corners,
and said to you: "You are my servant,
I have chosen you and not cast you off;
10. fear not I am with you;
be not apprehensive, for I am your God;
I will strengthen you, yea, I will help you;
I will uphold you with my victorious right hand."

Verse 8. It has been rightly claimed that the style of speaking in this passage is marked by special solemnity. The main point at issue is indicated by the honorable title that is used in regard to Israel — "servant." Note the frequency of its use by the prophet: cf. 42:19; 44:1, 2, 21; 45:4; 48:20; as also Jer. 30:10; Ezek. 28:25; 37:25. When it is used, even though the basic meaning of the term is "slave," yet here its connotations are entirely honorable. This servant is the one who enjoys a relation of close intimacy with his master and has major assignments laid upon him. In fact, the title runs a close parallel with words: "Jacob, whom I have chosen." The election of Israel to be the Lord's own people is being discussed. What gives rise to the subject is that another "servant" of the Lord has just been brought into the picture, Cyrus. The fact that servant-functions can be ascribed to Cyrus, does not cancel out Israel's election by God. In a very special sense Israel too remains God's servant. Note here how frequently Isaiah makes reference to the election of Israel: cf. 43:1 f; 44:1 f, 21, 24; 45:11; 48:12; 49:7, 13; 55:5. Many are the passages in Scripture that associate Israel's election with the time of the Exodus — when in reality the already existing election was confirmed. Isaiah prefers to trace it back to the earlier event, the promise made to Abraham (Gen. 12 and 15, etc.). Note the words, "the descendants of Abraham, my friend" (Cf. II Chron. 20:7; James 2: 23). What far-reaching activity was involved in this call and election is indicated by the clauses of v. 9: "whom I fetched from the ends of the earth, and called from the remotest corners."

Verse 9. Though no passage can be cited where the words occur: "You are my servant; I have chosen you and not cast you off," this statement is nevertheless an effective summary of God's sentiments toward Abraham and to his whole people. Of course, the particular thought associated with "I have not cast you off" is: by now choosing Cyrus as my servant, *your* initial call is not revoked. When the claim is advanced that Abraham was called "from the ends of the earth" and "from the remotest corners," that certainly agrees better with the approach that these words were written in Palestine than in Babylon, and so may with some justification be ascribed to Isaiah, the son of Amoz.

4. God's Further Reassurance That Israel's Opponents Will Not Prevail against Her (vv. 11-13)

41:11-13 11. Lo, all who are incensed at you will be ashamed and confounded;
those who strive against you, will be as nothing and shall perish.
12. As for those who quarrel with you, if you look for them, you will not find them.
They will be as ciphers and nothing, the men that make war against you.
13. For I, Yahweh, your God, am making your right hand strong;
I, who say to you: "Be not afraid, I myself will help you."

Verses 11-12. Where the preceding three verses laid down general principles defining God's attitude toward his people, these three verses now give the practical application of these principles. Reassurance is the essence of both sections. Though the opposition involved seems to be very generally all forces that might be arrayed against Israel, it is in reality *Babylon* that is under consideration. A new pattern of sentence-structure prevails: the subjects all stand at the end of each line. Besides the strophes mostly follow the 2:2 pattern instead of the 3:2 that had preceded. Furthermore, a climax is marked by the verbs describing the activity of those hostile to Israel. First they are described as being "incensed," i.e., filled with some kind of anger against this little Israel. Then they begin to "strive" with her; then an actual "quarrel" breaks out, which in turn develops into actual "making war." But in each case the form of hostility displayed is said to prove ineffective and futile. Some statements go so far as actually to describe the foe as vanishing off the scene, or as becoming "ciphers and nothing." Words more disparaging could hardly have been used.

Verse 13. The reason for the ineffectiveness of all this opposition is now disclosed: Yahweh, their own true God, is "making (their) right hand strong." He himself is breathing courage into them, saying: "Be not afraid, I myself will help you." So Israel faced catastrophe after catastrophe and came through it all victorious, although these words were in the first instance designed for the heavy days of the Captivity.

5. Rather, Israel Will Be Victorious over Her Foes (vv. 14-16)

41:14-16 14. Fear not, you worm Jacob,
          you men of Israel.
I myself will help you, says the Lord,
     and your redeemer is the Holy One of Israel.
15. Lo, I will make you a threshing sled,
     a new one with many teeth.
You shall thresh mountains and crush them;
and you shall make hills like chaff.
16. You shall winnow them and the wind shall sweep them away,
     and the storm shall scatter them.

But as for you, you shall rejoice in the Lord,
  in the Holy One of Israel you shall glory.

Verse 14. The opposite of a defeatist attitude is here suggested to small and seemingly unimportant Israel. The words, which as to form are a *Heilsorakel*, i.e., a salvation oracle, aim to inculcate a sense of victory over foes that seem practically insuperable. Israel's own lack of strength, as she stands alone by herself, is conceded. She is so small that she may be classified as being only a "worm." This is however not to be construed in a derogatory sense, even as in the German the diminutive *Luther* uses (*Wuermlein*) serves to indicate. Rather it is even a term of endearment. Parallel runs the expression "men of Israel," implying that there are not too many of them. But the Lord places himself at their side and promises to lend his aid. He describes himself as their "redeemer" and "the Holy One of Israel." A redeemer in the original is one who stands in a relation of obligation to help, over against him whose redeemer he is. God stands obligated, for he has taken Israel to be his own. Strangely, this combination of the term "redeemer" (*go'el*) with the "Holy One of Israel" appears seven times in these chapters, and in the use of the word "redeemer" as such lie the roots of the whole New Testament doctrine of redemption.

Verse 15. Now the prophet lists the achievements that God's people will be capable of, as they proceed to move forward in alliance with him. A bold figure is employed. Israel is likened to a "threshing sled," or board, an instrument drawn by oxen, which is used as a sled by the driver and with its sharp attachments fixed in the under side of the board, manages to break the ears of grain spread on the threshing-floor and set loose the kernels. The nations, strong and mighty as they seem, are the grain; Israel is the sled. This instrument is particularly effective. It is new and its teeth are many. Though the amount to be threshed seems high as a mountain, it still shall be controlled. For when it is said: "You shall thresh mountains" that can only mean: huge masses of the enemy, especially in the light of passages like Matt. 17:20; Zech. 4:7; Mic. 1:4; cf. also Mic. 4:13. But assuredly the thought of the writer is not that Israel shall achieve physical conquests of enemies in war, but rather that she shall achieve moral victories of the highest sort, especially in the face of the present difficulties that confront her.

Verse 16. Staying within the limits of the figure that is being used, the effectiveness with which Israel disposes of her stronger enemy is described as a winnowing, in the process of which the enemy, like the chaff and dust of threshing, is swept away by the wind and scattered. But Israel on her part, when she sees the outcome of her conflict with her strong opponents, shall "rejoice" and "glory," in the Lord. The sense of this last statement is that Israel, in her intimate connection with the Lord, shall be filled with great happiness over the outcome of her struggle.

6. Israel, Suffering in Captivity, Will Dwell in a Paradise Rather Than in a Wilderness (vv. 17-20)

41:17-20 17. when the meek and the poor seek water, and
there is none,
and their tongue is parched with thirst,
I, I the Lord, will answer them;
I, the God of Israel, will not forsake them.
18. I will open streams on the bare hills,
and fountains in the midst of the valleys.
I will make the wilderness a pool of water,
and the dry land springs of water.
19. I will provide in the wilderness the cedar,
the acacia, the myrtle and the wild olive tree.
I will set in the desert the cypress,
the plane tree and the larch together;
20. that men may see and know
and may note and understand together
that the hand of the Lord has done this,
and the Holy One of Israel has created this.

Verse 17. Everything is highly figurative in this passage. The chief question is: Is this, like 35:8-10, a passage that again describes how the Lord will transform the *route* along which Israel travels as she returns to her native land? Or is this merely a poetic way of describing a beautiful metamorphosis that will take place in Israel's *condition*? We prefer to stress the second possibility. For there is no reference, even a remote one, to a nation on the march. So v. 17 then is to be regarded as first a description of the pitiful state of Israel as a captive nation: she is like a people that are dying of thirst in the wilderness. When the terms "the meek and the poor" are used to describe those who are suffering, these words would seem to carry the connotation of awareness of spiritual poverty, even as in Matt. 5:3, 5. Here are souls longing for the Lord's deliverance. First of all the strong reassurance is given them by the Lord that he will respond to their need and will not forsake them to their desolate lot. Yet behind the terms used there appears to be a reference to the wilderness experience, where Moses smote the rock.

Verse 18. The prophet now stays within the limits of the figure just introduced: water in abundance will be provided. That signifies all manner of spiritual blessings of which they stand in such sore need. These are then, words spoken to penitent souls, by implication. "Bare hills," which are never the source of water, are here spoken of as opening up with "streams" of water. In addition, down in the valleys where fountains would naturally arise, they do spring forth. Dry areas, which never produced water will stand in "pools of water." So also the "dry land." In the Near East the blessing of water is always appreciated to the utmost. This prerequisite to growth and productiveness now having been met, luxuriant growth can begin. It does in the next verse.

Verse 19. But this productiveness is painted in colors of trees and forests rather than in terms of crops and fields of grain. The emphasis just happens to be on the beautiful rather than on the utilitarian. That certainly will mean the transformation of the "wilderness" and the "desert." Although there may be a small measure of doubt on the exact identification of some of the first of these trees, the translation given is sufficiently close for all practical purposes. On the "plane tree" and the "larch" the identification is very dubious.

Verse 20. In any case, though a picture of verdant beauty was unfolded, the emphasis, as usual, is less on the beauty of the scene than on the hand of God who wrought these things. This picture eloquently describes how the Lord loves to deal with his children when, in their need, they feel moved to call upon him.

7. The Gods of the Nations Are Challenged to Give Proof of Their Divine Powers by Divulging the Future (vv. 21-24)

41:21-24   21. Present your case, says the Lord;
         produce your strong arguments, says the King of Jacob.
22. Let them produce them and tell us what will transpire.
As for the former things, make known to us what they are,
    and we will take note that we may know the outcome.
23. Make known to us what will come hereafter,
    and we shall know that you are gods.
Yea, do something good or something bad,
    and we will both be properly amazed and will see it.
24. Lo, you are less than nothing,
    and your work is less than nought,
    an abomination is he that chooses you.

It must be said at the outset that there is more involved here than just ability to foretell the future. The Lord can indeed do that. But at the same time he also has control of all the issues that the future may bring.

Verse 21. From v. 23 we gather that all these remarks are addressed to the *gods* of the heathen. The trial, from which the line of thought departed with v. 5, for the purpose of reassuring God's chosen people, this court-trial is here being resumed. Another point has to be made. True, God is indeed the attorney for the defense as well as the presiding Judge, but he is very fair and is giving the opposition every opportunity to present all available evidence. It is as though he said to them "tell . . . tell . . . tell," if you have anything to tell. If they have perhaps any "strong arguments" which have not yet been submitted as good evidence, now is the time to set them forth. That the judge is called "the *king* of Jacob" reflects both his great authority and his close relation to his own people. This title appears also in 6:5; 33:22; 41:21; 43:15; 44:6, etc. "Jacob" is merely a synonym for "Israel."

Verse 22. When he challenges them to "produce" what they may have in reserve he seems to intimate that till now they may have had misgivings about the validity of their own arguments and so were reticent about submitting them. But the challenge is "tell us what will transpire." There are two areas where evidence might be adduced. One is concerning the "former things," which in this connection seems to refer to predictions concerning Cyrus, made in the past and now obviously fulfilled. Such evidence will be duly noted if it can be adduced. The term "former things" is repeatedly used (cf. 42:9; 43:9, 18; 46:9; 48:3; 65:16 f.). Not in every case does it refer to things done by Cyrus. But there is still another possibility. Perhaps they could furnish advance information about things that Cyrus, a man of many achievements, may yet accomplish in the future. Therefore the challenge: "Declare to us things that are to come."

Verse 23. Much in the same vein is the challenge: "Make known to us what is to come hereafter." This is not a vague and general challenge but stays within the context of what *Cyrus* may yet do. Such knowledge will indicate that you have some measure of control, you idols, over the things that you predict, "and we shall know that you are gods." The challenge moves over into a third area, the most general of all: It says in effect, at least do *something*, for that is what the expression "do something good or something bad" means (cf. Gen. 24:50; 31:24, 29; II Sam. 13:22; Jer. 10:5).

We promise due amazement, virtually says the next remark. For it will be most remarkable if you can be proved to have accomplished something. There is a veiled sarcasm behind this statement. At this point in the discussion a long

and embarrassing silence sets in. Not a sound, not a movement, nothing, on the part of those who have been summoned to this court-trial of the Almighty!

Verse 24. So the verdict has to be spoken. What is it that
has been proved by the evidence, or lack of it, submitted?
It is this: "Lo, you are less than nothing." This is the claim
advanced with reference to the idols. They are a totally
minus-quantity. So is their "work," and the futility of all
that they stand for is reflected in those that worship them,
for of such it must be said: "An abomination is he that chooses
you." Not a mere blunderer; not a simpleton; but an abomination. As *North* aptly translates: "He that chooses you is
as loathsome as you are." That concluding statement makes
the clear outcome of the court-trial quite plain.

8. On This Score the Gods of the Nations Fail Utterly (vv. 25-29)

41:25-29 25. I have stirred up one from the north, and he
has come;
from the rising of the sun one who proclaims my name.
And he shall come upon rulers as upon mortar,
as a potter tramples clay.
26. Who has declared it from the beginning that we might know,
and beforetime, that we might say: "Right!"?
Yea, there was not a one that declared it;
Yea, there was none that proclaimed it;
yea, there was not a one that heard words of yours.
27. I first have declared to Zion, Lo, lo, here they are;
and I give to Jerusalem a messenger of good tidings.
28. But when I look there is no man,
and from among them there is no counsellor,
that I might ask them and get an answer.
29. Lo, all of them are nought, their works are nothing;
their molten images are wind and confusion.

Verse 25. The issue involved is of sufficient importance to
warrant an official summary of the outcome of this court-
trial. This summary appears in this last section. God reiterates that he has "stirred up one from the north" that is from
Media, which lies more to the north. Or the one called

could be said to have been called from "the rising of the sun," i.e., the east. For if one regards the land of his birth i.e., Persia, this lies more toward the east. But what this one thus called actually does, is that he *proclaims* the name of Yahweh (cf. II Chron. 36:23). For so the expression which seems to say: "one who calls upon my name" is best rendered (cf. Exod. 33:19, 34:5). When this agent of Yahweh appears, opposition to him will be so ineffective that the leaders of it will be so completely at the mercy of the conqueror that they will be trampled under foot as mortar, or as the potter stamps on the clay.

Verse 26. Is there clear-cut evidence that anyone, god or man, foreknew, foreordained, and forecontrolled events to show that this situation was under his control? Did the words and the outcome so correspond that the conclusion had to be drawn: "Right," so it was? Not only was no declaration of a formal sort forthcoming; in fact, not a sound was heard.

Verse 27. Almost everyone admits that this verse poses difficulties. It appears to be extremely elliptical. But if it be viewed in its context some such obvious statement as "I have declared" must be supplied. So our above translation results. God had declared to Zion that the Conqueror would come, has pointed out: Here is the evidence. But for Jerusalem this news was like "good tidings" because it spelled the end of the Captivity. On the Lord's side, the facts are foreknown and the outcome is determined.

Verse 28. But to look at the opposition in this court-trial — No intimation, even the slightest, of awareness of what was to transpire may be detected. There simply is "no man," and "no counsellor." Only an embarassed silence. No answer was forthcoming. So the people on that side are "nought," "their works are nothing; their molten images are wind and confusion." Finis! The case and the trial are closed.

Notes

Verse 1. For "Listen unto me in silence" the Hebrew has a more compact form of statement, saying only: "Be silent unto me." This is properly classified as an instance of the *constructio praegnans*. Cf. *GK*, 119 gg; *KS*, 213 a. The words "Pick up fresh strength" also *Muilenburg* admits, are "not entirely out of place." As our interpretation shows, the peoples are thought of as frightened by the challenge from the Almighty. The verse begins with an address in the second person but almost immediately switches over into the third person.

Verse 2. *Tsédheq*, though it commonly means "righteousness," is best translated here as "victory." *KJ* makes of it an adjective, referring it to the one who is stirred up. In reality a relative pronoun could have been inserted immediately before this word. Then the translation used above results. The term connotes something that comes as a gift from God and is earnestly sought after by men.

Verse 3. *Shalom*, usually translated "peace," is best taken as an adverbial accusative and translated "safely." *GK*, 118 q.

Verse 4. In the expression "from the beginning" the Hebrew omits the article before the noun, thus, according to Hebrew usage making the noun practically a proper noun, and thus referring to the *absolute* beginning of things. See *KS*, 294 g.

Verse 5. When quite generally the words "they drew near and came" are treated as a gloss, they who do this seem to fail to see that men are being described as gathering together to perform a certain task. By these terms they are represented as coming together. That is the beginning of a colorful description. It is quite proper to have men assemble before they do their task.

Verse 6. These references to the futility of the manufacture of idols are by some called "idol interludes." *North* claims with regard to them that they read like "fugitive pieces," meaning apparently that they have been slipped in by editors but do not really fit where they stand. We believe it can be shown in each case that they fit well into given situations.

Verse 7. The "craftsman" is the smith who does heavier work in iron over against the one who does more delicate work and is termed the "goldsmith." Before the latter noun stands the sign of the definite object (*'eth*) usually used only when the noun has the article. Here this sign is used to avoid confusion as to which of the nouns is the object. See *KS*, 288 g.

Verse 10. *Tishta'*, according to a root found in the Ugaritic, should be derived from *shatha'* and is a Kal form. In the latter part of this verse all the perfects are perfects of confidence (*GK* 106 n). Or, according to *KS* 131, perfects of promise.

Verse 14. *Tola'ath* is in the construct state and therefore the next noun is a genitive of apposition. See *KS* 337 d. There is no need to change the next noun into "maggot" instead of "men." Least of all does the translation "louse" have good warrant (*contra Knight*).

Verses 14-16 are given an unusual interpretation by E. J. Hamlin (JNES, XIII, Jul. 1954, pp. 189 ff.) in that the "mountains" and "hills" of v. 15 are construed to signify figuratively the idolatrous religions of the nations. The evidence adduced from Accadian sources may establish the fact that such an interpretation was current in the religious literature of some nations of days of old. But it is none too likely that Israel's prophets were close students of all this literature or familiar with every bit of Accadian lore. Besides, looking at the context of our passage, especially v. 13, the enemies that threatened Israel's safety were the mighty empire like Babylon and Persia.

Verse 17. In the statement "their tongue is parched with thirst," five long *a*'s (*qametz*) appear, a king of *onomatopoea*, representing the stammering effects at speech made with a parched tongue (cf. *North*).

Verse 20. The *yachdaw* is a device often used by Isaiah to bind things together, something like a "once and for all" (*North*). Cf. also at the close of v. 23.

Verse 23. At the close of the verse, the word "and will see it," can be supplied with different vowels and then reads "and will be terrified." (*RSV*). We feel that "see" fits better in the present context.

Verse 24. In *me'ayin*, the *min* used is the *min* comparative. See *KS*, 352 z.

Verse 25. For *wayyabho'* ("and he shall come upon") many conjecture that it should be altered to *wayyabhas*, from *bhus* "to trample." But it can be shown that *bho'* ("to come") can also be used transitively (cf. *North*).

Excursus to 41:21-24

Above we gave the caption, "The gods of the nations are challenged to give proof of their divine powers by divulging the future."

If the question be raised: Is there any indication that in the religions of the nations round about Israel there was the possibility of foretelling events that were yet to come to pass? it must be admitted that a spirit of divination (foretelling the future) did manifest itself. It is true that preponderantly it was some form of doom (death, disaster, etc.) that was foretold. It is also true that in many an instance deception was practiced. False prophecies were submitted. It is equally true that oftentimes the oracular pronouncement was intentionally equivocal, allowing for an obvious double meaning, so that whatever the outcome, the word of the oracle still covered the case. But it must be admitted that sufficient evidence is available to demonstrate that mantic foretelling did occur. See Guillaume's *Prophecy and Divination among the Hebrews and other Semites,* Harper and Brothers, New York and London, 1938.

But does not this admission invalidate the prophet's challenge addressed to the gods of the surrounding nations to produce clear-cut instances of prediction? By way of answer it has been pointed out that there is every indication that the prophet knew of the existence of mantic powers among the heathen cults round about Israel. But it has also been shown (*Westermann*) that Isaiah is not interested in abstract prediction, that is, in bare foretelling. His challenge includes the predictive word and the actual subsequent fulfillment of the word, that is to say, realized prophecy.

In further substantiation of mantic phenomena among neighboring nations one may compare Claus Westermann, *Forschung am Alten Testament* (24) Theologische Buecherei, 1964, Chr. Kaiser Verlag, Muenchen, the essay, *"Die Mari-Briefe und die Prophetie in Israel."*

Chapter XLII

C. THE WORK OF THE SERVANT OF THE LORD (Chap. 42)

A break occurs between Chaps. 41 and 42: there is no transition made from the one to the other. This is the first of the so-called "Servant of the Lord" passages. Since these passages seem to fit a bit loosely in some cases into the context, some have assumed that they stem from some other writer and were merely inserted casually and without sufficient cause or motivation. The passages under consideration are 42:1-9; 49:1-7; 50:4-11; 52:13–53:12. But for the present let it suffice that good arguments can be adduced why these passages may be thought of as original parts of the book and not later insertions. *Muilenburg* indicates that without this strophe the poem would be incomplete.

As the chapter opens, the Lord is speaking as in 40:1 and in 41:1. But to whom is he speaking? Is it perhaps, as some suggest, to his heavenly council? We hardly believe so, for the heavenly council is largely a figurative representation employed for embellishment. As in Chap. 40, all who will take heed are being addressed.

But who is the "servant"? There has long been a division of opinion among commentators dating back to the Septuagint, which identified him with Israel, the nation. But as we proceed, we hope to offer sufficient arguments for maintaining that in the passages listed above, the person under consideration is none less than the one who in the New Testament goes under the name of Jesus the Christ. Other views, such as he is Deutero-Isaiah, or some ruler of Judah, etc., are quite unsatisfactory. And though it is true enough that in a certain sense Israel herself may be thought of as the servant of the Lord, as is the case in the second half of our chapter, nevertheless there are too many references of the New Testament that support our view of his identity with the Messiah. Yet we should note at the very outset that a certain "duality" runs through the Old Testament already, so that on the one hand the servant's work is done by a human agent, but on the other hand it is viewed as the work of God himself. The New Testament truth is therefore prepared for, which says with unmistakable clearness that this task is the task of the God-man, Jesus Christ. Let us note already that the Servant is thought of very clearly as distinct from the nation Israel, for in v. 6 he stands over against the nation as the mediator of the covenant and as its light.

By taking this position we do not rule out the fact that in a certain sense Israel, the nation, also shares in the work that the Lord would have his Servant do. But this is an achievement on a much lower scale, and this accounts for the fact that on the one hand the Servant can meet with God's fullest approval in his work, but yet (vv. 18-22) God may find his servant highly inadequate. Matthew sees the fulfillment of this passage in Christ's withdrawing himself from the multitude (Matt. 12:18-21).

1. The Servant of the Lord, Meek and Unassuming, Yet Successful (vv. 1-4)

42:1-4 1. Lo, my servant, whom I support,
my chosen one, in whom my inmost soul delights.
I have put my spirit upon him
that he may bring forth justice to the nations.
2. He will not cry out or raise his voice,
nor make it to be heard in the street.
3. A crushed reed he will not [utterly] break,
and a dimly burning wick he will not quench;
he will faithfully bring forth justice.
4. He himself will not be dimmed or crushed,
until he has established justice in the earth;
and for his teaching the coastlands do wait.

Verse 1. Though the word "servant" in the original does mean a slave, it is in this connection an entirely honorable term. If he is the Lord's servant, his is an honored task. Many have been designated by this title: Abram (Gen. 26:24), the patriarchs (Deut. 9:27), Moses (Num. 12:7), David (II Sam. 3:18), prophets (Amos 3:7), even Nebuchadnezzar (Jer. 27:6), so the individual connotation of this title is far more common than the collective; in a few instances Israel is referred to by this title. So then we place this passage by the side of those passages which refer to the individual Messiah, passages like 7:14; 9:1-6; 11:1-9. Neither can we find that interpretation satisfactory which finds here the description of some prophet. Several assertions are made about this servant. First of all he is the Lord's own servant ("my"). Then he is a man whom the Lord upholds or "supports." He needs help in his task and he enjoys the very maximum of help in that the Lord upholds him in every difficulty. This is further indicated by the fact that the Lord calls him "my chosen one." In fact he does his assigned task so well that the Lord can say of him, He is the one "in whom my inmost soul delighted." In Matt. 3:17 and 17:5 the reference to this passage is so obvious that the evangelist must be viewed as indicating that this passage is a distinct prophecy concerning the Messiah. The past tense in this case ("delighted") is to be taken as stating that the Lord has taken delight in everything that his chosen one did. As a further description of what equipment the Lord gave him for his work there comes the claim, "I have put my spirit upon him." On the Old Testament level the reference to the "spirit" almost invariably connotes "power." So this statement means that the Servant is richly indued with power. But the particular task that is assigned to him is "that he may bring forth justice to the nations." It is almost impossible to find an adequate equivalent for the word that we, with many others, have translated as "truth," as "a norm of judgment," or even as "the true religion." None of these is quite satisfactory. The term implies all that the nations need for their salvation, the blotting out of their spiritual ignorance. But this much is clear, he is not to confine his activity to the children of Israel. In fact, this is the big part of his assignment, this bringing forth justice to the nations, for in these verses (1-4) the matter appears three times. For further instances where the equipment of men with the "spirit" is referred to, cf. 32:15; 44: 3; Ezek. 36:26; 39:29; Joel 2:28.

Verse 2. From assignment and equipment a transition is made to the manner in which this chosen Servant of the Lord will do his work. A contrast seems to be implied, particularly with that conqueror from the north, or east (41:2 ff.), who is ruthless and cruel, trampling the vanquished ones under his feet. This Servant is modest and meek. He is not loud and boisterous, he does "not cry out nor raise his voice, nor make it to be heard in the street." He is so sure of himself and of the cause he represents that he can well expect his message to carry itself successfully through every test. How often Jesus shunned publicity, even though his aim was to carry his gospel to all men! This description is hardly intended to be a contrast to the ecstatic prophets of days of old.

Verse 3. We move into the area of pastoral care, so to speak. Wherever he finds men wounded and bruised by the harshness of life's experience, or wherever he finds wounded and bruised consciences, whether among the Gentiles or in Israel, there he is most tender and delicate in the gentle handling of these souls. Such individuals are likened in the first place to a "bruised reed," bent but not quite broken. He takes care that such a one is not utterly broken. In the second place such persons are likened to a "dimly burning wick." The flame of faith and hope has begun to flutter but is not quite gone out. He cups his hand around the flame that it may not be "quenched" or, as one writer has put it, "snuffed out." This will be the manner in which he "will faithfully bring forth justice." What a contrast such dealings are with 41:15 f.! But how in harmony this is with Matt. 5:3! Never did a servant acquit himself better in the achievement of a difficult assignment.

Verse 4. This assigned task was by no means an easy one. The Servant might have been overwhelmed by its enormity. But no! "He himself will not be dimmed or crushed" — the same verbs being intentionally used here as in reference to the afflicted ones whom he himself helps — as he goes about his task. Here for the first time comes a faint indication in the Servant Songs that this will be a *Suffering* Servant. Again, with emphatic repetition, he will carry on his work "until he has established justice in the earth." But it will not be universal hostility and opposition that he encounters. Prevenient grace will have been doing some work on the hearts of men in the distant coastlands. So the encouraging word is added: "for his teaching the coastlands do wait." Sometimes their longing will be dimly and not consciously defined. But it will be there, even if at times it is little more than a negative preparation. The next portion, vv. 5-9, may be regarded as also belonging to this Servant Song. It certainly is closely connected with it.

2. The Lord's Relation to His Servant Defined (vv. 5-9)

42:5-9 5. Thus says the true God, the Lord,
who created the heavens and stretched them out,
who spread out the earth and what it produces;
who gave breath to the people upon it
and spirit to those that walk in it:
6. "I the Lord have called you in righteousness,
and grasp you by the hand and guard you,
and give you as mediator of the covenant to the people,
and as a light to the nations,
7. to open blind eyes,
to bring prisoners from the dungeon,
from the prison-house those that sit in darkness.
8. I Yahweh, that is my name;
and my glory I will not give to another
nor my praise to graven images.
9. The former prophecies, lo, they have come to pass,
and now I declare new things;
before they spring forth, I let you hear of them."

Verse 5. Here the Lord himself defines his relation to his Servant, addressing him in person. To try to relate all these pronouncements to Cyrus falls far short of the great things that are here set forth. Not just any god is the speaker (if the gods of the nations could speak!); the article used before the word "God" gives the sense of the "true and only God." He is about to speak of achievements so great that men might have doubts as to whether he is able to fulfill them. Therefore he reminds them of the fact that he is none less than the very Creator himself, who has power to make the earth of nothing. Here, as so often, the Creator-character of God is the guaranty of his power to achieve any and all of the things he proposes to undertake (see 40:12, 13, 26, 28; 41:20; 43:1, 8, 12, 13, etc.). Besides, he is the one who also stretched out the heavens, with the ease with which a man spreads out a cloth. He also spread out (literally "hammered out") the earth and made it to bring forth what it produces; for it is no sterile earth. He did greater things even than these. He put animating breath into bodies so that they became living animated beings, and even higher than that, put spirit, a capacity for higher things, into these beings. Four tremendous achievements of the Almighty are here called to mind. You might well expect of such a one that he could produce great things to this day as he did in days of old.

Verse 6. He now envisions his Servant as standing before him. First of all, the call of this Servant to the task that he has, emanated from God, and it was transmitted "in righteousness," that is, with saving purposes in mind. More, from the very outset, when the Servant appears on the scene, God is grasping his right hand to uphold and strengthen him for the seemingly impossible great task which is his. At the same time he is continually guarding him against the many dangers that would assail him and thwart his work. And now the ultimate purposes for which all this is set in motion are delineated: First of all he is to serve as a "mediator of the covenant." There once was a covenant made with Abraham. This covenant was significantly expanded to involve all Israel at Mount Sinai. A greater covenant is now under consideration, one that involves "the people," that is all the nations on the face of the earth. In some mysterious way the Servant himself is the essence of that covenant, not only the one who transmits it. Some have tried to capture the force of the statement by defining this title as "truth personified" (*Volz*), which is helpful but not broad enough. This new covenant is spoken of also in 54:10; Jer. 31:31 ff.; Ezek. 16: 60 ff. But even this significant epithet says too little. He and his work may further be defined as being "the light of the nations." There is no real truth by which men can walk aside from him. He lightens the darkness of the natural mind of man. Jesus claimed this role for himself (John 8:12; cf. also Luke 2:32). Isaiah 49:6 again alludes to this outstanding work. But no less than "the nations," that is to say, all of them, are the beneficiaries of his great work.

Verse 7. But having once gotten on the rich subject of the work outlined for this Servant, the Lord himself cannot soon drop it, for it involves infinitely more. A few bold strokes fully round out the picture. He will come "to open blind eyes." Obviously this refers to more than occasional instances where he restored sight to eyes physically blind. Imparting insight into saving divine truth is what is primarily under consideration (cf. 29:18; 35:5 ff.). Or, completely altering the figure, his task is "to bring prisoners from the dungeon." Again the spiritual interpretation of the task described alone fits the needs of the case. For prisoners in dungeons often must be kept in such confinement for the safety of mankind. But when the parallel statement speaks of liberating those that sit in darkness, again some sad spiritual plight is under consideration.

It must freely be admitted that taken all together, these are achievements which only Christ, the Savior, was able to accomplish and still does on a grand scale. At this point attempts to interpret the passage in reference to a collective object like Israel, completely breaks down.

Verse 8. The Lord is still speaking. By raising up and sustaining this Servant of his the Lord achieves great honor, honor of the highest sort, which he desires to achieve, as he now asserts. He who bears the distinctive name of the God of Israel, the name "Yahweh," is jealous of this honor of his, and will not allow it to be snatched from him or awarded to any other, because this honor is so intimately tied up with the salvation of mankind. Least of all can "graven images" ever match what he does with comparable works done in their name.

Verse 9. But what does the prophet mean by the statement, "the former prophecies, lo, they have come to pass"? What are the "former prophecies"? Much perplexity has been caused by this expression. Perhaps it is best after all to follow the lead of those who refer to distinct passages in Isaiah and Jeremiah, which declared beforehand that Babylon would fall at the hands of the Medes, passages like Isa. 13 and 14 (esp. 13:17); 21:1-10; Jer. 50 and 51 (esp. 51:11, 28). No one could have foreseen that the Medes would be successful in this direction. But the prophets, by the spirit of the Lord, foretold that it would come to pass, and it came. And now the prophet is foretelling restoration from Captivity for Israel and salvation unto the ends of the earth through the Servant of the Lord. "Before they spring forth" the Lord tells of them. These are the "new things" here referred to. These future events will come to pass as certainly as did the predictions of days of old. This is one of the distinctive achievements of the God of Jacob and the great Lord of Israel. All this makes the work of the Servant of the Lord more glorious.

3. A Summons to Praise the Lord for the Work of His Servant (vv. 10-12)

42:10-12 10. Sing to Yahweh, a new song,
his praise to the end of the earth,
they that go down to the sea and that which fills it,
you coastlands and they who dwell in them.
11. Let the wilderness and its cities raise their voice,
the villages that Kedar inhabits.
Let the cliff-dwellers exult;
let them call aloud from the mountain-tops.
12. Let them give glory to the Lord,
and make known his praise in the coastlands.

Here, as pointed out by *Westermann*, occurs for the first time in the second half of the book "an eschatological hymn of praise," further examples of which are to be found in 44:23; 45:8; 48:20-21; 49:13; 52:7-10.

Verse 10. *G. A. Smith* at this point very appropriately remarks: "God's commission to his Servant is hailed by a hymn." So this summons to praise the Lord looks back at the commission as such and regards it as being of such supreme benefit to all mankind that they should all break forth into singing at what is here being done for the good of all. As so often in the Scriptures, a new work that God does for the children of men is to be greeted with a new song (cf. Ps. 33:3; 40:4; 96:1; 98:1; 144:9; 149:1). But in this case the blessing under consideration is so vast that it affects all of mankind, and only praise from all can begin to do justice to its magnitude. So praise is to come forth and ring out "to the ends of the earth." They who are to participate include certain ones, here enumerated as being persons whom we are likely to overlook in so general a summons — persons that sail the seas, or to use the idiom of a people who lived in the hills and whenever they betook themselves to the sea had to "come down" from the hill country. Add to the sailors all the various kinds of creature-life that exists in endless variety in the waters of the sea, all forms of aquatic life, strange as it may strike us that they should contribute their share of the praise due to the Lord. Then there is, of course, the vast expance of "the coastlands," i.e., the very irregular Mediterranean shoreline, where people of many races live. What this Servant of the Lord will do, bears very great meaning for them also. They should join in offering praises for these benefits. But a still larger chorus and symphony orchestra are to be enlisted to make the praises worthy of him to whom they are directed.

Verse 11. So even "the wilderness" where people are comparatively few, yet even, by way of exception, "cities" (like Tadmor, I Kings 9:18) are to be found, are summoned to bear their share. So too "the villages (or 'tentdwellings')

that Kedar (perhaps Arabia) inhabits" and which represent
the eastern fringe of the nations with whom Israel had contact, even as the "coastlands" represented the western borders. Add to this the very isolated groups like "the cliff-
dwellers" (or "denizens of the rocks" as *North* calls them).
They are to be exuberantly glad ("exult") for the Servant's
work is for their good, too. They are to ascend high mountains and from there "call aloud" that they may be heard far
and wide. All these are called upon to praise, for a work of
most tremendous proportions, affecting the wellbeing of all
of them, is being achieved.

Verse 12. All this praise is to be tendered to the true God
of Israel, Yahweh, who alone can do such wonderful things
that affect the destiny of all.

4. How the Lord Himself Will Participate in the Achievement of His Servant's Tasks (vv. 13-17)

42:13-17 13. The Lord will go forth as a mighty man,
like a man of war he will stir up his fury.
He will raise the war-cry, he will roar;
he will prove himself victorious over his enemies.
14. For a long time I have kept silent,
I have been still and restrained myself.
As a woman in childbirth I will groan,
I will gasp and pant together.
15. I will lay waste mountains and hills,
and dry up all their vegetation;
I will turn rivers into islands,
and dry up the pools.
16. And I will lead blind people in a way they have not known,
and in paths unknown to them I will let them go;
I will turn darkness before them into light,
and rough places into level country.
These things I will do and not leave undone.
17. They that trust in graven images shall be turned back,
and utterly put to shame;
they that say to molten images,
"You are our gods!"

Verse 13. Another way of looking at what is now portrayed is to regard this as a description of the Lord's activity

about achieving his objectives. Or looking back at v. 9, our verse now begins to picture the eagerness with which the Lord takes his projects, the "new things," in hand. The Lord really appears now in a new role. He is no longer so much the deliverer as the successful conqueror. Those familiar with Akkadian and Ugaritic literature find many parallels here as to the role in which God pictures himself as a mighty warrior. In fact biblical parallels are not wanting (see Judg. 5; Ps. 18; Hab. 3; Zech. 14:3). *North* ventures the rather bold observation that the Lord is represented as stirring himself up to a kind of "berserker" rage, and offers as further biblical parallel Isa. 63:1-6. Note the "holy war" language.

From the very first word on, military language is being employed; for the verb "to go forth" is the technical term for venturing forth to battle (cf. II Sam. 11:1); and "mighty man" is merely another title for "warrior." Language here goes as far as it possibly could without impropriety in picturing one who will be terrible to encounter as he goes against his foes. He is said to work himself up into a veritable passion (*Kampfeslust*) (cf. I Sam. 17:20). When sufficiently aroused, "he will raise the war cry," challenging his foe to the conflict. He will even "roar" in his anger. Then he ventures to assert before the conflict has even started that "he will prove himself victorious over his enemies." In this whole section it has been noted that there are no less than fifteen verbs used in reference to the various forms of activity in which the Lord engages. The whole scene is packed with action.

Verse 14. This is still a description of the change in policy from former inaction to present, intense activity. The Lord is like a man who for good reasons of his own has refrained from action. This has been difficult with a situation that seemed to clamor for intervention. Still "for a long time, he kept silent," he has "been still," and "restrained" himself. Now he can hold back no longer. *Volz* goes so far as to claim (and to us the claim seems justifiable) that this inaction sums up the whole space of time up till this moment. Now comes the birth-hour of a new aeon. In the colorful portrayal of the strenuous activity now getting under way, the words beat a kind of staccato tempo indicative of intense action. But the figure of the warrior is abruptly abandoned for one which well covers the other aspect of this new activity. The new figure is that of a woman in travail. So God travails to bring forth the new: he groans, gasps, and pants. Certainly the least one can claim is that these verbs reflect the intense concern that God has for the achievement of his goals. The final "together" of the verse seems to lump all activities together into one and to impart to the various verbs used a kind of superlative intensity.

Verse 15. This verse seems to fit badly into the picture, whether we look at the warrior aspect of God, or the woman-in-childbirth aspect, or also when we think of the deliverance-of-Israel approach. Perhaps the solution lies in the thought that this is all eschatological language, the final-judgment aspect of history, all blending together into one vast scene of divine activity without regard for the time sequence. Mountains and hills are being devastated, as it were, by the hot blast that goes forth from his mouth. Vegetation withers. Where rivers ran, now islands appear; the waters having been driven away by the hot blast of the Lord's anger. Pools also disappear. But at this point things seem to blend into another kind of perspective.

Verse 16. The destructive work of v. 15 was preparatory to making a road that the captive people might travel as they go back to their old homeland. As so often, the Exodus tradition of Israel's past comes to the forefront: a new Exodus is in the making. God appears as leading his once captive people through a wilderness again, as he led Israel from Egypt to Canaan. He calls them "blind people" because they are not yet able to see God's great purposes that he has in mind for their good. Some measure of the blindness of unbelief is still upon them. They cannot for themselves detect the way they are to take, nor do they know the road to restoration. But he promises to give them light as the cloud of God's presence guided them in the way through the dread wilderness of old. So to speak, he will even make the rough places plain. And if these promises seem grand and unbelievable, he gives the nation the assurance, like as by an oath, "These things will I do and not leave undone."

Verse 17. What is deliverance for Israel at the same time becomes a defeat for her idolatrous enemies. They will not prevail against Israel any longer. The magnificent display of power on God's part will mark an hour of disgrace and impotence of her enemies, who, like true idolaters say to the molten image, "You are our gods."

5. The Blind and Deaf Servant Who Failed God and Suffered the Consequences (vv. 18-22)

42:18-22 18. Hear, you deaf,
and look, you blind, that you may see!
19. Who is blind but my servant,
and deaf as my messenger whom I send?
Who is blind as my trusted one,
and blind as the servant of the Lord?
20. You have seen many things, but you took no note of them,
I opened (his) ears, but he did not listen.
21. The Lord was pleased for his righteousness' sake
to make his instruction great and glorious.
22. But this is a people robbed and plundered;
men have ensnared them all in pits,
and they were hid away in prisons.
They have been given over to plundering, with none to deliver,
for spoil, and no one says, "Restore!"

Verse 18. The "servant" now encountered is an entirely different person than the one met with heretofore in the chapter. He stands in sharpest contrast to the Lord and his zeal for Israel. This servant is blind and deaf. He is a collective personality. The note of comfort that is so outstanding since 40:1 ff., recedes into the background, and the Comforter becomes the Rebuker and Educator. For him this servant now is Israel, an Israel marked by one most serious shortcoming, blindness. It is not an excusable blindness but a reprehensible one which merits sharp rebuke. Perhaps no one questions that the servant here spoken of is unbelieving Israel. The nation is here sharply challenged for its lack of receptivity. It is blind, not by accident but through fault of its own. Cf. the situation of Isa. 6.

Verse 19. Though in a sense the whole nation appears to be indicted, no doubt the unbelieving exiles in Captivity are primarily under consideration, and that in spite of the fact that the Lord can refer to the nation as "*my* servant," and also as "*my* messenger whom I send." For this latter claim does apply to Israel: she was always a nation with a distinct mission from God. Other honorable titles may be used in reference to the nation. She is God's "trusted one," a one to whom important tasks were entrusted. She is still, summing it all up, "the servant of the Lord." She has never been dismissed from this post of honor. The blindness she is charged with appears to be chiefly her failure to recognize her commission as servant. To this must be added the resultant blindness that grows out of misunderstanding her assignment. Lack of all deeper spiritual perception grows out of this root-oversight.

Verse 20. This failure of the nation dare not be attributed to any failure on God's part to do for her what needed to be done. The Lord displayed mighty acts, especially acts of deliverance in great number before the eyes of his chosen people. But Israel saw what was done but failed actually to take note of what it meant. God could even go so far as to claim that he "had opened [his] ears, but he did not listen." The change in person within the compass of this one verse is very significant. At first Israel is addressed directly. Then the Lord, in a somewhat cool manner, appears to turn away from the more intimate second person to the impersonal third. This we have sought to indicate by inserting a parenthetical "his" before "ears."

Verse 21. At this point the Lord makes reference to the greatest of the gifts that he bestowed upon Israel to fit the nation for its task. "He was pleased . . . to make his instruction [Hebrew: *torah* in the broadest sense of the word] great and glorious." The reference is to all the instruction that was in God's providence bestowed upon the nation. And this favor was granted "for his righteousness' sake," that is to say, with saving purposes in mind. No nation was ever so richly and so graciously endowed. Many have claimed that this verse does not belong here but is a later addition. The connection indicated above shows that it fits admirably into the picture.

Verse 22. So, from having been a nation with a high potential for blessed activity, she became disobedient and unresponsive, with the result, she had to be given over to God's judgment. So she became a "people robbed and plundered; men have ensnared them all in pits, and they were hidden away in prisons." All the needs of the figure used seem to be met if we think in terms of a caravan that was attacked by marauders out in the desert and cruelly deprived of all their goods and of their very liberty, being allowed to languish in places of captivity. This figure is still being followed in the remainder of the verse: "They have been given over to plundering with none to deliver; for spoil, and no one says: 'Restore!' " For the present at least no indication of a deliverance from this sorry lot is discernible.

6. An Indictment of the Deaf Servant for His Failure (vv. 23-25)

42:23-25 23. Who among you gives ear to this,
hearkens and listens from now on?
24. Who gave Jacob up to be plundered
and Israel to robbers?
Was it not the Lord against whom we have sinned,
and in whose ways men were not willing to walk,
and whose instruction they did not obey?
25. So he poured out upon him the heat of his anger
and the fierceness of war;
and it set him on fire round about,
but he did not note it;
and it burned him,
but he did not take it to heart.

Verse 23. It is as though this section (vv. 23-25) were saying, O that Israel might recognize that the present disaster, the state of exile prevailing, is a just judgment of God! Looking forward to 43:1-7, we might say that the present portion is a preparation for the mercy about to be proclaimed. Or thinking in terms of the form in which these words are cast, it would be quite in order to describe vv. 23-25 as an invective, but 43:1-7 as an oracle of redemption (*Muilenburg*). In any case, when the prophet wrote there was as yet no evidence of a spirit of repentance on the part of the nation Israel for its infidelity to the Lord. Surely here it cannot be claimed that the restoration came as a result of Israel's repentance. Much as in the preceding section, v. 23 charges the nation with dullness and lack of perception. The Lord was saying something to the nation by the way in which he was treating them, but no man listened. No one was paying close attention ("hearkens and listens") to the Lord's words, at least "from now on," careless as they may have been previously.

Verse 24. The Captivity of Israel was not something that just happened. By the form of question used the prophet indicates that a divine act of giving up the people was the cause of it all. That was how Israel got into the hands of "robbers," an allusion to the figure used in v. 22. Sin was the major cause, and this sin was against the Lord (cf. Ps. 90: 11 ff.). When the prophet uses the first person plural ("against whom *we* have sinned") and includes himself, he is leading the nation to admit that here lies the root of their misfortune and seeks to induce them to make a frank and free confession. The sin involved could also be described as stubbornness ("in whose ways men were not willing to walk"), the right way was not unknown but the nation was not minded to go according to the course prescribed. The last statement adds a significant thought ("whose instructions they did not obey"): God had virtually spelled out for them what course his people should follow. This put them under obligation to obey; but they were at heart a stubborn and disobedient people.

Verse 25. What else was there left for God to do than to chastise them? And it was chastisement of the most severe sort: "he poured out upon him the heat of his anger and the fierceness of war." The figure is a telling one, emphasizing the painfulness of the experience. Wars are not primarily the result of economic, industrial and nationalistic causes, or of misdirected diplomacy. They are judgments upon the guilty. The heavier the crime, the greater the judgment of God. But Israel, in the midst of it all, could be described as a person actually set on fire and not noting what had happened; or as a person who was being burned but did not take it to heart. Physically such an attitude would be unthinkable, spiritually it was a fact.

Notes

Verse 1. The *Septuagint* already indicates what interpretation was much in vogue in the Jewish circles B.C. when it inserts the word "Jacob" before "my servant" and "Israel" before "my chosen one." The verb "I support" is construed with a preposition in Hebrew (cf. *KS*, 215 h). Both "my servant" and "my chosen one" are absolute nominatives in the original.

Verse 4. The construction "until he has established" — *'adh* with an imperfect — practically equals a future perfect (cf. *KS*, 387 g).

Verse 5. The participle *noteyhem* ("stretching them out") may be viewed as only seemingly a plural (*GK* 93 ss) or as a plural of potency (*KS*, 263 b and d; also *GK* 124 k). The expression "the true God, the Lord" occurs only here in the second half of Isaiah.

Verse 6. On the verbs from *we'achzeq*, where *we* is regularly used as connective (not *waw* conversive) the major versions, *Septuagint*, *Vulgate*, *Syriac* and *Targum*, do read the text as though it were the connective *wa*. It is better to let the masoretic text stand. These are all acts of the Almighty that are still going on and do not only lie in the past.

Verse 7. For *'asir* read *'asirim*, *m* having fallen out through haplography. The sense demands the plural. The subject of the infinitives may be Yahweh or the Servant.

Verse 10. *Miqtseh* should not be rendered "*from*" but "*to*" "the end of the earth," according to the common point of view reflected in the Hebrew approach in such instances. At first glance the emendation *yir-am* ("let roar") for *yoredey* ("they that go down") according to Ps. 96:11 seems attractive. But some of the color of the verse is lost by this emendation.

Verse 13. The context would suggest that *yetse'* is better rendered as a future than a present (*Koenig*). The comparison "as a mighty man" uses an article before the noun, as is pointed out and explained *GK* 126 or *KS* 299 m.

Verse 14. After the perfect, follows a series of unconnected imperfects. They constitute what is called "a synchronistic asyndeton," *GK* 120 c.

Verse 18. The vocative may use the article. *GK* 126, e, f.

Verse 19. The *Septuagint* not inappropriately read the plural "my servants" for the singular, as the Hebrew text allows.

Verse 20. For "*he* did not listen," some 60 manuscripts render "you." But the more difficult reading deserves the preference and shows the Lord, as it were, turning away from more intimate address to objective impartiality.

Verse 22. Before "plundering" the *le*, appearing before *baz*, is still in force (*GK* 119 hh).

Verse 24. The *zu* used here is really a demonstrative pronoun, which is here used as a relative. See *KS* 51, 385 b; *GK* 138 g. The *athnach*, marking the middle of the verse (under *Yahweh*) is usually regarded as being out of place in this verse; it should stand two words earlier. For some reason *bethoratho* is by some regarded as a "pious gloss." This is purely subjective opinion. Obedience is clearly related to the keeping of the law. Disobedience is the lack of it. As the verse swerves from the address of the second person to the objective style of the third person ("men were not willing") it marks a kind of estranged aloofness on the part of the Lord.

Verse 25. At the close of the verse the expression, "heat of his anger" does not offer the usual relation of the first noun being in the construct state ("heat of"). This is explained either as a kind of apposition: the heat, which was his anger (*GK* 131 k); or it is thought of as an instance where the north-Hebrew construct state on long *a* is used (*KS* 285 f).

Chapter XLIII

D. RESTORATION BY DIVINE GRACE (Chap. 43)

This caption only roughly gathers together what is covered by this chapter. For there are diverse elements pieced together here, diverse but not unrelated, as the outline demonstrates.

The tone of the chapter, as indicated by the opening words, is not at all what would be expected after the somewhat sharp close of the preceding chapter. For, to use some of the terminology employed by form criticism, the preceding chapter has closed on the note of a rebuke (*Scheltwort*). But rebukes are, as a general rule, followed by threats of disaster (*Drohwort*). But to our surprise we find a gracious promise (*Verheissung*). But this is only a seeming irregularity. For the prophet is a man with a message primarily of comfort. He delights in transmitting messages of grace. He can be, and is, a man of sharp rebukes on occasion. But his book (chaps. 40-66) is primarily a comfort book, as is commonly conceded. The antithesis between the close of the one chapter and the opening of the next is indicated by the opening particle, "but now." Besides, though addressing the nation, these words have a singularly personal tone (cf. *Westermann*).

1. Restoration of Israel Impending (vv. 1-7)

43:1-7 1. But now, thus says the Lord,
who created you, O Jacob, and formed you, O Israel:
"Fear not, for I have redeemed you;
I have called you by your name; you are mine.
2. When you pass through the waters, I am with you,
and through the rivers, they will not sweep you away;
when you walk through fire; you will not be burned,
and the flame shall not scorch you.

77

3. For I, the Lord, am your God,
the Holy One of Israel, your Savior.
I give Egypt as your ransom, Cush and Seba in place of you.
4. Because you are precious in my eyes,
    honored, and I love you;
therefore I will give men in your stead,
    peoples for your life.
5. Fear not, for I am with you;
from the east will I bring your descendants,
    and from the west I will gather you.
6. I will say to the north, Give up!
and to the south, Keep not back!
Bring my sons from afar, and my daughters from the end of the
    earth;
7. every one who is called by my name,
and whom I created for my glory,
    whom I have formed and made."

Verse 1. That a new oracle is about to be presented is indicated by the formula "thus says the Lord," as well as by
the adversative "but now." To give a solid basis for the claim
that the Lord is about to make to the effect that he will not
fail Israel in the present emergency, the word of the Lord
points to two major activities that may also be ascribed to
him in connection with his people — he "created" them and
"formed" them. They owe their origin as a nation to him as
well as any substantial thing that they have become (for in
spite of the disaster of the Exile, Israel was still a nation with
perhaps more than ordinary potential, at least as far as the
divine purpose was concerned). The essence of the particular word to be imparted at this time is "fear not." Israel may
have been very dubious as to her future as nation. Many may
have seen nothing less than national extinction staring them in
the face. Any people would view such a prospect with fear.
In Israel's case such fear is groundless. It is for this reason
that the divine "fear not," runs like a continuous thread,
through these oracles (see 40:9; 41:10, 13 f.; 44:2; 54:4).
To the two outstanding favors already mentioned, two
others are added: (1) "I have redeemed you," one of those
perfects that the Hebrew uses to indicate that an event is as
good as already done. The verb here implies that Israel has

been freed from a threatening danger by one upon whom she has some well-established claim for help. (2) "I have called you by your name," an idiom which means about as much as: I have appointed you for a very special purpose in a very direct way. The expression occurs in Exod. 31:2; 35:30; Isa. 45:4. In other words, summing up: Innumerable ties bind the Lord and his people to one another. To this must be added the statement in which the prophet himself sums it all up: "You are mine" (Exod. 19:5). That is to say: I have special claim on you, and you on me.

Verse 2. This is now spelled out by way of practical application. This verse is a kind of generalization. It applies not only to the prevailing crisis but to the entire history of the nation. No matter what kind of dangers are encountered, Israel can survive. Two types of danger are mentioned for the whole catalogue of them that might be enumerated — passing through water and through fire, as in Ps. 66:12. The nation is thought of as on a journey. She may have to ford streams — there were no bridges in those days. Should the waters prove dangerous, her comfort is: The Lord will be with her. His mere presence is the epitome of safety. The waters will not be able to sweep her away. Should a fire in the wilderness be encountered, like our prairie fires, she will not be burned or scorched. This last statement seems to be a kind of reverse of what was said in 42:25. When God's displeasure had to be vented on his people, they were burned. In the season of compassion that is about to begin, such suffering shall not overtake them.

Verse 3. That such assurance is well founded is here undergirded by several of the choice names by which the Lord designates himself: "your God, the Holy One of Israel, your Savior." As God he stands related to them as their proper head; as the Holy One he is devoted to their welfare; as Savior he can be depended on to deliver from every extremity. This last title is a favorite one of the prophet (see 45:15, 21; 49:24; 60:16; 63:8).

Perhaps it is best to construe the rest of v. 3 as implying

what God would be ready to do, should emergency demand it. That Israel might go free he would give up other nations as substitutes. Or, so to speak, the Lord is ready to pay a high ransom for his people. In this verse even three nations are mentioned: Egypt, Cush (sometimes translated Ethiopia, or even Nubia) and Seba. These three constituted all that was known of Africa in those days. So God is practically ready to sacrifice a continent to rescue his people. *Muilenburg* does well to point out that a "literalistic interpretation" would do violence to the meaning of the passage. But still it should be noted that if the passage should imply that the Lord would reimburse Persia, or Cyrus, for liberating the Jews and restoring them to their independence, then it did at least happen that Cambyses, the successor of Cyrus, conquered Egypt. But it may also be noted that physical dominion is not promised to Israel in reference to the nations of the earth. Strange to say, Ezekiel (29:17-20) has a similar passage in which Egypt again is promised to Nebuchadnezzar for Tyre.

Verse 4. These totally unmerited favors that God is willing to bestow upon his people are now traced down to their deepest root — the love of God. For reasons that man will never be able fully to fathom, the Lord loved Israel: she was "precious in [his] eyes," she was also "honored" and he "loved" her. Our prophet is not the only one who knows of this remarkable love that God bears to his people (cf. Hos. 11:1; Jer. 31:20). It is this love that prompts the Lord's redeeming activity. Expanding the thought of v. 3, the prophet claims that God will "give men in [her] stead, peoples for [her] life." There is, as *Wright* says, something "highly metaphorical" about this statement, which forbids putting a "precise historical interpretation" on these words. But there is at the same time something of a divine mystery here involved. It lay entirely in the free choice of the Lord whether he would select one people to be his own in a distinct sense, preferring them to others, even, as here claimed, sacrificing others in their behalf. But Israel was given preferential treatment, even though she certainly did not merit it. This passage is one of the strongest statements on the mysterious subject of the election of Israel. But the dominant tone of it all is not speculation but solid divine comfort. As *Westermann* rightly remarks, in v. 2 the Creator, the Lord of the elements, speaks; in v. 3b-4b, the Lord of history.

Verse 5. Therefore the prophet goes on with strong words of reassurance. However, little Israel may have merited it, God's attitude is still: "Fear not for I am with you." His presence is enough to allay all fear. But translating the election into terms of restoration, it implies that he will gather her scattered remnants from all quarters of the globe. For here "descendants" does not refer to future offspring but to her present membership. Each of the cardinal points of the compass is expressly given orders to give back what has been scattered there in any form of captivity due to historical circumstances. Apparently many cases of deportation of captives of war from Israel had taken place of which we have no record even in the sacred Scriptures, as would appear from 11:11, and from the findings of archaeology (cf. the discovery of the one-time existence of a great colony of Jews in Elephantine on the Nile). The diaspora was quite widely spread already in Isaiah's day. This is now quite generally conceded.

Verse 6. In highly poetic terms these various areas are commanded to restore these captives to their native land. As special motivation mention is made of the fact that the persons involved are really God's "sons," or children, a point of view that found expression also in passages like Exod. 4:22, 23; Hos. 11:1; Isa. 1:2, etc. By specifying "sons" and "daughters" separately, the Hebrew language would cover the *totality* of the nation. However, it could hardly be asserted that the prophet actually expected these nations personally to escort Israelites back home.

Verse 7. Still the prophet cannot refrain from indicating to his own people how deeply concerned the Lord is about this restoration and how profound his love for them is, stating the case in rich and expressive terms that are calculated to make Israel aware of her rare prerogatives. So, for example, the chosen people may be described as being "called by [his] name." He is uniquely associated with them as with no other nation. Besides, they are "created for [his] glory." No ground here for nationalistic, chauvinistic pride. All this was undertaken by the Lord to display his glory in reference to Israel. Note the progression of the verbs used: created, formed, made. From his first contact with them to the last act that he does for making them to be what he has destined them to be, his divine activity centers about them historically. Here *Delitzsch* suggests that the three verbs involve the ideas of "produce, shape, finish." But the Lord's ultimate goal is his own glory, not Israel's, as has been correctly observed.

2. A Court Trial of the Idols (vv. 8-13)

43:8-13 8. Bring forth the people who are blind and yet have eyes,
who are deaf and yet have ears.
9. And all the nations have already gathered together,
and the peoples have assembled.
"Who among them can declare this,
and is able to show us former things?
Let them bring their witnesses to justify them,
and let them hear and say: "That's true!"
10. You are my witnesses, says the Lord,
and my servant whom I have chosen.
that you may know and believe me,
and that you may perceive that I am he.
Before me no god was formed,
neither shall there be any after me.
11. I, I am the Lord,
and apart from me there is no savior.
12. I declared and I saved and I let it be known,
and there was no strange god among you;
and [so] you are my witnesses, says the Lord,
and I [only] am God.
13. Also from henceforth I am he;
and there is none that can deliver out of my hands.
When I act, who can reverse it?"

The prophet has a special liking for presenting his material in the form of a "court trial." One whole chapter (41) used this approach. Here it appears again. But it should be noted that the tone of the passage is not that of calm, legal investigation, but rather one of passionate speech. The whole transaction may be conceived of as taking place in a court-room.

Verse 8. The author's particular concern is his own people. They are the ones who are to be brought into the court-room. They are a group who have long languished in a dungeon, where the light was exceedingly dim. Still the thought is that as such the Babylonian Captivity was not a season productive of repentance and deeper insights. As in 42:18 ff. there is reference here to a reprehensible blindness. The capacities that the nation has for grasping the truth offered, have not been utilized. Such persons will always be found everywhere. They were the object of deep concern on the part of our Lord, who, basing his call on words like those here used by the prophet, often exhorted men: "He that hath ears to hear, let him hear." But the summons, "Bring forth" in the present context involves the idea of bringing the nation into the court-trial which is about to take place. Verse 8 refers to the summoning of Israel; v. 9 to that of "the nations."

Verse 9. Where v. 8 set the scene, v. 9 now quickly advances to the second stage: All persons concerned are thought of as having been notified and as having given heed, and as being now "already gathered" and "assembled" for the impending transactions. At once the Lord launches into the case in hand. What he said is not formally introduced by some familiar statement such as, "The Lord said." The verse suddenly veers over into direct discourse with the words, "Who among them can declare this?" The investigation which is getting under way is reflecting on two areas, first "this" and then "former things." The first seems to refer to the present situation where a restoration is getting under way. The second has in mind past instances of foreknowing the future and controlling it. The pronoun "them" in the question "Who among them . . . ?" may refer to such persons as were found in practically all nations of antiquity, namely soothsayers, men who claimed ability in some way to foretell the future. In the two areas just named not a one of the heathen soothsayers ever produced anything at all. They are challenged if they have any witnesses anywhere who can produce proof that the future was forecast; they are given free rein to produce their proof now. Then they might be justified in claiming that they have occult power of some sort. Now is the time and the place. Those standing by will themselves be able to render the verdict in such an event and say: "That's true!" — Utter silence greets this challenge.

Verse 10. All rivals to the honor of being God having been eliminated, Yahweh now moves the trial on to its proper conclusion. "Witnesses" for the opposition could not be found. Yahweh has such available — his own people. In fact that is in a sense their very destiny. Israel is not to be a mighty worldly power dominating other nations and exercising world-empire. She is to be witness to what God has done for her, witness by her very existence and witness by the testimony that she can bear orally. By thus witnessing she fulfils her calling of being God's "servant," whom he has chosen. First of all she must come to the overpowering conviction that Yahweh is the one that alone deserves to be called God. Monotheism is Israel's most precious insight. Whatever indications along this line had begun to glimmer here and there in divine revelation, all this now comes to clear expression and is finalized by our prophet. When he claims — letting the Lord speak the words — that no god was formed before him, he is not conceding that gods can be "formed." He is using about the only verb that can be used in a context like this. Before him no other god ever existed. None will ever spring into being in times to come.

Verse 11. Or, formulated very precisely, "I, I am the Lord." But this is not a barren monotheism, predicating sole existence of Yahweh. This is all extremely practical, one

might say existential. For the rest of the statement is: "apart
from me there is no savior." He is a God who acts. The
consistent purpose of his mighty acts bears testimony to his
essential unity.

Verse 12. Now the prophet is back on a favorite subject
of his — the foretelling and execution of the restoration of
his chosen people. He (God) saw it coming; he made it
come to pass. "I declared and I saved and I let it be known"
refers just to this issue alone. This constitutes overwhelming
proof of his being. None could share in this honor: "There
was no strange God among you." The approach is the same
as in 45:5 f., 18, 22. There is not and there cannot be a god
who shares even the least bit of the honor of the work done
in behalf of Israel. And Israel knows this. So the author
brings the matter to a conclusion: "And [so] you are my
witnesses, and I [only] am your God. The words we have inserted in brackets are not expressed in the text but they represent the manner in which the case would be formulated
in our day and language. Strangely the prophet does not
quite say, "There is but one God." But he implies it. In a
sense he says more than such a claim. He says: "I am he."
In these verses (11-13) as *Muilenburg* has observed, there are
twenty-nine words, twelve of which are in the first person.

Verse 13. Thus far the eyes were directed primarily to the
past, to things accomplished. There comes a brief glance into
the future: "Also from henceforth I am he." Gods cannot
spring into being. *He* always was. But this again is not pure
theory but the substance of Israel's experience. For "there is
none that can deliver out of [his] hands." As he has sole
existence so he has sole power. Therefore "When I act who
can reverse it" (cf. also Amos 1:3, 6, 9, 11, 13, etc.). How
strongly all this stands contrasted with what the heathen
believed, appears from the fact that rank and power among
the gods of the heathen was continually in flux. As has
been remarked, in Egypt Amon replaced Re; in Babylon,
Marduk replaced Bel, etc.

3.　The Captivity of the Chaldeans (vv. 14-15)

43:14-15 14. Thus says the Lord, your Redeemer, the Holy
One of Israel;
"For your sake I will send to Babylon,
　and I will bring low as captives all of them,
　namely the Chaldeans, in the ships of which they were so proud;
15. I, the Lord, your Holy One,
　the Creator of Israel, your King."

In the court-trial of the idols (vv. 8-13) a note that had
stood out prominently was the summary and description of
the great things God had done in behalf of, and in control of,
his people. By way of contrast a brief section now follows,
in which the Lord indicates how he can, and does, control the
fortunes of other nations, even mighty Babylon.

Verse 14. This brief oracle is full of difficulties. We shall
briefly set forth how it may be construed, and briefly sub-
stantiate our interpretation. One writer has labelled it "Babylon in Panic" (*North*). This approach summarizes our understanding of the passage. Solemn introduction is made to
the passage by familiar formulas and names: "Thus says the
Lord, your Redeemer, the Holy One of Israel." This last
title does not stress the metaphysical attribute of holiness,
but marks God's "ethical activity."

But when the oracle that follows is introduced by the
phrase "for your sake," it should be noted that in the view of
the prophets the big movements of history center around
God's people and take place, under divine control with the
purpose of furthering God's designs in reference to his own.
The somewhat vague statement, "I will send to Babylon,"
involves perhaps the sending of Cyrus, who became the conqueror of Babylon. Not the instrument but the control of
history is stressed by this form of statement. That all the
Babylonians will be involved in what God does is indicated
by the statement, "I will bring low as captives all of them."
The verb used is usually translated "I will bring down."
"Bring low" seems to cover the issue more adequately.
These Babylonians are in the parallel statement described ac-

cording to the older geographical designation "Chaldeans." The point seems to be that when the city falls, sooner or later, Babylonian captives will be transported away on ships, on the very ships "of which they were so extremely proud." Literally this last statement reads "on the ships of their exultation." Babylon, on the Euphrates, controlled a tremendous world-trade. For this many ships were used. Any nation would be proud of its merchant marine. But there is a strange irony about having the objects of their pride become the means of their grief.

Verse 15. In concluding this brief oracle, the Lord uses a very solemn identification of himself, as the one who does all these things for the good of his people. He created them; he still is their "King." Though now in Captivity, Israel is still not without a king, and her King will assert his effective rule of his people.

Practically all interpretations of this passage portray, in one form or another, the defeat of the Chaldeans, the great super-power that had dominated a good part of history so successfully in the days of Isaiah and thereafter. *RSV* arrives at a feasible interpretation, largely by extensive textual emendations (always a somewhat dubious procedure) on the basis of too much confidence in the versions.

4. The Remarkable Exodus (vv. 16-21)

43:16-21 16. Thus says the Lord, he that made a way in the sea,
    and a path in the mighty waters,
17. he that brought forth chariots and horses,
    an army and warriors together, —
there they lie and can't get up,
    they are extinguished, they are put out like a wick:
18. "Remember not former things;
do not consider things long past.
19. Lo, I am about to do a new thing;
now it is already springing up; haven't you noticed it?
    I am also making a way in the wilderness,
        and streams in the desert.
20. The wild beasts shall honor me, the jackals and the ostriches;

for I give water in the wilderness,
   and streams in the desert,
to give drink to my people, my chosen ones;
21. a people whom I have formed for myself shall declare my
   praise."

Verse 16. It may be that *North's* caption is even better
than ours for this section — "Wonders of the New Exodus."
The old national traditions of his people live strong in the
remembrance of this prophet. "He that made a way in the
sea" reminds at once of the happenings that took place in the
days of Moses at the Red Sea. The parallel statement indicates what a remarkable work this was, for it actually involved the parting of "mighty waters" even though an area
was involved where the waters were comparatively shallow,
yet with a sudden change of the wind they may become the
equivalent of a mad tide. "Mighty waters" is no "exaggeration."

Verse 17. More of the ancient story is recalled. A turn is,
however, given to the thought which goes deeper than the
familiar historical account. The bringing forth of chariots
and horses, armies and warriors is attributed to *Yahweh*,
even as in Ezek. 38:4 it is *he* who leads the armies of God.
All this is merely a drastic way of saying that even the most
hostile forces that rage "against the Lord and against his
anointed" are still only doing the behest of the One True
God. That does not mean that Pharaoh, in sending forth his
chariots, was not a free agent. But it does mean that the in-
comprehensible God, who controls all things, was manifest-
ing his mysterious control even when the Egyptians went
out with hostile intention. Yahweh was leading them to their
doom. For "army and warriors together" *North* suggests
"armies in mass formation." By a sudden change of the
Hebrew tense (?) we are introduced into the very midst of
the developing situation: without any agent apparently having been at work, the hosts lie low: "There they lie and can't
get up." Then by another sudden change of the Hebrew to
the perfect, marking the abruptness of the action, the whole

episode is over, done, finished: "They are extinguished, they are put out like a wick," even as Exod. 14 so dramatically pictures the incident.

Verse 18. The next step in the prophet's thinking is almost the very opposite of what we might have expected. He says not: "Remember," He says: "Remember *not* former things." Extreme forms of statement must always be regarded with due caution. In 46:9 Israel is bidden to "remember the former things." So the present statement must be meant in the sense of letting the memory linger on the events of the past, of dwelling nostalgically on what happened in the good old days. So the thought is this: Let the grand past be over-topped by the more glorious future. Cultivate hope, not re-membrance. The "new thing" that is to be eagerly antici-pated is the impending exodus from Babylon.

Verse 19. It is on the verge of happening. Alert minds can already discern traces of its coming: "It is already spring-ing up." Indications of its coming must already have been discernible. Israel could be challenged: "Haven't you noticed it?" Now comes the statement of what the prophet had in mind: "I am also making a way in the wilderness, and streams in the desert," for those returning from Captivity. Once it was a way through the waters; now it is a way through seemingly impassable dry, desert land. Then he re-moved the water; now he will furnish it.

Verse 20. But for this prophet, the area of grace and the area of what we call nature is a unit. Even the wild beasts have an interest and a share in what happens to God's people. It will make them glad to behold what God does for them, so glad that they, in their own way "will honor" him, even "jackals and ostriches" — creatures notoriously shy and un-friendly. The language is rhetorically rich and colorful: "I give water in the wilderness and streams in the desert, to give drink to my people, my chosen ones." Streams may never, in the course of this exodus have sprung up miraculously; but Israel never lacked for what was necessary for her subsis-tence during the return from Exile. In reality these statements cover the entire sweep of God's gracious dealings with his own for all times. They are truly eschatological in their scope.

Verse 21. God's people shall acknowledge the greatness of his works in their behalf. The future has mighty things in store according to the rich plans of the Lord.

5. Israel's Guilt — Yahweh's Grace (vv. 22-28)

43:22-28 22. "Yet you, O Jacob, did not call upon me;
but you have been weary of me, O Israel.
23. You have not brought me a sheep for a burnt offering,
nor have you honored me with your sacrifices.
I have not burdened you with offerings,
nor wearied you with [the demand of] frankincense.
24. You have not bought me sweet cane with money,
nor sated me with the fat of your sacrifices;
but you have burdened me with your sins,
and wearied me with your iniquities.
25. I, I am he who blots out your transgressions for my sake,
and will not remember your sins any more.
26. Remind me, and let us argue it out together;
you declare your case that you may be proved right.
27. Your first father [already] sinned,
and your mediators transgressed against me.
28. Therefore I profaned the princes of the sanctuary,
and gave up Jacob to utter destruction, and Israel to scorn."

How does this section (vv. 22-28) stand related to the one that preceded (vv. 16-21)? The connection is traced in so many words, but apparently the pattern: effect — cause, is in evidence. The effect, the new exodus, has just been emphasized. Now that which is *not* the cause is being reflected upon. There are times when the people of God are exceedingly prone to attribute favorable developments within the kingdom to some measure of worthiness or desert on their part. The prophet may have sensed something of that spirit among those to whom his message was being transmitted. Since such an attitude tends to the corruption of faith and is full of spiritual dangers of all sorts, he promptly launches into an invective (*Gerichtsrede*, like 50:1-3 — *Westermann*) which is strangely followed by a sweet declaration of divine grace (v. 25). We say "strangely" because grace is not the logical answer to a sharp denunciation. But God's grace so far transcends human logic that we shall never be able to grasp its full magnitude.

Verse 22. What follows is not a rejection of formal worship or a repudiation of the sacrifices of Israel, any more than is the case in Jer. 7:21-23; or Amos 5:21-25; or Isa. 29:13. But it is certainly a repudiation of the type of soulless worship that prevailed in those days. Priest and prophet were not pitted against one another in sharp antithesis, as they are so frequently represented to have been.

The first count on which Israel is indicted is worthless prayer; for prayer may rightly be regarded as the soul of all true worship. Prayers were no doubt made publicly and privately; but they did not amount to a calling upon the Lord. They must have had something of the spirit of the Pharisee who went up into the temple to pray, according to Luke 18. That such was the case is indicated clearly enough by the parallel statement of this verse: "But you have been weary of me." The performance of the rite of prayer proved a boring thing. If that be the case, then nothing that follows as part of the rites of worship can have any validity.

Verse 23. They may have offered sheep, but they did not sincerely bring them to the Lord. So the words appear to be construed: "You have not brought *me* a sheep." Or the matter might be regarded from this angle: The true spirit that should have motivated "a burnt offering," was noticeably lacking. So also the next statement is to be construed: "You have not honored me with your sacrifices." Of course, it must also be remembered that Israel in captivity could not meet the requirements of the cultus because the temple was destroyed and the priests were scattered. But that is not a major consideration of the prophet here. Apparently an attitude is being described which prevailed abundantly already while the temple still stood and has not been remedied since. God's side of the matter is covered by the second half of the verse. This appears at first reading as a repudiation of all that the law of Moses ascribed to divine appointment in the days after the Exodus from Egypt. But since such a flagrant contradiction within the sacred Scriptures is hardly reasonable, apparently the statements are meant in the sense that the Lord did not require these ceremonial acts as mere outward performances devoid of soul and sincerity. God certainly had not made what would be burdensome demands of "offerings." What God had appointed, the true worshipper would present, not as a heavy duty but as a meaningful outlet of deep emotion and inner need. So the offering of frankincense could be either a dead chore or a spiritual experience, depending on the attitude of the heart of the worshipper.

Verse 24. The "sweet cane" referred to was a part of the sacred anointing oil that is described in Exod. 30:23. How it was assigned to some form of use in the cultus otherwise, we do not know. In any case it was a rare article that was used by some in cultic practices. It may have constituted a special part of an act of devotion resorted to by some of the Israelites and may have been part of a very special observance. It could be meaningful. Here the prophet rebukes his people for not having ventured to do anything special of this sort for their Lord. And since the "fat of sacrifices" was regarded as a choice gift specially devoted to the Lord, Israel is here charged with not having ventured to do any such special act in a spirit of deeper devotion.

Summing up at this point for the moment, we must emphasize that we reject as totally unwarranted the contention of *Volz* that the prophet did not regard the prevailing laws regarding sacrifice as divinely appointed. God had, in other words, given no appointments about sacrificial rites. But we do regard the remarks of *Fischer* as entirely proper — "This is by no means a total rejection of sacrifices." Even more to the point is *Skinner's* statement: "This hardly amounts to a repudiation of sacrifice *in principle* on the part of Jehovah." This approach would be further well expressed by *North,* when he suggests as translation for v. 22 the following: "Do not imagine that it was me you invited to your feasting."

The second half of v. 24 shows what their sacrifice in those days actually amounted to. Taking the words from v. 23, the writer suggests that "burdening" was done, but it was Israel who did it to the Lord with their sins. So also some "wearying" was done, but again it was Israel wearying the Lord "with their iniquities." What could have been a delight and a helpful sacramental experience, instead became something offensive to God as well as harmful to man.

Verse 25. At this point the turn of thought comes very abruptly. Here, if ever, the invective could have been followed by a word of threat. Instead there follows one of the most gracious promises of the whole book. With heavy emphasis on the "I" as the author of this grace, the word says in effect: I, the very one whom you offended; I who have just cause to vent my anger on you to the full; I am the one who blots out the very transgressions that have so wearied and offended me. God, as *Delitzsch* rightly asserts, is the one who here proclaims the *sola gratia* (by grace alone) and the *sola fide* (through faith alone). That the motivation and the whole approach rests solely with him and not on any merit or worthiness on the nation's part is contained in the "for my sake." Another of the standard expressions for forgiving is set forth in the parallel statement: "I will not remember your sins any more." Under the circumstances it is true that the statement totally passes by for the moment the need of expiation or the method of it. It is not the prophet's intention to offer the total theology of redemption. But he is the strongest exponent of justification by faith found in the Old Testament, and here fully vindicates his right to that title.

Verse 26. Having for the moment relieved the tension by the assurance of divine grace, the prophet drives home still more fully the point of Israel's grave guilt. He does it by the use of the means of a court-trial again. For that is what the words, "let us argue it out together" clearly imply. Half ironic comes the introductory summons, "Remind me."

That apparently means nothing more here than: You shall have a fair hearing; no evidence shall be suppressed. In that spirit the words are added, "You declare your case that you may be proved right." From the sequel it appears that in the face of this challenge Israel never even ventured a word of excuse. Total silence testified to total guiltiness.

Verse 27. Here Yahweh charges that their "first father" already was a guilty man, stained by major sins. We do best to regard this as a reference to Jacob (not to Adam — who lies too far in the past; not to Abraham — who was also the father of Arabs and Edomites; not to David — to whom a title like "first father" scarcely applies). But Jacob who secured the birth-right by subterfuge and did other deeds of questionable character, is truly the father of this people who have been guilty of double dealing with God throughout their history. When we come to the second statement, "Your mediators transgressed against me," a number of reasonable possibilities confront us. The "mediators" could be priests or prophets (cf. 28:7); or "kings and prophets (*North*); or Moses and Aaron (cf. Num. 20:12). Israel often stood in need of mediation. Her "mediators" were almost as fallible as the nation they represented. They almost may be said to have led the way for the nation in disobedience. In the face of such indictments, the people could hardly have an easy conscience about the way they had treated their God. They could hardly take forgiveness lightly just because God was so gracious. As has often been remarked: here too "free grace is not cheap grace."

Verse 28. That God did not take their sin lightly is driven home more effectively by a reference to the recent experience of the capture of Jerusalem, the destruction of the temple, and the dragging of the nation into Captivity. For the "profaning of the princes of the sanctuary" may refer to acts like II Kings 25:18-21, where the execution of priests is expressly mentioned. That "Jacob was given to utter destruction" most likely is a reference to the Captivity as such.

So too, "the giving of Israel to scorn," or "to reviling" (*RSV*).

Notes

Verse 1. Both "I have redeemed" and "I have called" are to be regarded as prophetic perfects.

Verse 4. The singular "man" and the plural "peoples" both together constitute one of those pairs that aim to cover the entire scope of a certain concept. Cf. *KS* 94. This approach makes it unnecessary to attempt any textual changes (like *'adhamoth* for *'adham*).

Verse 6. "Sons" and "daughters" again is a means for expressing totality of a given concept. Cf. *GK* 122 v.

Verse 8. *Volz* decrees, we believe rather arbitrarily, that v. 8 must be dropped. But if viewed, as set forth above, as referring to Israel and v. 9 as referring to the nations, the two approaches make very good sense together. The initial word *hotsi'* is most commonly regarded as an imperative, which is made possible by a vowel change — *hotse'*. Cf. *GK* 53 m.

Verse 9. The verb *niqbetsu* need not be changed into an imperative form. It may be regarded as a future perfect "will have already assembled themselves," as *KS* 172 a, points out. This approach ties up well with the further suggestion that before *kol* a *waw* may have fallen out through haplography. That could serve as further indication how the two verses belong together.

Verse 10. Before *tha'aminu* the customary *waw* conversive with perfects is not used because the two verbs are synonymns.

Verse 14. When *Muilenburg* takes the material from this verse on to 44:5 and arranges it as belonging into seven strophies, "of approximately the same length," this strikes us as too highly artificial. Certain broader thought patterns are lost by such an arrangement.

On this difficult verse *North* suggests the emendation "drive the Chaldeans downstream" — at least a possible translation for *horadhti*. *Volz* relates *rinnatham* to the "noisy bustle" at the wharves (*Weltgetuemmel*).

Verse 16. *Nothen*, the participle, stands in a past context, and so must be translated "made," as *KS* 237a shows.

Verse 17. The perfects *da'achu* and *kabhu* are used to indicate the abruptness of the event they describe (*KS* 119).

Verse 20. For "jackals and ostriches" — at best a questionable translation — *North* suggests "wolves and owls."

Verse 21. V. 21 does not appeal to the taste of some commentators and so they eliminate it. Such purely subjective criteria of judgment are inadequate.

Verse 24. The *be* before *keseph* is the *be* or price (*GK* 119 p).

The verb *he'bhadhtanni* literally means, "you have made me your servant."

Verse 25. The "any more" at the end of the verse appears in the Isaiah (I) scroll of Qumran as *'odh* and seems to be very much in place. For some the entire verse does not appear sharp enough in a context of rebuke. But in Isaiah this often is the case. Therefore the verse need not be regarded as a later addition.

Verse 28. The word for "scorn" (*gidduphim*) appears in the plural — an intensive plural — like "to much scorn." Cf. *GK* 124 e.

Chapter XLIV:1-23

E. THE GOD OF GRACE VS. THE IMPOTENT IDOLS (Chap. 44:1-23)

The preceding chapter had closed with a strong word of rebuke (*Scheltrede*). But in this rebuke was imbedded one verse that indicated that this rebuke was not God's last word to his people, namely v. 25. The note struck in that verse is now taken up in our chapter and developed more at length in sharp contrast to the preceding rebuke. This creates the impression that rebuke and promise are inextricably intertwined, if not dovetailed together in a rather surprising turn of thought.

But this approach does not yet indicate the character of the chapter as a whole, which is a sharp contrast between two widely divergent concepts of God, or gods. For the true concept of who and what God is, as Israel held the faith concerning him, and the view held by the typical non-Israelite of that day, the idolater, are presented in the sharpest contrast that could possibly be depicted, as our above caption sets forth: The God of (effective) grace vs. the impotent idols.

We may pause for a moment at this point to indicate the pattern of this chapter as form-criticism sees it. In this type of approach vv. 1-5 constitute a salvation oracle; vv. 6-8 constitute an oracle of judgment; vv. 9-20 is excised and treated separately, as a passage that does not have its setting in this chapter originally; vv. 21-22 constitute an oracle of admonition (*Mahnrede*); v. 23 is a hymn. Leaving aside the problem of vv. 9-20, the rest of this approach gives the reader a feel of the nature of the chapter as a whole.

Centering again on vv. 9-20 for the moment it may be noted how *G. A. Smith* evaluates this section in particular.

He uses terminology that at least effectively catches the unique character of this passage, when he says: "A burst of laughter comes very weirdly out of exile." Though it may be sharp satire rather than "laughter," still one is made to feel the uniqueness of the passage. While engaged in evaluating this large sector of the chapter we may also now already take note of the fact that, as the same writer says, the style is not as smooth as the *KJ* version makes it. It does indeed have some irregularities about it. Many find it difficult to determine whether this piece is to be classified as prose or as poetry. *RSV* prints it as prose. Some measure of parallelism is no doubt to be detected throughout. Nevertheless we cannot help but feel that the grounds for denying this section to the author of the rest of the chapter are none too solid.

1. The Blessing of the Spirit to Be Poured on the Unworthy

44:1-5 1. But now hear, O Jacob my servant,
and Israel whom I have chosen!
2. Thus says Yahweh, who made you,
who formed you from the womb, who will help you:
"Fear not, my servant Jacob,
Jeshurun, whom I have chosen;
3. For as I pour out water on the thirsty land
and copious rains on the dry land,
so I will pour out my spirit on your descendants
and my blessing on your offspring.
4. And they shall spring up in the midst of grass,
as willows by the streams of water.
5. This one will say, 'I belong to the Lord,'
and another will call himself by the name of Jacob;
and still another will write on his hand, 'I am the Lord's'
and shall surname himself by the name of Israel."

Verse 1. The "but now" sets this new section off sharply from what preceded. "Jacob" and "Israel," being used together, in parallel lines seem to signify, as elsewhere, the entire nation. The lamentable division of the days of Jeroboam I, will be a thing of the past. Israel's role as God's "servant" is again stressed. The fact as such is held parallel to the fact that God has freely chosen this people as his own. Again and again God's choice of the nation as his people is the foundation of his further kindly dealings with them.

Verse 2. Other favors included in the original choice are brought to the fore. For one thing God "made" them to be what they are, the only nation enjoying this unique distinction. Or to stress still further God's favors, he may be said to have "formed [them] from the womb," which here means from the very beginning of their national existence. Therefore it follows freely that he will "help" them whenever help is needed. It may well have been that in the days of the captivity many a "fear" assailed the hearts of the godly in Israel whether they still had any future whatever to look forward to. Therefore the kindly assurance: "Fear not, my servant Jacob." In the parallel statement Israel is now addressed as "Jeshurun," a name which already appears in Deut. 32:15; 33:5, 26. It appears to be related to the name Israel, but no one seems to know just how. The idea that it is a tender diminutive has now generally been abandoned. It could be traced back to the root meaning "righteous," and then might be designed to describe the nation as righteous in God's sight rather than the "conniver" which is the root meaning of the name Jacob. But all this is dubious. At least it must be classed as a term of endearment. To it is added a second reference to God's free choice of the people.

Verse 3. Now comes the issue toward which this elaborate introduction has been leading. We follow the approach of those interpreters who see the first half of the verse as correlated to the second (as — so). One thing God is known to do the world over: he provides water and rain for the thirsty land and more often than not, does this work of his in a very generous fashion; he "pours out water." So in days to come (here indicated by the terms "descendeants" and "offspring") he will "pour out [his] Spirit." The divine power that created physical life will also be the source of spiritual life. For Spirit here, as so frequently, connotes the acme of divine power. This gift is also described as being a "blessing" which term again signifies an effective form of divine enrichment. The prophet had previously expressed a similar thought in 32:15 (cf. also Ps. 104:30). Ezekiel 37 also stands related to this approach. Again we recall in this connection that in the background some emphasis lies on the fact that a gift such as this to be bestowed upon the unworthy nation was a gift of free grace.

Verse 4. Rounding out the figure employed, the prophet now indicates that as a result of God's abundant outpouring of water a tree is to spring up, and the tree is Israel. More is meant than the mere fact that the growth involved merely germinates. It is implied that it will continue to grow and prosper. The fact that it is to spring up "in the midst of grass," would seem to imply that it stands in an area rich in other vegetation, which also thrives because of abundant water. In all this approach, though we recognize the figure of a tree, it may still be said appropriately "they [plural] shall spring up," because the tree idea covers the multitude of the members of the nation. Thus far the idea seems to limit itself to the nation Israel. *It* shall again grow and thrive and flourish and be a mighty tree.

Verse 5. Now the emphasis changes and the thought is stressed that outsiders shall take pride in becoming affiliated with this ancient and marvelous people on whom God's blessing rests in such abundant measure. The term "Israel" takes on new dimensions. It is no longer limited to the purely national; it takes on possibilities of an expanded concept of, shall we say, the congregational. It blossoms out into the super-racial. Several examples are given. One man will say: "I belong to the Lord," that is to say, to Yahweh, who was once regarded as the national God of *Israel* and no more. Now he will take pride in being under the authority of this God, whom he no doubt recognizes as being beyond such limitations. Another person will feel honored to be identified with the ancestor of the nation, Jacob. Still another will even "write on his hand, 'I am the Lord's.'" This could mean that he tatoos Yahweh's name on his hand that he may carry it before his eyes and see it continually as a reminder of his allegiance to the God of Israel. The fact that tatooing was forbidden in the Mosaic law (see Lev. 19:28; 21:5) was connected with the fact that this practice was associated with idolatry. But here it is regarded as the very antithesis to such a connotation. Even a fourth possibility is suggested: a man may "surname himself by the name of Israel." In addition to his native name, a man shall give himself the surname "Israel" as indicative of the highest honor that any name can bestow.

2. Redemption Guaranteed by Yahweh, the Only God Who Can Foretell (vv. 6-8)

44:6-8 6. Thus says the Lord, the King of Israel
and his Redeemer, the Lord of hosts:
"I am the first and I am the last
and apart from me there is no god.
7. And who is like me? Let him proclaim it;
let him tell it, and set forth before me what has happened
from the time when I set up nations in days of old.
Let them tell us what is yet to be.
8. Be not afraid nor perplexed.
Have I not told you from of old and declared it?
And you are my witnesses! Is there a god apart from me?
There is no Rock; I know none."

The emphasis now lies on the fact that the God of Israel in anything but one of the impotent idols. He works by grace but it is effective grace. And so the redemption that is held forth in prospect for God's people is a thing that will be definitely achieved. So a word is given from the mouth of the Almighty that sets forth this thought effectively.

Verse 6. The formula introducing this word from the mouth of the Lord first centers attention on three titles that fitly apply to him. He is first of all "King," one who administers affairs efficiently. But above all — here comes a favorite title — he is the "Lord of hosts," the one who has the entire host of things always under total control. When such a one speaks he merits attention. What he says will assuredly come to pass. All this adds up again to the claim that he is the only one deserving of the name God — monotheism. The same approach was used in 41:21-29 and 43:9-13. When he claims that he is "the first and . . . the last" he represents himself as functioning throughout the entire course of history. He was on the scene when things began to be made. He will still be on the scene when the stage of history is cleared for the last time. The same statement appears also in Rev. 1:8, 17 and 22:13. All of which amounts to the claim that "apart from [him] there is no god."

Verse 7. This involves not only his exclusiveness but also his being totally other than the rest of those who are called gods. This verse would seem to be a challenge addressed to the so-called gods. They are invited to a court-trial again. If any one of their number is in any sense like him, let such a one stand forth and say so, and tell it. The one area in which this test can prove decisive is the ability of these who are challenged "to set forth . . . what has happened," that is to say, give instances where a coming event was predicted and then came the fulfillment of the prediction. Perhaps God, the challenger, has in mind cases like the foretelling of the Flood in the days of Noah, an event which indubitably came to pass just as it was foretold. We go back as far as this because rather remote time seems to be under consideration, as the somewhat difficult statement indicates: "from the time when I set up nations in days of old." But here again Yahweh is in a class by himself, just as he is distinct from all others in that he can tell "what is yet to be" in reference to the things that lie in the future. The Lord keeps making this point because the proof employed is distinctive and powerful.

Verse 8. Now comes the practical application of all this. If these claims of the Holy One be true then there is no ground for fear or perplexity. For even though the heathen gods look very impressive in the light of their massive temples, their splendid processions, their costly images, their rich ceremonial worship, the apparent success of the arms of their worshippers, all this is nothing more than a fleeting shadow when subjected to the test of time. God keeps reiterating that *he* told and declared things from of old and of that Israel in its long and impressive history is witness, a history that allows for only one conclusion: There is no god "apart from [him]." Or to phrase it all in terms hallowed from days of old: "There is no rock." He knows of none, and his knowledge is more comprehensive than theirs. (On "rock" cf. 26: 4; Deut. 32:31; it is a term used 33 times in reference to God in the Old Testament).

3. Idolatry, Empty Folly (vv. 9-11)

44:9-11 9. The makers of idols are all of them numskulls,
and their darlings [the idols] are useless;
and their witnesses neither see nor understand.
So they must be ashamed.
10. Whoever has formed a god,
well, he has cast an image to no avail.
11. And behold, all who are attached to them, will be ashamed,
and the workmen, they are but human beings.
Let them all assemble, let them step forth;
they shall be terrified and put to shame together.

In addition to what was said before on this section a few remarks are in order. Very much to the point is *North's* description: "the stupidity of idolatry." Furthermore the fact that vv. 9-20 may be omitted and then v. 21 will follow readily after v. 8 and make good sequence, that claim, we say, proves nothing. For any writer may interrupt a line of argument for a momentary digression, then continue with his former line of thought. What the critical claim says in effect is: Writers dare not make digressions. The sequence going from v. 8 to v. 9 is also readily seen to be a good and coherent one. If the subject under consideration had been "Redemption guaranteed," obviously v. 9 brings in a contrast: The useless idols could not work any redemption.

In approaching this section it should be noted, as again *North* has well said: "The Old Testament knows nothing of the distinction between an idol in which the god is supposed to reside . . . and the symbol." In other words, the Old Testament writers identify the image with the idol. For in practice that is the way the matter works out. The philosopher's reflections together with those of the historian on the subject were not to be found among the people at large. So the same approach prevails in each of the passages that satirize idolatry (cf. 40:19, 20; 41:6, 7, 29; 45:16; 46:5-7).

Verse 9. It must be borne in mind that it took courage in the face of strongly intrenched idolatry to make remarks such as are about to be examined. Idolatry seemed the very embodiment of success. Now comes the prophet and says the idol-makers are "numskulls." He goes farther: "Their darlings," i.e., the very idols themselves, are "useless." All who are addicted to idolatry (for they are the ones meant by the name "their witnesses,") "neither see nor understand." "So they must be ashamed" as is now historically the case virtually with all idolaters the world over. Idolatry stands discredited as utter folly.

Verse 10. Aside from the senselessness of the practice of it all there is the complete futility of it. This the prophet sums up in the claim that all who have made images have done something that was done "to no avail." No idol ever did anything.

Verse 11. He sees the day coming when all devotees of the idols will be ashamed. So will the workmen and all who commission them to produce an idol. For the workmen are "but human beings." But water cannot rise above its level. So the human cannot produce the divine. If a test case were to be made of it and all who had ever made idols were to assemble as one unit group and were to try to step forth in support of what they had produced, they could furnish nothing by way of upholding their bold claims about what they manufacture; they would all "be terrified and put to shame together." The whole crew of them would have been engaged in a totally futile project.

4. A Satirical Description of the Manufacture of Idols (vv. 12-17)

44:12-17 12. The ironsmith [makes] an axe and works it over
the coals;
with the hammer he shapes it,
and works it over with his strong right arm.
Then he grows hungry and has no strength left;
he drinks no water and is faint.
13. The carpenter stretches the measuring-line over it,
then shapes it up with a pencil.
He works with a scraping-tool and shapes it up with a compass.
He makes it to be like the figure of a man,
with all the beauty of a man —
to take its place in a dwelling.
14. He went out and cut down cedars for himself,
or he took a holm-tree or an oak,
and lets it become sturdy among the trees of the forest.
Or he even planted a fir and the rain nourished it.
15. Then it serves as fuel for a man.
Namely he takes some of it and warms himself;
he kindles a fire and bakes bread;
also he makes a god and worships it;
he makes an image for himself and falls down before it.
16. A part of it he burns in the fire
and over another part of it he eats flesh.
He prepares a roast and satisfies his hunger.
He also warms himself and says:
"Aha! I am warm; I feel the warm glow."
17. And the rest of it he makes into a god, his idol.
He falls down before it and worships it,
and he says: "Deliver me, for you are my god!"

In expounding this passage we are beset by two major difficulties. One, the names of the tools and implements used
by craftsmen in days of old are not very familiar to us. Two,
the writer does not follow through on the process of manufacture of the idol in strict sequence, but reaches back, it
seems, to a certain point; then reaches back even farther;
then even farther still. He reverses the procedure that we
would have been inclined to pursue. We may indicate at this
point that at least in the Apocrypha (Wisdom 13:11 ff.) a
fairly close parallel to this account is to be found.

Verse 12. Two types of craftsmen are depicted in their
respective activities — "the ironsmith" and (v. 13) "the carpenter." This is due to the fact that images, as has been long

understood by now, in days of old were so constructed as to consist of a metal plating over a wood framework. So a kind of cooperation between the two types of craftsmen is taken for granted in this description. We are not even sure of the meaning of the term we have translated as "axe." The point of the writer seems to be that even the necessary tools used in the process have to be manufactured before the task can be taken in hand. But even that part of the assignment makes the smith to grow weary with hunger and faint with thirst. So the basis of it all is clumsy tools and weak workmen. They are the source from which an idol springs.

Verse 13. Now it is as though the prophet says: Let us examine how the carpenter goes about his task. The measuring-line is stretched. Whether the idol has an inch or two more of height depends on that measuring line. His general shape depends on the "pencil" used. Lack of skill in this direction could result in a disfigured god. Then the carpenter works with a "scraping-tool" — perhaps a plane; and uses the "compass" to round out perhaps the shape of the head. Always in the back of the craftman's mind is the "image of a man," and not just any man, but one who has some measure of "beauty" or attractiveness. And in the process of all this work from time to time the workman already envisions the finished product occupying its place "in a dwelling," or a shrine. We failed to take note of the possibility that the carpenter may have had as basis for the entire model a solid tree trunk, rather than a light frame of wood.

Verse 14. Now the investigation into the procedure involved is pushed back a little farther, into the time when the idol to be was still in the tree-state, and the tree had not yet been cut down. Then the woodsman may have started out with several trees, "cedars" perhaps, intending after they were cut down to decide which would be best suited for his purpose. It might have been "a holm-tree or an oak," that was cut down, but even there some deliberation was involved. These last two mentioned may have been good prospects but were not quite tall enough. So they had to be nursed along for a while till they became "sturdy among the trees of the forest." So much were these idols creatures of chance; they could have turned out quite a bit different from what actually resulted in the end. To such an extent are the idols victims of circumstance. They do not control circumstance. Circumstance controls them. Or for that matter, the craftsman may even have supervised the process of selection back from the point where he even "planted a fir and the rain nourished it." The whole destiny of the idol was at each of these junctures hanging in the balance.

Verse 15. Now a number of possible uses to which the wood that made the body of the idol *might* have been put, and always it might have been the idol that was put to such uses. It could have been, as parts of it certainly were, used "as fuel for a man." The craftsman did actually use some of this same wood for kindling "a fire and [baking] bread," Such purely utilitarian uses! But the sentence goes on in one breath: "also he makes a god and worships it." It's all in a day's work, this manufacture of idols. Just to repeat: "he makes an image for himself and falls down before it." It's such a senseless thing to fall down before that which is the work of his hands, achieved with so much toil and trouble.

Verse 16. The particular point to be made is spelled out so that it may by no means be overlooked. Note the various uses to which "a part" of the wood has been put. It need not always be the same pattern. Not all men would necessarily do according to the letter of what is here outlined. But the uses involved could include: burning some in the fire; eating flesh over some of it; preparing roast over another portion; satisfying his hunger; warming himself, and expressing his satisfaction at having taken the chill out of his bones.

Verse 17. Now comes what to him was the climax: "the rest of it he makes into a god, his idol." Really that is a ludicrous anticlimax. The writer repeats, as much as to say: "He *actually* falls down before it and worships it." His prayer and confession follow: "Deliver me, for you are my god!"

5. The Idle Folly of Idolatry (vv. 18-20)

44:18-20 18. They still have not known and have not understood;

for their eyes have been smeared shut so that they cannot see,
and their minds so that they cannot understand.
19. No one gives the matter any thought,
nor has any one knowledge or insight enough to say:
"Half of it I burned in the fire,
    and I also baked bread on its coals;
    I am now roasting flesh and eating it;
and shall I now make the rest of it an abominable idol,
and shall I fall down before a block of wood?"
20. If a man feeds on ashes,
    a mind that has been deceived has led him astray,
and he cannot deliver himself,
    or say: "Am I not holding fast to a delusion?"

The heading we have set down for this section is practically the same as for the section 3. above. Repetition for the sake of driving a point home to the utmost! A bigger piece of folly can hardly be conceived of. Perhaps now a little more emphasis is put on the aspect of the *delusion* involved.

Verse 19. In this verse the use of the term "abominable idol" may seem a bit out of place. In fact, this is not a term that the idol-worshipper would actually have used. The writer has merely substituted a word out of his own vocabulary. Or else he feels so strongly that if the man were but honest he would himself feel impelled to use a term like this.

Verse 20. The opening of the verse sounds like a kind of proverbial saying. One feels instinctively that some form of self-deception is under consideration. Some have thought that the figure is derived from the idea of trying to graze sheep on a barren ash-heap. So the mind of the idolater is dealing with empty, fruitless concepts and is not doing any solid reasoning. Or it may be thought of as involving an attempt at self-help. But who could "deliver himself" by manufacturing an idol, who cannot even deliver himself when dangers draw near? The conclusion of the verse actually runs thus: "Is there not a lie in my right hand?" We have chosen one of the several translations which have been offered for this line in the words: "Am I not holding fast to a delusion?" It might be to the point to indicate that the "right hand" referred to in the text often involves the idea of a position of honor, and the word for "delusion" is literally "a lie." The whole attitude of the idol-worshipper then boils down to this: In his life and thinking the position of honor is occupied by a lie.

6. The Effective Pardon Bestowed by the Lord (vv. 21-23)

44:21-23 21. Remember these things, O Jacob,
and Israel, for you are my servant.
I formed you, you are my servant;
   O Israel, you will not be forgotten by me.
22. I have blotted out your transgressions like a cloud,
   your sins like a mist.
O return to me, for I have redeemed you.
23. Rejoice, O heavens, for the Lord has done it;
shout aloud, O depths of the earth.
Break forth into singing, O mountains,
   your forest and every tree in it!
For the Lord has redeemed Jacob
   and will be glorified in Israel.

Verse 21. Now comes the practical application of the above. The issue of idolatry is so important, for the sin is so devastating and foolish. Demonstrations like the one just presented should not be forgotten. It is as though the words "these things" demanded some such unique presentation as the one just covered. This shows how well the entire section (vv. 9-20) fits into this context and is by no means extraneous material. Israel in her role as "servant" of the Lord has a high honor and should heed all things that contribute to her successful fulfillment of this role. The Lord is beginning again to set forth how different a God he is. His people "will not be forgotten" by him. He remembers them even when they have forgotten him. The idols, when appealed to, cannot remember, cannot, in fact, do anything at any time. There is a wealth of comforting assurance in words like these. They reveal God's heart.

Verse 22. But more than vague generalities are involved in Yahweh's attitude toward his people. It involves effective dealing with the most crucial issue of the lives of men — sin. And what does he do about sin? He "blots it out," even as the morning mists are dissipated by the heat of rising sun, and are dispersed so effectively as to be no more. They vanish. Clouds, higher up in the atmosphere and mists, clinging close to the earth, are both disposed of. That is the kind of God that mankind needs above all other needs. That more is involved than some kind of juggling of balances, in fact that a corresponding attitude, or reaction, to this forgiving grace is necessary, is suggested by the last line: "Return to me, for I have redeemed you." Unless there be a decisive personal turning to God, there is no receiving of pardon. Not that man's attitude gained the slightest merit in the transaction. In the whole context of Isaiah only grace without a particle of human achievement can be involved. Again Isaiah has proven himself to be the outstanding evangelist of the Old Covenant.

Verse 23. Again and again men have pointed out that the hymnic conclusion of this section is characteristic of the prophet. God does so many things for which he is to be praised resoundingly. To such praise the prophet not only admonishes but provides the very terms to be used convenient at hand for immediate use. Again the feeling that the mercy bestowed is so great that it calls for more praise than man is normally capable of offering, and so all of nature is summoned to contribute its share: heavens above and the depths of the earth beneath; mountains and forests and trees. This praise is due to him for on the one hand "He has done it." In this context that seems to refer to the fact that he has effectively acted. He has actually bestowed pardon. Or it can also be stated in terms like this: "He has redeemed Jacob and will be glorified in Israel." More than national restoration is under consideration here, though that too is reflected upon. And so once again a section has been concluded on the "theocentric" note. It may even be, as *North* suggests that the Lord "points to Israel as his crowning achievement."

Notes

Verse 3. Though it is not fully expressed in the Hebrew, the nature of the two successive clauses is clearly correlative, and may well be translated in this way: "as . . . so" (Cf. *KS* 371 l).

Verse 7. After "Who is like me?" the *Septuagint* inserts the verb, "let him step forth" which fits very appropriately. The clause beginning *missumi* is admittedly very difficult, but may be construed as an infinitive clause of time (*KS* 401 d).

Verse 9. The pronoun *hemah* has a row of points over it in the Masoretic text, apparently to indicate that the very presence of the word in the text is questionable. It may safely be omitted. At the close of the verse the clause introduced by *lema'an*, would seem to express purpose, but is one of the many instances where purpose should rather be construed as *result*.

Verse 10. The word *chabheraw* ("who are attached to them") in its root meaning appears with about the same connotation in Hos. 4:17.

Verse 11. We have translated *me'adham* as "but human beings"; the expression may also be rendered "despised of men" or "less than human." Cf. *KS* 402 e.

Verse 12. The verb is missing at the beginning of the verse and so the *Septuagint* already inserted one (*"sharpened"*). We preferred to use "makes."

Verse 13. In this verse too there are the names of tools and instruments which do not appear elsewhere in the Scriptures: "Pencil," and "scraping tool." The last word of the verse is construed without a preposition, something like "to occupy a shrine." *KS* 211 e.

Verse 14. In this verse the initial word apparently has to be supplied, "he went out."

Verse 16. What we translated "a part of it" actually says in Hebrew "half of it." Then the second half is referred to, then that which is left over. Apparently terms are not being used with mathematical exactitude. Therefore our translation.

Verse 18. "Smeared shut" does not agree with its subject in gender and number, a common observation in Hebrew when the verb stands first and the gender and number of the subject have not yet been determined. See *GK* 145.

Verse 21. In the last word *tinnascheni* the pronominal suffix is dative in character (*KS* 21; *GK* 117 x).

Chapter XLIV:24—XLV:25

F. THE COMMISSIONING OF CYRUS, THE AGENT OF THE RESTORATION (Chaps. 44:24—45:25

There have been two references to Cyrus in the second half of Isaiah's book thus far (41:2-4, 25). In neither case was his name mentioned. The references were vague in character. He was the man of mystery. Now his name is prophetically disclosed; he appears as the one whose success was so miraculous. We still hold to the view of the fathers that it was Isaiah, the son of Amoz, who made these prophecies more than 150 years prior to the time they came to pass. In God's sovereign control of history this is merely the agent who carries into effect plans and purposes long prepared for by the Lord. Cyrus makes the liberation of Israel from Babylonian Captivity a reality.

But it is a strange thing how Isaiah envisions these things that shall come to pass. Like so many other Biblical writers he sees the Cyrus-epoch and the End-time flow together into one. The time-sequence is unimportant, in fact, it is very likely not even discerned by the prophet. He merely knows that these things will come to pass. He seems to have no knowledge in what order or after how much time has elapsed these things will come to pass. Their coming is certain; their sequence is not yet clearly seen.

In fact, Isaiah seems to think in terms of a conversion of Cyrus to the true God, Yahweh, and as subsequent result to this conversion, the acknowledgement of Yahweh by all the world. Neither of these two hopes was realized, nor are they to this day. Was the Prophet in error? We shall attempt a solution of the difficulty as we come to the specific verses that are involved.

But another matter may be disposed of now, the similarity

of the statements of this chapter with the statement made about Cyrus and the relation of the gods, Marduk, Bel, and Nebo, to him. There are three statements in particular that call for examination. We cite as parallels to the Biblical text from *Ancient Near Eastern Texts* by Pritchard (Princeton, 1950). 45:1-2 give the words "whose right hand I have grasped" and "I will go before you." The Cyrus cylinder says "going at his side like a friend." 45:4 says: "I call you by your name" and "I surname you." The cylinder reads: "He pronounced the name of Cyrus." Again 44:28 says: "He is my shepherd" and the cylinder: "Whose rule Bel and Nebo love." Is the Isaiah material after all perhaps dependent upon the Cyrus cylinder? In the first place, it is commonly acknowledged that the Cyrus cylinder is later in point of time than the Biblical passage. And in the second place it will have to be conceded that the statements involved are of a general character that might have been used quite commonly in all languages when the relation of a victorious ruler to some god is being described. For aside from these three parallels the material in the two documents involved has precious little in common.

1. The Commissioning, a Work of the All-powerful Lord (44:24-28)

44:24-28 24. Thus says the Lord, who has redeemed you, he who formed you from the womb,
"I am the Lord who made all things,
   who stretched out the heavens, I alone,
   who spread out the earth (who was with me?);
25. who nullifies the omens of the charlatan prognosticators,
   who makes the diviners appear as fools,
   who refutes the wise,
and shows up their knowledge to be folly;
26. [but] establishes the word of his servant,
   and fulfils the purpose announced through his messengers;
who says to Jerusalem, 'She shall be inhabited,'
   and to the cities of Judah, 'They shall be built,'
   and their ruins I will raise up again.
27. who says to the ocean-deep, 'Be dry,'
   I will dry up your rivers;

28. who says to Cyrus, 'He is my shepherd,
    he will execute my whole plan
        by ordering Jerusalem to be rebuilt
    and the temple-foundations to be relaid.' "

Verse 24. This section is one sentence, one of the longest in the Old Testament, each clause practically beginning with a participle (there are nine participles involved). Some classify the piece as a *Selbsthymnus*, a hymn in which God sings his own praise. The connotation is unfortunate; a better designation will have to be found. God does proclaim his own honor, an entirely proper procedure, for he is in reality all that he predicates concerning himself. He proclaims with authority things he has done, is doing at the present, and will yet fulfill in the future. The emphasis is strong on history, which is entirely under God's control without being predestined. The first reference is to Israel's redemption from Egyptian bondage, the one great act that welded Israel into a unity and gave her her national existence. Parallel runs the statement "he who formed you from the womb." The reference is to all the things done in the grand and glorious days of Moses. At this point the pronouncements veer over into the first person. When he claims that he is the Lord "who made all things" two areas are apparently under consideration — creation and history. For he created all things that are and still majestically controls them by determining the outcome of history. Other works of creation that fit very properly into the picture here are: (he) "stretched out the heavens alone" (cf. 40:22). And he similarly "spread out the earth" and there was no one who was needed to be of assistance. Creation is the sole work of God. Here we have a brief assortment of the most marvelous achievements attributable to God alone.

Verse 25. Now a second area in which Yahweh's all-powerful character is discernible is subjected to scrutiny. It is the area of magic, divining, astrology and kindred pursuits. For activity in these fields all the nations of antiquity were known. Babylon perhaps excelled them all. "Omens" were

carefully observed. Prognostications were continually resorted to. "Diviners" were even officially appointed by the
state. Since all these activities lay outside the field of the
exact sciences, many a "charlatan" would be found studiously
framing double-talk. All of them could take refuge behind
their ambiguous prognostications. Perhaps the prophet is
here thinking of efforts along these lines spoken at the approach of Cyrus to Babylon. Success for the Babylonians
was abundantly foretold. Even if that had not been the case,
God had still made all the efforts of the fortunetellers of
none effect. He "nullified" the omens to which they attached
so much importance, made their authors appear as fools,
refuted the wise and made all their "knowledge appear to be
folly." So lengthy a refutation of the hollowness of their
endeavors was quite in keeping with the importance men
attached to this subject.

Verse 26. What now follows further establishes how all-
powerful the Lord is. His effective work is contrasted with
the futile efforts of their pseudo-science. Therefore we inserted an adversative "but" in our translation. The Lord also
has men who deal with the possibilities that the future holds.
There is first of all his "servant," the prophet himself,
through whom he had repeatedly made his purposes and the
future outcome of things known. All his messages are
summed up as being a "word." But this prophet is not the
only one whom he has in reserve; there are also his "messengers," the men of whom Israel's tradition and Israel's
sacred writings had many a clear-cut word on record.
Through these he had announced his "purpose" and what
had been announced had invariably come to pass. Now
comes the comfort that the prophet was strongly setting
forth for Israel. He is on record as having promised to his
people that Jerusalem would again be inhabited and that the
cities of Judah would again be built, and the ruins would
again be raised up. This is the first clear prediction of the
restoration of Jerusalem, the name of the city being plainly
indicated (*Westermann*).

Verse 27. The negative (v. 25) having thus been met by a positive (v. 26), the prophetic word moves on, building up to a skillful climax. Men are not quite sure how they should construe the meaning of the "ocean-deep," perhaps all needs of the case are best met if it be thought of as a historic reference to the crossing of the waters of the Red Sea in the days of the Exodus, and if the drying up of the rivers be thought of in connection with the crossing of the Jordan, all in highly poetic terminology. The reference then appears to be to the validated acts of a historic past. They abundantly testify how all-powerful the Lord is, whose acts are now under review.

Verse 28. Now the climax! The mysterious personage, whose coming has repeatedly been alluded to, is now mentioned by name. It is a man called Cyrus. According to our position (whose merits we shall not argue here) it was granted to the prophet by the omniscient God to foretell the coming and the name of the deliverer from Babylonian Captivity more than 150 years before these things transpired, an approach that the heathen idols through their priests and prognosticators could not make, as the prophet had contended again and again. This Cyrus now functions as the Lord's "shepherd." This is a name frequently used in the Scriptures for rulers (see Gen. 48:15; II Sam. 5:2; 7:7; Jer. 3:15; Ezek. 34:23; 37:24, etc.). The care and guidance of a nation are conferred upon its shepherd. Whatever the relation of Cyrus to his own nation may be said to be, for Israel he distinctly functions as shepherd. He, whether he is aware of it or not (both possibilities may be urged) "will execute (God's) whole plan." In essence this will involve that the capital city of Israel be rebuilt and that the temple-foundations be relaid. These are the tasks that are assigned to Cyrus by the Lord at the time when he commissioned him, an act which he himself ascribes to himself in this verse. It may yet be added that the emphasis in the matter of the restoration of the temple at Jerusalem is not on providing a place for authentic cultic worship — though this too is by no means unimportant — but chiefly to provide a place where Israel can have assurance that the Lord's presence is in the midst of his people.

It must yet be added that when it is said of Cyrus that he will "execute the Lord's whole plan" that form of statement need not be taken in the sense that whatever plans God has even down to the end of time for his people and for the whole world will, in the thinking of the prophet, come to total fulfillment in the days of Cyrus. Eschatological statements are sometimes cast into a somewhat loose form and dare not be pressed with undue emphasis on the very letter.

2. The Resultant Success of Cyrus Attributable to Yahweh's Dominion (vv. 1-7)

45:1-7 1. Thus says the Lord in reference to his anointed one,
to Cyrus — "whose right hand I have grasped,
in order to trample down nations before him,
    and to strip kings of their weapons;
to open doors before him,
    that gates shall not be shut.
2. I myself will go before you,
    and level off the hindrances that would block your path;
I will shatter doors of bronze,
    and hew in pieces iron gate-bars.
3. And I will give you treasures stored up in dark chambers
    and such as are buried in secret hiding-places;
that you may know that I am the Lord,
    the one who has called you by your name, the God of Israel,
4. For the sake of my servant Jacob,
    and of Israel, my chosen one,
I call you by your name,
    indeed I give you a title of honor,
    although you did not know me;
5. I am the Lord and there is no other;
    apart from me there is no God;
I arm you though you did not know me;
6. in order that men may know from the rising of the sun
    and from the west that there is none besides me.
I am the Lord and there is no other God.
7. I form the light and create the darkness,
    I make weal and create woe.
    I am the Lord who does all these things."

Here Yahweh presents Cyrus to his people as the "agent of her salvation." Because he is addressed in terms of intimacy some read into the text that Cyrus is to be thought of as going over to the faith of the children of Israel and accepting the worship of their God. Then they add that the prophet expected this step to sweep all the nations along with him. Such an approach claims more than the evidence of the case here warrants. But this much is clear that the success that Cyrus had is attributed to Yahweh's dominion. So much the prophet clearly claims. Throughout the passage terms are used that are proverbial for the ceremony of the crowning of kings both in, and outside of, Israel (cf. *Westermann*).

Verse 1. Here Cyrus is mentioned by name a second time. He is even given a most distinctive title, the "anointed one." The word used happens to be the word that coincides with the name Messiah, although it should be remarked at once that this title is never used in the Scriptures of the Old Testament for the Christ that is to come. That usage developed in the time between the Testaments. It is however used for kings like Saul (I Sam. 12:3, etc.); for the people of God (Hab. 3:13); and even for the patriarchs (Ps. 105:15). It does not necessarily imply that an actual anointing of the person in question took place. It is a designation of honor. Here now it is used of a heathen ruler whom God is employing for a very special purpose. To say then that Cyrus was God's Messiah is technically correct but very misleading. God has a proclamation to make with reference to this Cyrus, a proclamation which is lengthy and weighty. It discloses things that neither Cyrus nor Israel nor the Gentiles could have sensed. The first claim is that in the work of conquest which Cyrus is engaged in, God is upholding him ("whose right hand I have grasped"). By thus being upheld by God, Cyrus is enabled to have success wherever he goes. But it is the Lord who "tramples down nations before him," a colorful way of describing the success that Cyrus had. The same Lord "strips kings of their weapons" before him. The verb for "strips" really is "ungirds," that is to say

either: "loosens the girdle" and so lets flowing garments
hamper his activity; or it means "loosen the belt to which
the sword is attached" and so disarm the man. We prefer the
latter interpretation. (cf. I Kings 20:11). A third form of
activity that Yahweh engages in for Cyrus' benefit is "to
open doors [of cities] before him that gates [of cities] shall
not be shut."

Verse 2. It is as though the Lord himself personally took
a hand in the issues involved, came down from heaven, led
the way for Cyrus and cleared away the obstacles that
towered in his path. To make it all more personal and intimate, at this point the Lord addresses himself to Cyrus
directly. In other words the Lord's proclamation moves
over into the second person. In highly effective figures, the
Lord represents himself as actually battering down strong
bronze gates that seemed to guaranty the safety of the cities,
and actually hewing in pieces iron gate-bars, and all this in
the interest of Cyrus, "his anointed one."

Verse 3. A further item of God's guiding of the destinies
of this servant of his is that he allows the conqueror to amass
rich treasures, such as are wont to be kept for safe-keeping
in dark, sometimes subterranean, chambers, or may be buried
in secret hiding-places — so to speak, the Fort Knox-in-
stallations of days of old. The treasures amassed by Babylon
must have been fabulous, for they are also referred to in
Hab. 2:6-8; Jer. 50:37; 51:13. The purpose expressed in
reference to Cyrus' acquisition of treasures is quite unexpected and a bit unusual. It is that Cyrus may know that
Yahweh is the Lord, the one who has called him by his
name, the God of Israel. The difficulty here involved is unduly increased if these expressed results are associated only
with the acquisition of treasure. It is rather the sum total of
all the things that the Lord did for Cyrus, from vv. 1-3, that
bring home a more intimate knowledge of the Lord God of
Israel to the Persian conqueror. This almost seems to demand
something that the Hebrew tradition, as reported by Jose-
phus, brings to our attention, that namely these prophecies

concerning his success were shown to Cyrus by the Jews and were known to have deeply impressed the monarch. In any case, at least in some way, not disclosed to us, Cyrus became aware of the fact that the God of the Jews had willed and contributed to his success. The verse before us does not directly say that Cyrus confessed the monotheistic faith, or his acceptance of it, but he came close to taking this step as the two passages II Chron. 36:22 f. and the parallel Ezra 1: 2 ff. indicate. But perhaps this particular decree is to be rated no higher than an analogous one, which Nebuchadnezzar in his day set forth, as recorded in Dan. 4:1-3. For from the Cyrus cylinder, referred to above as given in Pritchard's *Ancient New Eastern Texts*, we learn that Cyrus attributed his success in his enterprises and in the capture of Babylon to the Babylonian god, Marduk. It is entirely possible that both the Biblical and cylinder accounts come from Cyrus, and that from his polytheistic point of view he was able to make these, to us, conflicting statements.

Verse 4. The previous verse indicated what purpose the Lord had in mind with regard to Cyrus when he gave him Babylon and all the rest of his phenomenal success. Now the Lord adds what it was that he had in mind with regard to his own people Israel. It may be said to have all been done "for the sake of my servant Jacob." This honorific title ("servant") for Israel occurs often enough in the course of the book (see 41:8; 42:1; 43:10; 44:1-2; 49:3-6). To it is added the further title "my chosen one." Both together show how high Israel stands in the Lord's esteem. True this is traceable to the covenant relationship. But it still makes it apparent why he will use so select an instrument for the liberation and restoration of his people as Cyrus. He has much at stake as Lord of his people. In addition he honors Cyrus by calling him by his name, even as he did Israel (43:1), and also asserts that he has given to this instrument that he uses "a title of honor." That the personal merits of Cyrus were not the determining factor in God's choice of the man, good though he otherwise was, appears from the further assertion here made: "you did not know me." God's dealings with man can never be motivated by the merit and achievements of man. That thought bridges over to the next verse.

Verse 5. This type of dealing with man on the basis of pure grace is then the distinctive mark of his dealing with all mankind. In a sense that is the mark of the monotheistic Lord. In all relations between men and gods, so called, merit is the distinguishing factor, at least to some extent, passing by for the moment the occasional strange whims of these same gods. But grace is the determining issue between the *Lord* and men. We might then well say that sole grace and sole deity are factors that mutually determine one another. On this basis one more of the favors bestowed on Cyrus comes to the forefront: "I arm you though you did not know me." The total sovereignty of God must be maintained at any cost. Therefore this additional reminder.

Verse 6. One further factor that entered into the choice and equipment of Cyrus is added here: the impression that all this is calculated to make on men the world over, from "the rising of the sun and from the west." Somehow God's choice and guidance of Cyrus will bring his sole claim to deity to the attention of men, wherever they may dwell. Though we have no corroborative material available from historical sources, it is still possible that results and effects were produced at that time that are far in excess of what we might have thought likely. That men will then follow through logically on this basis and will, the world over, renounce their inferior gods and turn to Yahweh, that is not claimed by the prophet, although some men feel that this is actually his position. This subject may be explored a little more fully. Two claims at least may be made in this connection. One is that Cyrus does appear in this passage as a kind of pioneer in advancing the claim of monotheism. Yet as noted above from the historical records it appears that his own insight was a bit confused: Cyrus ascribed his success to Marduk also. It would then appear that in his better moments he championed to an extent the monotheism of Israel. The other claim that may be made on the basis of this passage is that Cyrus is represented hopefully as a possible convert to the Lord of Israel. This is in reality merely another form of the first of these two claims.

Verse 7. This verse attempts to further clarify the big issues that are at stake. Monotheism involves that Yahweh must be regarded as sole ruler and controller of the universe. Of course, he is never the source of evil. But both good and evil, no matter with whom they originate, are never out of God's control. Basic are the two elements, light and darkness, and all that they represent in common parlance. Equally basic almost are the two possible types of deeds of men, the good and the bad, or as here stated: "weal" and "woe." All heathen systems of religion were basically dualistic, having two separate sources for all that is done, one good and one evil, and one as powerful and efficient as the other. This dualism is disavowed strongly by this text. We have here then not a disavowing of the position of the dualistic Persian religion only, but of all systems that were known to antiquity outside the revelation and faith of Israel. The form in which this claim was cast in the old King James version could well prove disturbing, when it said: "I make peace and create evil," although the Hebrew would allow for such a translation. But it is not the morally good and the morally evil that are being attributed to Yahweh, but things good and bad are said to lie totally in his power, as far as their physical aspects and consequences are concerned. The *RSV* version does full justice to the issues involved when it says: "I make weal and create woe." Note similar statements in Amos 3:6b; and Isa. 14:24-27. "I am the Lord who does all these things" aptly sums it all up, and obviously ties back to 44:24 — obvious evidence of careful composition.

3. A Prayer for the Realization of This Work (v. 8)

45:8 8. Distil moisture, you skies above,
and let the skies rain down success!

Let the earth open, that salvation may grow forth,
   and let it cause success to spring up also!
I the Lord have created it.

Who is speaking? We seem to have one of those situations where the prophet so completely identifies himself with the objectives of the Lord that the words of the Lord and his servant merge into one. The opening line of the verse may well be classified as "the yearning cry of the prophet," and so may be regarded as a prayer. The last line represents the Lord as speaking. In any case, poetically both heaven and earth are appealed to to bring to pass the good blessings that the Lord has in store for his people. The world is a unit. Heaven and earth are sympathetically thought of as both interested in the achievement of the Lord objectives. These objectives are "success" and "salvation." Both are regarded as being furthered by the coming of a fructifying rain and by the springing forth of a growth of God's blessings. The injection of this touching prayer indicates how deeply the prophet was concerned about having the good things of which he prophesied come to pass. A kindred approach is to be seen in Ps. 85:12 and Hos. 2:21 ff.

4. Rebuke of Those Who Are Critical of Yahweh in His Use of Cyrus (vv. 9-13)

45:9-13 9. Woe to the man who would find fault with his Maker,
   a piece of mere pottery among pieces of earthen pottery.
Dare the clay say to the potter, "What are you making?"
   or your work say: "He has no hands?"
10. Woe to him who says to his father: "What are you begetting?"
   or to his mother: "To what are you giving birth?"
11. Thus says the Lord, the Holy One of Israel,
   and he who formed it:
"Inquire of me concerning things to come?
   give orders concerning my children
   and about the work of my hands?
12. It is I who made the earth
   and created man upon it;
it is I whose hands stretched out the heavens
   and appointed all their host.

13. It is I who raised him up for a saving purpose,
   and will make straight all his ways.
It is I who will build my city
   and liberate my exiles;
   not for a price and reward," says the Lord of hosts.

Verse 9. So it has just been indicated that the Lord is going to use as his instrument for restoring Israel the conqueror Cyrus. That purpose may indeed meet with some measure of disapproval on the part of some of the children of Israel. Their attitude would be: A heathen like that is not worthy for the achievement of God's high purposes. This objection would not be raised, as has been indicated, by faint-hearted unbelief, but the very verb "find fault" may also be translated "strive." That would imply stubborn opposition, an attitude of knowing things better than the very Lord himself. The prophet cannot but denounce such an attitude. He points out several analogies, each of which would be equally reprehensible. Such a man would be like a "piece of pottery among pieces of earthen pottery" — that means: a mere potsherd — finding fault with the potter. Not a complete finished article, but the mere remains of a broken dish. The "potter" in this instance, of course, is God. This approach is found in 29:16; Jer. 18:1 ff.; Rom. 9:20.; cf. Isa. 10:15. Carrying this approach farther — would there not be a strong impropriety about having a lump of clay remonstrate with the potter, if it could speak words, and say by way of criticism: "What are you making?" Or to make the insolence of it still more apparent — what if some cup or saucer ("your work") were to take the potter to task for making it, charging him with incompetence ("He has no hands!") or lack of skill, implying that for hands he has mere clumsy stumps (or, as we might say of a man: "He is all thumbs").

Verse 10. The prophet is so indignant with the impudence of the critics of the Almighty that he must carry this line of reasoning a few steps farther. He continues in a strong vein of indignation, as the second "woe" indicates. It is as though a child were questioning the propriety of having a father beget it and bring it into the world, an uninformed, inexperienced child. It is as though at any point in childhood any youngster were to remonstrate with his mother: "To what are you giving birth?" As unheard of as that is and as unthinkable as it should be, so is Israel's criticism of the means God employs for the achievement of his sovereign designs.

Verse 11. In a tone of solemn majesty the prophet continues: "Thus says the Lord, the Holy One of Israel and he who formed it," as much as to say, it is this Lord whom you are in fact belittling. What follows is difficult of interpretation. We take the two verbs as they stand, as imperatives, spoken, however, with strong indignation as a question in the sense: ("Will you) inquire of me concerning things to come?" i.e., will you remonstrate with me about things that have not yet come to pass? i.e., sitting in judgment upon them before they have even happened? Or the second question is in the nature of the protest of an astonished parent whose dealings with his children are being questioned by an outsider: ("Will you) give me orders concerning my children and about the work of my hands?" For an outsider to interfere with a parent dealing with his children in a case of discipline is usually rightly resented. So here.

Verse 12. The Lord now proceeds to indicate what manner of works he is in the habit of engaging in, in order to make the conclusion obvious that if he resorts to the use of certain minor plans in readjustments among the things that need readjustment in his creation, he surely must be entirely capable of making the proper choice of means and agents. Here are the things that he lists as being in the ordinary range of the projects he engages in: Making the earth; creating man upon it; stretching out the heavens with his hands; appointing all the host to their proper place and sphere. Who would even dream of advising one who is capable of handling issues of such dimensions?

Verse 13. Once again the Lord patiently defines his purposes and the place of Cyrus within these purposes of his. Though the term is not used it is made very plain that Cyrus merely functions as agent of the Almighty. What things he accomplishes the Lord does through him. The project on which the Lord is working is described by a number of terms: "a saving purpose," "his [Cyrus'] ways," "build my city," "liberate my exiles" — all of which have been previously set forth and are now being re-enumerated that one may see that they are projects vitally related to the future of Israel and well worthy of the best thoughts of the God of Israel. The closing remark of the verse presents a difficulty. All this is being done in Israel's behalf "not for price nor reward." If this be construed to mean that neither Israel nor any man or group of men are producing something that could be valued as a due and proper payment for so great a favor, and so God is not in any way being repaid for what he does, this is a proper statement which no man could call into question. Construed thus, as referring to a ransom that might be paid by man to God, this passage presents no problem over against 43:3 f., as *North* has claimed it does. This previous passage speaks of the reward that the *Lord* either would be ready to pay, if it were necessary, or that he would be ready to provide to offset what Cyrus loses by giving up his claim on Israel.

5. The Submission of Nations Validates God's Work (vv. 14-17)

45:14-17 14. Thus says the Lord:
"The wealth of Egypt and the merchandise of Ethiopia
and of the tall Sabeans shall come over to you and be yours.
   They shall follow you [Zion], they shall come fettered;
   They shall prostrate themselves before you
      and make supplication to you:
   'God is only with you, and there is no other;
      no God besides you!' "
15. Surely thou art a God who conceals himself,
   thou God of Israel, the Savior.
16. All of them are put to shame and confusion,
   the manufacturers of idols shall be totally confounded.

17. But Israel shall be saved by the Lord
   with an everlasting salvation;
you shall not be ashamed or confounded
   forever and ever.

Verse 14. Men cannot agree how they are to label this section. *Haller* says it is one of the songs of Zion. *Volz* calls at least vv. 15-17 a word of prayer and a prophetic word of doom. *Begrich* sees here only an oracle of salvation. The piece evidently does not fit into the usual categories. *Skinner* regards v. 14 in particular as addressed to Cyrus, which sounds very strange for the end of the verse. Zion is being addressed. When different national groups with their treasures are pictured as coming to Israel in a spirit of submission, this is analogous with what is stated in 2:2-4; 18:7; 23:18; 60:5 ff. First the bringing of treasures is stressed — treasure from Egypt, from Ethiopia and from the Sabeans, from southwest Arabia (cf. 43:3). Also the "merchandise" that is the exportable articles from these nations. Israel is then regarded as heading a march of the nations; the others follow. Besides "they shall come fettered." This is either a hyperbole used to express total submission, or better still, this indicates "a deference approaching worship." They have manacled themselves voluntarily. Political domination by Israel is not even remotely thought of. Their cheerful prostration before Israel shows a spirit of submission like that described in 2:2-4. When these nations are said to "make supplication" to Israel this statement seems to regard them as imploring Israel to be allowed to share her spiritual treasures and to accept the treasures they bring in gratitude. The words, "God is only with you, and there is no other, no God besides you," are the confession of a faith and an insight which stands behind their present approach. Insight has come to them that there is only one nation whose God has true existence; all other gods so-called are fiction. This then describes the marvelous day, even now but partially realized, when the knowledge of the living God shall have spread to all nations and shall have been accepted as the treasure that it is. This statement of the case does not necessarily mean that *all* men will at some time actually accept what is told them of this saving truth. That possibility is not reflected upon.

Verse 15. Now the prophet breaks forth into a prayer of adoration, moved by the mysterious character of God's dealing with Israel. Above (vv. 9 ff.), an unwholesome attitude toward God's dealings with Israel was repudiated. Here a right attitude is pictured: falling down, as it were, before him and singing his praises. The word could perhaps be construed as reflecting the attitude of the nations mentioned in v. 14. But it seems better to think of it as a prayer in which the prophet leads his people in veneration of the Lord. Yahweh is a "God who conceals himself," a concept for which *Luther* employed the classical title *deus absconditus* ("the hidden God"). He conceals himself, as it were, behind the fact that he lets Jerusalem be destroyed; or by the mysterious manner in which he lets history develop. Several Scriptures have the thought of his self-concealing, as Ps. 97:2; Exod. 33:17-23; cf. also, for the more positive side, Rom. 11:33. But this concealing of himself does not cancel out the constructive side of this attitude; for he still is for Israel "the God of Israel, the Savior."

Verses 16, 17. But even as v. 14 showed that God's dealings would bring about the submission even of the distant Gentiles, so the negative may properly be brought into the picture. They who are in their native benightedness, or refuse to come out of it to the light, that is to say, "the manufacturers of idols," they shall be totally confounded, they "shall be put to shame and confusion." But still reflecting upon the fact that God's ways with Israel have been productive of good, the prophet sums up the good that will be achieved (v. 17). She shall "be saved by the Lord with an everlasting salvation." She shall not be "ashamed or confounded forever and ever." The outcome will prove how well the plans of the Almighty were laid. So God's work is fully validated.

6. Appeal to the Survivors of the Nations to Acknowledge the Only God (vv. 18-21)

45:18-21   18. For thus says Yahweh, who created the heavens
— he is God —
who formed the earth and made it — he established it —
  he did not create it to no purpose;
  he formed it for men to dwell in,
"I am the Lord and there is no other.
19. I did not speak in secret,
  in some place in a land of darkness;
  nor did I say in vain to the offspring of Jacob, 'Seek me.'
I am the Lord, I speak the truth;
  I declare what is right.
20. Assemble yourselves and come;
draw near together, you survivors of the nations!
  They who carry their wooden idols are utterly without knowledge,
  as are they who pray to a god who cannot help.
21. State your case and present your arguments —
  yea, let us have a conference together —
  Who has made this to be heard long ago
    and declared it long since?
  Was it not I, the Lord?
  and there is no God besides me;
  a righteous God and a Savior;
    there is none except me."

Verse 18. Two points are stressed in this and the following verse, creation and revelation. Both are clear and orderly. The Creator did not form this world of his "to no purpose," or as some translate, as "a chaos." "He formed it for men to dwell in," and it gives overwhelming evidence of being adapted to that purpose. It also bears testimony to the oneness of God, a truth, which the prophet presses home at every possible point. Both these great truths find their oneness in God himself. They reinforce the faith of Israel in monotheism.

Verse 19. Whenever God has spoken it was done with such clear light that his meaning was immediately apparent to all who would lend an attentive ear. No veiled disclosures! No need of groping around in "a land of darkness" where the disclosures of heathen prognosticators so often left men. In other words, God did not deal in esoteric knowledge which was available only for a select few. When God said "Seek me!" that involved that he could be found, "seeking" here being taken in the sense of seeking his face in worship, as "seek" so often signifies. One major trait of God's deity was that what he spoke was "truth" and "right."

Verse 20. This much was needed to provide a solid foundation for the appeal to the "survivors of the nations" which was about to be made. A sort of court-trial comes into the picture. A test is to be made openly and publicly. The survivors of the nations are those who have lived through the recent major world-wide upheavals, contingent upon the conquests made by the Persians under Cyrus. In the midst of the readjustments that come after such an upheaval the minds of many may be ready for new things, open for new truths. The idols and faith in them are inadequate for trying times such as those that had befallen men. So it is quickly pointed out that they who "carry their wooden idols," cannot seriously expect these helpless blocks of wood that have to be carried about, help those who have to carry them. So the idol-worshippers "are utterly without knowledge." They are as badly off as any who keep on praying "to a god who cannot help."

Verse 21. But these persons are not merely to submit unconditionally. They are to present their arguments and state their case in a public examination of the issues involved. In the prophet's mind there is no doubt as to how such a test, honestly conducted, must turn out. He cheerfully invites the opposition to "a conference." But immediately he produces the strong argument with which he has operated successfully so many times in the past: "Who has made this to be heard long ago and declared it long since" (cf. 41:22). The answer is, of course, Yahweh, the God of Israel. He has declared things beforehand, also the coming and the success of Cyrus, as Chaps. 41-44 have so conclusively demonstrated, especially 13:2-4, 17-25; 21:1-10. This the survivors of the nations are asked to take under advisement. If they do and examine Yahweh's claim, "Was it not I . . . ?" they should be moved to the acceptance of him, as v. 14 already indicated that this outcome would be the result.

The broad outlook and the high hope for the nations outside of Israel, as reflected in this chapter, make this section to be one of the high points of the message of the prophet.

7. God's Objectives Reach to All the Ends of the Earth (vv. 22-25)

45:22-25 22. Turn to me and be saved, all the ends of the earth;
for I am God and there is no other.
23. By myself have I sworn;
truth has gone forth from my mouth,
a word that shall not be nullified:
"To me every knee shall bow
and every tongue shall swear allegiance!"
24. Only in the Lord [men shall say]
do I have full righteousness and strength;
to him shall come, utterly ashamed,
all that were incensed against him.
25. In the Lord all the offspring of Israel
shall be justified and shall glory.

Verse 22. If a large segment of mankind was under consideration in the preceding section, now the prospect widens still farther. All the ends of the earth are taken into the picture. This verse might have been tied up with what preceded by the use of a "therefore." For if God's concern is so warm for the "survivors" then it is but logical to assume that it is without limit. In fact, as *Haller* rightly remarks, the "door of salvation is thrown wide open" at this point. Or as *Volz* suggests, "universalism follows from monotheism," but, mark well, universalism in the Biblical sense. All nations, ignorant of the living God and his ways, are thought of as all faced in the wrong direction and going in this direction. They are invited "to turn," which definitely here involves a reversal of their direction. If they turn and throw themselves upon the mercy of the Lord, in one word "be saved," God will receive them. The verb involved could more ac-

curately be rendered "let yourselves be saved." For in conversion as such, man is completely passive. He contributes
nothing to his salvation. When the "ends of the earth" are
referred to, that approach does not eliminate those areas
that lie in between. So the appeal is truly universal. God
would have all men to be saved. No narrow nationalism
blurred the vision of men like our prophet. The supporting
argument should be noted: "for I am the Lord and there is no
other." Since he is God alone, his interest in mankind is a
unit interest that involves all mankind.

Verse 23. This is an issue of such tremendous moment
that the Lord supports his invitation by a solemn oath. Since
there is no one greater by whom he could swear (see Heb.
6:13) he swears by himself. The parallel statement ("truth
has gone forth from my mouth") clinches the point being
made. A third parallel ("a word that shall not be nullified")
makes assurance doubly sure. The truth that is being uttered
is still that of v. 22, that God's mercies are all-inclusive. But
the emphasis now rests not on the fact that God can rescue
those whom he invites, but on the other side of the matter,
that these people shall be brought to the point where in adoration they acknowledge his sole lordship and saviorhood.
"Every knee shall bow" for there is no other posture permissible for man nor worthy of him when he steps into the
presence of the All-holy (cf. also Rom. 14:11 and Phil. 2:
10 f.). This might all be misread as supporting an unbiblical
universalism. The two New Testament passages cited indicate that in this connection men must still think in terms of
a final judgment. So that we might interpretively paraphrase:
"To me every knee — of those who are ready to acknowledge the Lordship of the Christ — shall bow; but even they
that do not acknowledge him as Christ, must admit his sole
sovereignty, though perhaps grudgingly." For, to be exact,
the verb "swear" that follows does not of itself mean "swear
allegiance," but merely swear in the sense of acknowledg-
ing the highest authority and appealing to it.

Verse 24. Still on the same high level of confessing the

breadth of the purposes of God is the claim, "Only in the Lord (men shall say) do I have full righteousness and strength." The one Lord is set forth as the only source of help and deliverance. At this point the prophet is speaking. The aspect of the word "righteousness" that is here under consideration is the righteousness that justifies, even as this appears in Holy Writ from Gen. 15:6 on. And where faith grasps this righteousness a new hidden source of "strength" opens up that man can appropriate in no other way. From this point onward the pronouncement of the prophet drops to lower levels of enthusiastic insight. This drop is unduly magnified when it is claimed that the rest now "limps along lamely" and this rest is even discarded as a poor afterthought of an uninspired glossator. For the things referred to are still great and glorious. Is it not indicative of a great victory when those "that were incensed against him" now approach "utterly ashamed," convinced of the utter folly of their former ways? This new attitude grows out of the clear insight how wrong they once were, how far removed from the true center of life.

Verse 25. The prophet also deems it worthy of mention that Israel herself shall occupy the same position as the rest of the saved and "shall be justified and shall glory" in what they again possess. When this attitude of Israel is ascribed to "all the offspring of Israel" it is difficult to determine whether this refers to the entirety of the nation of Israel, which is to be thought of as involved in an almost national conversion, or whether the *spiritual* Israel is under consideration.

Notes

Verse 24. We prefer to follow the marginal reading on the last word of the verse, as suggested by the Jewish scribes, namely *two* words, *mi 'itti*, "who (was) with me."

Verse 25. The word *baddim*, "empty talk," or "empty talkers," is in our day frequently taken in the sense of a known type of Babylonian priests, namely *barim* priests, an interpretation requiring the change of *d* to *r*. These *barim* priests were regarded as great prognosticators. But something vital is lost in making this change, the fact that they are really "charlatans."

Verse 26. Should we read the consonants as involving a singular
or a plural in the case of the word we have rendered "his servant"? Parallelism would suggest the plural. The singular, supported by the Hebrew tradition, makes the word refer to the
prophet himself. The decision is difficult. We prefer the latter
sense.

Verse 27. Does the reference to the "ocean deep" here inject the
"chaos-dragon" motif? Many hold that to be the case. We believe
that the mythological approach is being sadly overworked and that
such an approach contributes nothing helpful to the interpretation.

Verse 28. For the opening word of the second half of this verse
where the word *le'mor* (infinitive) occurs, the *Septuagint* and the
Vulgate have the participle, in line with the type of construction
which appears from v. 24b onward. Much may be said in favor of
such an emendation. The last two lines of the verse are regarded
with suspicion as being repetitious. We believe they should be
retained, for they re-emphasize an important point. It has been
noted that this is the only occurrence of the word "temple" in the
second half of the book.

45:2 In the case of the verb "level off" we feel that the *Keri*
should be followed *'ayyasher* (*Piel* imperfect).

Verse 4. It is believed by many that vv. 4-6 are more or less in
a state of confusion. We believe that our interpretation shows
that a good measure of coherence marks the passage.

Verse 8. In approaching the verb "open," some hold that it
should be thought of as assuming as its object the words "her
womb." Then this would be a kind of carry-over, having "erotic
associations" with Baal religion, which however are here rather
"sublimated." Such assumptions are neither helpful nor can they
be demonstrated to be valid.

Verse 9. The *RSV* seems to have an attractive solution of the
difficulty at the end of the verse when it renders, "Your work
has no handles." But as has been pointed out that translation
would require the *masculine* plural form rather than the *feminine*.

Verse 10. On the somewhat unusual ending for the verb "begetting" see *GK* 47 o.

Verse 16. In this verse the *athnach* should stand with *yachdaw*.

Verse 19. For "right" the Hebrew has "right things" — an ampli-
ficative plural (*GK* 124 s).

Verse 22. "Let yourselves be saved" is a *Nifal tolerativum*, see
GK 51 c. The imperative conveys a note of assurance, see *GK* 110 f.

Verse 24. Where we have rendered "men shall say" the Hebrew
has the plain perfect, 3. singular *'amar*, here used impersonally,
"one says" or "men shall say."

Verse 25. It will remain an open question whether the first verb
should be translated "triumph" (*RSV*) or "justified" (*McKenzie
et al.*). Usage allows for either.

Chapter XLVI

G. YAHWEH AND IDOLS CONTRASTED (Chap. 46)

We now move a step forward after considering how Cyrus was to be commissioned as the agent of the restoration of Israel. The other side of the coin is looked at: after Israel's restoration comes the story of Babylon's downfall — to be more exact, first the downfall of her gods, then her own collapse in Chaps. 46 and 47 respectively. But just as Yahweh was a vital factor in the restoration of Israel, so Babylon's idols are a factor — purely negative of course — in the overthrow of the greatest city of the then-time world. We say "negative" because they are totally impotent to avert the impending downfall.

It is for this reason that some of the following captions have been devised for this chapter: "Bel cowers, Yahweh sustains to eternity" (*Volz*); "Gods impotent and the Lord God omnipotent" (*North*); "Bearing or borne" (*G. A. Smith*). Though there is a high strain of victorious faith in evidence in this chapter and though the heathen idols are spoken of in a somewhat derogatory manner, this is hardly "a mocking-song" as *Muilenburg* has rightly pointed out.

As *North* again has maintained, the chapter is easily discerned to be a unity. There is no need to attempt to eliminate certain verses, as many writers are only too prone to do. The coherence that pervades the chapter is made obvious in part already by the outline.

1. Babylon's Gods Will Be Borne into Captivity (vv. 1-2)

46:1-2 1. Bel will bow down, Nebo will stoop;
their images will be consigned to beasts and cattle;
your items of baggage will be loaded up

as burdens for weary beasts.
2. They [the gods] will both stoop and bow down;
   they will be unable to save their load;
   they themselves will go into exile.

It has been rightly pointed out that this chapter begins like
a proclamation of victory, the defeated ones being Babylon's
gods.

Verse 1. Bel was the principal god of the Babylonians. He
is usually identified with the Greek god Mercury, who was
the spokesman for the gods. Nabu (or Nebo) was his son.
When in the course of time Marduk became the chief divinity of Babylon he was also called Bel, by that convenient
identification of old gods with new that was achieved so
easily among the ancients. Bel, of course, is only a variant
from of the Canaanite Baal. When however Marduk became so prominent the rank of his son Nebo became more
outstanding, as is indicated by the frequency with which
names were compounded with Nabu (Nebuchadnezzar,
Nabopolassar, Nabonidus). Bel's major temple was in Bor-
sippa, which lay twelve miles to the south of Babylon. According to Herodotus the image of Bel found in this temple
was gold and twelve cubits (*ca.* eighteen feet) tall.

Now of these two outstanding Babylonian gods it is said
that they "will bow down and stoop." This is meant in the
sense of being carried away *by their worshippers* into safety
at the time of the approach of the enemy to capture the
city and its idols. The words could be interpreted as referring
to the fact that the images would be carried away by the
victorious enemy as booty of war. In either case the great
Babylonian gods will suffer a shameful humiliation. Not
only are they to be a burden to weary beasts and cattle, but
they will be loaded up unceremoniously on these baggage
animals and suffer all the indignities of such treatment. These
two are mentioned as examples of how all Babylonian deities
will be treated. (*Pritchard's* ANEP, No. 538 gives an apt
illustration from the monuments.)

Verse 2. The impotence of these two gods in this time of

extremity is now further indicated. When the two verbs "stoop" and "bow down" are used a second time it is to stress the utter humiliation that they will experience. They (the idols) can contribute nothing to their own salvation. They are just so much dead weight. Being unable to deliver their worshippers from exile they must themselves experience that very fate.

But at this point attention is commonly drawn to the fact that Cyrus in his capture of the city of Babylon did nothing by way of humiliating the city's gods, nor did the inhabitants transport them away at the advent of Cyrus. In fact the capture of Babylon was not marked by the customary plundering and destruction and loss of life. As far as the Babylonian gods were concerned, Cyrus not only let them remain in their temples, but besought that prayers be made in these temples for his own success and that of his son Cambyses. So Isaiah erred in his prediction? That is a hasty conclusion. Fact of the matter is that the prophet had not specifically said that the downfall of the Babylonian deities would take place when Cyrus captured the city. He merely asserted that it could take place. Of their overthrow he was entirely certain. We do not even know whether he perhaps personally expected that the two events would coincide. This chapter may rightly be said to be marked by supreme confidence in the downfall of these impotent idols, and fall they did.

2. Yahweh Has Borne His People Faithfully (vv. 3-4)

46:3-4 "Hearken to me, O house of Jacob,
          all of you of the house of Israel who are left;
you who have been borne from birth,
          carried ever since you came forth from the womb.
4. Even to your old age I remain the same,
          and till your hairs are grey I will support you.
I have done so and I myself will carry you,
          yea, I myself will support and save you.

Verse 3. At this point without formal introduction direct discourse begins, God addressing his people. Two names are used for this people — Jacob and Israel. Both, of course, in this context refer to the same group, being used in parallelism for variety's sake. The clause "who are left" really is made up of the noun "remnant" (found only here in chaps. 40-66) which here is not used in the customary sense of "the remnant of Israel," but merely to indicate that the persons involved constituted a pitifully small group. When it is said that from birth they have been "borne" and "carried," this is merely a repetition of the two verbs that appeared in the first two verses in reference to the idols: *they* were borne; *God* bears his own. "From birth" and "from the womb" merely signifies: from the time when Israel became a nation, she has been the object of God's solicitous care and protection (cf. 44:2, 24; 49:5; also passages such as 63:9; Deut. 1:31; 33:27; Isa. 40:11).

Westermann very aptly draws attention to the fact that it is a stylistic peculiarity of the prophet to begin larger sections of his material with imperatives ("hearken", cf. v. 12, etc.).

Verse 4. When it is asserted that God will remain the same in his attitude toward his people "even to your old age" that surely does not imply that when they come to the point of old age his care for them is terminated. So the faithfulness of God is not set forth in terms of abstractions but in a practical and most comforting manner, as is often the case in this second half of Isaiah's book. When the word "carry" is used, the root meaning involved means to bear a heavy burden. There is a half-reproachful note in this, for God had often found Israel very burdensome in her self-will and stubborn pride. But the major emphasis lies on the fact that it is Yahweh himself who has taken these obligations upon himself for his people; for five times the emphatic personal pronoun "I" appears in this verse.

3. The Idols Are Utterly Impotent (vv. 5-7)

46:5-7   5. "To whom then will you liken me, or equate me, or compare me that I will really be like?

6. Those who pour forth gold from a purse
   and weigh out silver in balances
   and hire a goldsmith to make a god of it,
and then prostrate themselves before it, yea, worship it;
7. they lift it up upon their shoulders and laboriously transport it;
   they set it down in its place and it stays there.
      He cannot move from his spot.
   Even if one cries out to him he cannot answer;
      he will not deliver him from his distress."

Is this section perhaps an intrusion or a later addition?
Some claim this to be the case because the polemic against
idols has now been repeated a number of times since 40:18-
20. But it must be obvious that this section forms a strong
contrast to the faithfulness that Yahweh displays over against
them that truly serve him. Besides should not a vital point
be driven home again and again? This is a fresh statement of
a point that has indeed been previously made. A number of
commentators strongly defend the authenticity of these verses.

Verse 5. Yahweh is in a class entirely by himself. That
Israel understood well and the prophets taught it with emphasis. There is no being that can even remotely be compared with him. A class word for Yahweh and other beings
cannot be found.

Verse 6. So the way is prepared for a realistic estimate of
the heathen idols. They are of man's manufacture. The
process may be thought of as beginning at the moment when
a person, having a sufficiency of precious metal, pours it
forth from the money-bag that it may be weighed in the
balances. Coined money was not yet in common circulation
in the days of the prophet: metal had to be weighed out in
balances. An additional amount has to be weighed out to
hire the goldsmith "to make a god of it." Till now it was
merely a mass of metal. The rest of the process is in this case
passed by, having been described sufficiently already in 44:
12 ff. We move up at once to the use to which the finished
object is put. That use is this: they "prostrate themselves before it, yea, worship it." Combining the two ideas, *North*
comes up with the rather apt translation: they "prostrate

themselves full length." They adore and implore the work of their hands, of which they can rest assured, they may expect nothing by way of help. Not after such an origin of the object involved! Perhaps there never was a greater folly than idolatry. But before he drops the subject, the Lord, here still speaking, expands one feature that clearly reveals the ridiculousness of it all, viz. v. 7.

Verse 7. The whole approach centers around the fact that the idols can become so heavy a burden for a man. He "lifts it up upon his shoulders and laboriously transports it" to the place destined for it. The sweat streams from the face of those who do the work. Finally they get to their distination. There "they set it down in its place and — what else could be the result? — it stays there." The god is rigidly held in place by the law of gravity; "he cannot move from his spot," in fact cannot budge so much as an inch by his own power. Let the worshipper now step before him; let him present his petition modestly. Or, if he pleases let him "cry out." Still "he cannot answer" or give any token of having even heard the voice that cried. Summing it up: "he will not deliver him from his distress." Idolatry is the height of futility. — This portion is immediately followed by one of those striking contrasts so characteristic of the prophet (vv. 8-11).

4. Yahweh's Total Control of All Things Made Apparent by the Fact That He Can Foretell the Future (vv. 8-11)

46:8-11   8. "Remember this and show yourselves firm;
        lay it to heart, you rebels.
9. Remember the former things of long ago;
     for I am God and there is no other,
          very God and there is none like me,
10. declaring the end [outcome] from the beginning,
     and long beforehand things not yet done;
saying, 'My purpose stands,
     and I will execute all my good pleasure;
11. calling a falcon from the east,

from a far country the man who shall carry out my purpose.'
I have both spoken and will also bring it to pass;
I have formulated my plan and will also carry it out."

Another approach may be used in taking this passage in
hand. *Volz* captions it, "A warning addressed to rebels." It
is that too, for v. 8 calls those who are being addressed
"rebels." So this passage to an extent runs parallel with 45:
9-13, where those addressed also find fault with what the
Almighty is doing. But as to content the passage does set
forth Yahweh's total control of all things; and so our title
may be retained. In that the passage used the proof from
prophecy as indicative of the fact that he has all things
under his control, it presents a parallel to 41:22-24; 42:9;
43:9-13; 48:3-5.

Verse 8. Yahweh is still speaking. He is still addressing
Israel as was the case since v. 3. However it is only a portion
of the people whom he challenges. He calls them "rebels."
They seem to be an impenitent element in the nation that
in spite of all that God has done for his people still take a
critical attitude. The prophet falls into a tone of a somewhat
unusual severity not otherwise characteristic of him at all.
The same somewhat harsh tone appears again in v. 12. Apparently they wavered in their whole attitude and were far
from taking that trustful position that they should have.
Therefore the challenge: "Remember this and show yourselves firm; lay it to heart," spoken somewhat in the tone of
I Cor. 16:13. Continual vacillation, trusting the Lord one
day and being dubious about him the next, is most unwholesome and dangerous.

Verse 9. To reinforce this challenge, the prophet once
more resorts to the proof from prophecy that he seemingly
loves to operate with. He invites the rebels to turn their
thoughts back far into the past, recalling "former things" like
perhaps the Exodus, or other such mighty works of God
done for Israel. These works of his demonstrate, as nothing
else can, his consistent attitude toward his people, that he has

proved himself to be their God, and there is no other. He is "very God and none like [him]."

Verse 10. Now follows the rest of the proof built up on this fact. What he purposed to do for his covenant-people he also declared from the beginning, demonstrating his control by specifying what the end would be from the very beginning of time. The Lord's deeds are thought of as a series; the predictions that these deeds would come to pass are also a series. These two series correspond with one another: they match up. The foretelling always came "long beforehand." Only the Lord can do or has done things like that. The very magnitude of the conception of God that is displayed by all this guarantees for Israel what a reliable and able God she has. Another way of stating the case is: "My purpose stands and I will execute my good pleasure." Previous passages where this approach was used are 41:22 and 42:9.

Verse 11. Now the argument is brought down to the present instance: The Lord has called "a falcon from the east, from a far country the man who shall carry out [his] purpose." The reference is obviously to Cyrus, who previously was described as the man from the *north* (41:25). A specific bird is not really mentioned, for the original means a swooping bird; could be an eagle or any bird of prey. A similar figure is used in Jer. 49:22 in reference to a bird of prey coming against Edom. In the present instance a swift and deadly thrust against Babylon is under consideration. But the point is: this is not merely another conqueror. This is a divinely commissioned conqueror whose coming the Lord has foreseen and determined, guarantying his success at the same time. The full certainty of God's control of the situation is reflected in the concluding statement: "I have both spoken and will also bring it to pass; I have formulated my plan and will also carry it out."

This whole declaration (vv. 8-11) has aptly been described as a "superb expression of the prophet's theology," in other words, of his concept of God. The future lies in God's mind, but does not lie there "dormant." God foresees, predetermines, and brings his purposes to completion. More complete control of the issues of history could not even be visualized.

In conclusion it may yet be remarked that in the use of the figure of the eagle there is hardly an allusion to the fact that on the imperial standards of Persia the symbol of the eagle appeared, as it also did at a later date on the battle flags of Rome.

5. Yahweh's Deliverance Will Soon Take Place (vv. 12-13)

46:12-13 12. "Hearken to me you stubborn-hearted,
　　　　　you who are far from righteousness.
13. I have brought near my righteousness,
　　it is not far off,
　　　　and my salvation will not lag.
I shall give my gift of salvation in Zion,
　　for Israel my glorification."

Verse 12. The class who are now being addressed as the "stubborn-hearted" will most likely be the very "rebels" of v. 8. The two failings are akin, and they are still in the same general category. First this group is described as not submitting to the divine word but rebelling against it. Then they are thought of as having made their hearts obdurate against divine truth. Such an attitude puts them far away from "righteousness." Though the tendency is strong in our day to use the perfectly permissible translation "deliverance" for this word, still that aspect of the case seems to be covered by the word found at the end of v. 13 — "salvation." We find good ground therefore for taking the word in what many are pleased to call the "forensic sense," i.e., practically synonymous with "justification." For as long as men harden their hearts against God's promises and refuse to appropriate them they certainly are not in a situation in which God can pronounce them to be what they ought to be in his sight. They are "far from righteousness." Speaking more nearly in terms applicable to the Old Testament we could say, these persons are not obedient to the demands of the covenant of their God and to faith in its promises, as it has been aptly claimed.

Verse 13. But God's graciousness far exceeds what man might expect. So he still promises to grant unto them this righteousness, which he alone can impart or impute. It has, as it were, been brought so close by him that all they on their part need to do is to stretch forth their hand and take it. But he also has another gift at hand, the "salvation" they as a nation so badly need; for they are far from fully restored from the Captivity. This salvation is described as a gift by the use of the word "give." To make this apparent we have translated: "I shall give my gift of salvation in Zion," a promise which is further amplified by the parallel statement, "for Israel (I shall give) my glorification." Thus noun "glorification" has nothing to do with the glory of God, which in different instances he allowed to appear and to dwell among his people. This refers to the singular honors that he bestowed upon his people, giving them a glorious name. On this note the contrast between the mighty God and the impotent idols comes to a close. Yahweh is not only mighty but mighty to give whatever his people need or desire.

Notes

Verse 2. The two perfects *qaresu* and *kare'u* are used without conjunction (the customary *waw* consecutive) as is frequently the case with synonymns. See *KS* 370 h. "They themselves" in Hebrew reads "their souls," souls being used for persons.

Verse 4. In *'esbol* we have an instance of the growing usage in later Hebrew to avoid the *waw* consecutive construction. See *KS* 40. In *'asithi* (perfect) and *'essa'* (imperfect) we should note the distinction. The perfect expresses the nature of an act; the imperfect, the display of that nature.

Verse 5. The last verb *wenidhmeh* seems to coordinate this verb with the preceding by a *waw* consecutive, but this is really a consecutive clause "*that* I will really be like." *KS* 364 n.

Verse 7. When the construction switches to the singular with *yits'aq* it is the distributive singular ("any one") that is actually being resorted to. See *KS* 348 w.

Verse 8. There is no need to try to emend the text at this point when *hith'oshashu* is used just because this is the only instance of the use of this verb *'ashash*. The *Targum* already renders it "take courage." An Arabic parallel root would seem to confirm this approach.

Verse 10. *Re'shith* is used without an article; that virtually stamps it as a proper noun, the absolute beginning (*KS* 294 g).

Verse 11. We follow the *keri 'atsathi*, rather than "*his* purpose" which yields no usable sense. The threefold use of the *'aph* in the second half of the verse gives a kind of staccato effect.

Chapter XLVII

H. THE OVERTHROW OF BABYLON TRIUMPHANTLY PREDICTED (Chap. 47)

This overthrow is not just the overthrow of one more city during the course of history; it is the overthrow of the proud world-capital of the time.

We have before us a poem in the form of a "taunt song," or "mocking song." In mood and content it is like the preceding chapter, which told of the overthrow of Babylon's gods. Where however this type of poem might degenerate into something cheap and trivial and thus quite unworthy of being the utterance of a man of God, that is not the case here. The taunt is the taunt of faith; the mockery is based on the certainty of God's judgments. God has determined to overthrow a city marked by overweening pride; the author of this poem concurs fully in what is determined and sees both the justice and the wisdom of what God has determined. So, as *North* has said, this is a "magnificent taunt song." Nor should we think of it as offering a certain type of philosophy of history, namely an illustration of the validity of the ancient rule that things move in cycles, empires too. The kingdoms of this world keep rising and falling in a ceaseless round. True as that is to an extent, for the present writer, the prophet, Babylon's fall is an instance of the absolute control of history by Yahweh, the Lord God Almighty. A defeated God of a defeated people boldly asserts that he will take a victorious nation in hand and execute vengeance upon her, as *Westermann* points out. A striking thought!

When some claim for this song that it is not as vengeful as Nahum's song about Nineveh's overthrow, we fear that such a comparison is inept. As stated above, the writer concurs in the judgments of the Almighty and is glad over them

because they are right. The one to be punished has fully
merited the judgment contemplated. When justice therefore
is done, that is something to rejoice over. Such rejoicing can
be true and wholesome without the note of an unholy
gloating.

It is a bit difficult to determine who it is that is speaking.
Some think that it is God addressing Babylon. Others feel
it is the prophet. Still others, that it is the nation of Israel
itself. There is a propriety about each approach. It could
have been any one of these three. It really does not matter
in this instance which interpretation one prefers. It still
clearly is a prediction of what must befall Babylon.

Breaking the poem up into component parts is not easy, at
least not achieving an outline that is fully convincing. There
are advocates of a three part division, of a four, five, or six
part division. Again it does not matter too much which pattern is followed. The six-part division has the most enthusiastic adherents, calling it, in terms of pattern, "a poem of
outstanding artistry." That it is in any case. But where certain arrangements are arrived at by deletions and corrections,
we admit that such procedures may be classed as being questionable. All writers in our day practically agree that the
qinah (lament) meter is employed to a very large extent.
The artistry claimed for the poem involves such elements
as imperatives freely used, repetition, onomatopoeia, a striking introduction, a similar conclusion, and the like.

The thing at which this song strikes out sharply is the
overweening pride and heartlessness of the Babylonian empire, in controlling the destinies of the nations comprising her
empire. Some surmise that it was this factor that made Babylon the type of the Antichrist, as it is in the New Testament, rather than Assyria, an equally renowned empire (cf.
Rev. 17 and 18).

Comparing the taunt songs that stand out, we find in Isaiah
14 dealing with Babylon's wicked king, Chap. 46, with her
impotent idols, and Chap. 47 with the dethroned queen.

Let us underscore one point a bit more strongly. The fact

just alluded to is what we have in mind. In the Scriptures, Babylon is sometimes a historical entity, sometimes it is practically only a symbol of concentrated wickedness, ripe for judgment. She is a pattern how world empires grow, become exceedingly proud, and are drastically overthrown.

1. It Is Impending and Inevitable (vv. 1-5)

47:1-5 1. Down with you and sit in the dust,
          O virgin daughter of Babylon;
sit on the bare earth dethroned,
    O daughter of the Chaldeans.
For no longer shall you be in a situation that men
    shall call you tender and delicate.
2. Take a mill and grind meal;
remove your veil; strip off the train;
    lay bare the leg; wade through the streams.
3. Your nakedness shall be uncovered,
    and your shame shall be seen.
I will take vegeance; I will yield to no man.
4. Our Redeemer — the Lord of hosts is his name —
    is the Holy One of Israel.
5. Sit down in silence and go into darkness,
    O daughter of the Chaldeans;
        for you shall no more be called
        the queen of kingdoms.

Verse 1. It is a common practice to let a nation be personified as a woman. In this case the designation of "virgin" is added, signifying that she is to be thought of as sexually unconquered (cf. 23:12 — Sidon — and 37:22 — Zion). Whether this woman in question is to be thought of as a queen or as a prominent member of the royal harem, is not immediately clear; we feel the former possibility has greater likelihood. It is, however, quite clear that a severe humiliation is in prospect ("virgin daughter" regularly introduces doom oracles). So, being also the object of divine displeasure, she is somewhat rudely addressed: "Down with you"! and: "Sit on the bare earth"! and "Sit in the dust"! Sitting on the bare earth is sometimes to be construed as a gesture of mourning; here it involves humiliation, even as does the designation "dethroned." From being as high as women can rise, she is to be as low as they can descend. Perhaps *North* goes a little too far when he takes the second imperative to mean: "sit among the rubble." For the picture has not yet been developed enough to allow for the thought of ruins in the picture. "Tender and delicate" is virtually a quotation from Deut. 28:56, describing a pampered person, who has enjoyed every luxury. Some explain the terms as involving sensuous and sensual living in the extreme, which could certainly be asserted concerning Babylon of old.

Verse 2. Having been demoted, as it were, from queen to slave, she is next bidden to engage in the most menial of tasks — to "take a mill and grind meal." All pleasant and luxurious living is at an end: the garments of luxury must go, "veil and train." At this point the figure of the slave is abandoned and the woman is conceived of as being led away into captivity. In the course of being led away she must ford streams and in doing so must lay bare the leg and wade.

Verse 3. The figure continues in terms of wading across a stream. The water is thought of as deeper than was expected. So the garment had to be raised higher. Result: exposure, unavoidable, of "nakedness," and also (her) "shame" — genitalia — shall be seen. No need here to go to extremes of interpretation, as though rape, for example, were being described; or even, that the woman is being thought of as stripped like an adulteress, or that she shall be put on public display on the slave market, naked. Similar expressions are found in 20:4; Nah. 3:5; Jer 13:22, 26. All this that is thus figuratively described is now approached from another point of view: God is "taking vengeance." Here this noun is apparently being used in the constructive sense of righting wrongs long due for correction. What befalls Babylon is her just punishment and well deserved. The last statement of the verse — "I will yield to no man" — is merely another way of saying: Her doom is irrevocable; intercessions in her behalf will be of no avail. She has gone too far.

Verse 4. This verse looks like an uncalled for interruption of the train of thought, however, it is anything but that. It asserts that a higher point of view is to be noted in regard to what is happening to Babylon. The "Redeemer" of Israel, who, as "Lord of hosts" has all things under his control, and stands in a unique relation to his people, having set himself apart for their care and protection ("the Holy One of Israel") is the one under whose aegis all these things are happening to the once proud capital of the empire of Babylon. All history is God-related and remains totally under his control. Here there are no cheap and trivial retaliations. Here is controlled history. Nor should this verse be regarded as an afterthought. It reflects the very heart and soul of what happened when Babylon fell.

Verse 5. As this section began so it ends with a summons to step down and begin to lead a different type of existence. Babylon is to be removed from high station and is to "sit down." She is to move out of the spotlight of prominence and popularity and is to sit "in darkness," that is to say, in comparative obscurity. "Chaldeans" is here merely used as a synonymn for Babylonians. In one word, she is no longer to be a "queen" — a parallel to this would be the designation of Venice as "the queen of the Adriatic."

2. It Is Largely Due to Her Misunderstanding Israel's Overthrow (vv. 6-7)

47:6-7 6. I was indeed angry with my people,
        I profaned my heritage,
and gave them over into your hand.
    But you showed them no mercy;
    even upon the old men you made
        the yoke press very heavily.
7. You thought, "I shall be queen forever,"
    you did not lay these things to heart;
you did not consider how all this would end.

Verse 6. It is quite clear that Yahweh is now speaking. He is outlining for Babylon what it is that has actually happened. But what he claims happened is hardly what a nation like Babylon would have deemed possible. The little nation of God's people suddenly moves into the picture as a matter of even greater concern than mighty Babylon. History has as its very center God's people and not the mighty empires which seem to dominate the world. So what actually happened was this: Israel had led a life unworthy of her destiny as God's people. This called forth God's just anger. The nation persisted in its wilfulness, and so God had to act. He did act, and so doing "profaned his heritage." This somewhat weighty statement involved that he allowed his people to be profaned, which here means "polluted," or "defiled." He gave them over to the spoiler or plunderer. "Heritage" could here mean Israel itself. The term is sometimes also used for the Temple, or for the Holy Land. Which ever is thought of, the net result is about the same. But the Lord gives over his prized possession into the hands of the enemy. The ultimate control of what befalls nations in their conflict with one another rests with the Almighty. So Babylon conquered Judah. But in the process of working out the results of such a victory there were certain normal limitations that reason dictated for the conqueror in the treatment of the vanquished. These obvious humane limitations Babylon did not observe. She ignored what the natural law taught all nations. The victor cannot let his vilest passions rage against the nation overcome in war. But Babylon behaved very arbitrarily; she "showed them no mercy." One instance of such unpardonable behavior is cited: "even upon the old men you made the yoke press very heavily." Harsh cruelty was the order of the day as though Babylon could let its basest and most cruel passion have free range. Her success in war called forth the worst in her. There are indications also in the Scriptures that even heathen nations felt that they were instruments in the hand of God when they gained victories over other nations.

Verse 7. But Babylon thought that perpetual success was bound to be her destiny. In other words: "I shall be queen forever." Whatever lessons of history and suggestions of conscience there were, Babylon disregarded them proudly. She made her calculations without thinking "how all this would end." She should have known that if she played her role badly she would have to answer to the Deity himself. These aspects of history are obvious but they have been misread over and over again by the nations. The prophet has in these words allowed us a glimpse behind the scenes of history. Now we know why Babylon had to fall. She defied God's purposes with his people.

3. But It Is Also Due to Her Own Unseemly Pride (vv. 8-11)

47:8-11   8. But now hear this, you voluptuous one,
⠀⠀⠀⠀⠀⠀⠀⠀⠀who dwell securely,
who say in your heart:
⠀"I am, and there is none besides me;
⠀I shall not sit as a widow
⠀⠀or know the loss of children."
9. And yet both these things shall befall you,
⠀suddenly, on one and the same day:
⠀the loss of children and widowhood shall come upon you
⠀⠀in their full measure,
⠀in spite of your many sorceries,
⠀⠀and in spite of the great power of your spells.
10. But you felt secure in your wickedness.
⠀You said: "No one sees me."
⠀Your very wisdom and your knowledge led you astray;
⠀⠀and you said in your heart:
⠀"I am, and there is none besides me."
11. But there will come upon you evil,
⠀which you shall not know how to control.
Catastrophe, such as you have not known,
⠀shall suddenly befall you.

Verse 8. The key to this section lies in the fact that the proud claim of Babylon is presented twice, in v. 8 and v. 10. Twice she is represented as saying: "I am and there is none besides me." Still it is true that, as to form, this passage is introduced as a "prophetic oracle" in the form "of a threat," following "the invective" (*Muilenburg*). Babylon is addressed as "you voluptuous one." She may be harsh in her dealings with others; she pampers herself, as happens so often. At the same time she lives under the illusion that no evil can befall her, or "she dwells securely." (cf. Zeph. 2:15, where Nineveh is represented as taking the same attitude). When however Babylon makes her proud boast, "I am and there is none besides me," it should be noted first that elsewhere in the book this is the language used by none less than Yahweh himself (cf. 45:5, 21; 46:9). This therefore amounts to self-deification, as is also indicated by Ezek. 28:1-10, in the case of Tyre. This therefore is no ordinary boast but a most arrogant and presumptuous one. For sheer daring this boast cannot be matched. It defiantly challenges God himself. By way of further comparison, 14:13 f. may appropriately be examined. In her presumption the nation therefore likens herself to a woman who is happily married and has a goodly number of children and now regards her position as impregnable. The folly of such a boastful attitude is only too apparent. No position offers the promise of total security. The suddenness of the overthrow of proud Babylon is historically well attested.

Verse 9. So the prophet punctures the bubble of false security, proclaiming that the very thing the nation deems impossible will come to pass, yes, both things, "loss of children and widowhood," and that very suddenly. Babylon sat on top of the world one day and the next she was in the hands of the Persians. And all this in "full measure." Total collapse! Certain resources on which Babylon particularly prided itself would avail nothing when her time came upon her, resources such as "sorceries" and "spells." In these areas Babylon was known to be very much at home. These practices were assiduously cultivated by all nations of antiquity, and by none more than by the men of Babylon. *Haller* aptly described Babylon as "the promised land of astrology and magic." These pseudo-sciences were cultivated in a manner "incredibly elaborate" (*North*). In spite of all this, the *mass* of sorceries and the *great power* of the spells would prove utterly futile.

Verse 10. But such an attitude which assumed that one can get along well without God is more than a grandiose delusion. It is "wickedness." It sadly misleads him who harbors it. Yet there is something of an awareness of guilt involved in such an attitude. For when the remark is added: "You said: 'No one sees me,' " that very statement indicates that the speaker was aware that something reprehensible was involved. Superb pride also is one of those things that shuns the light because it is wicked, and seeks to remain hid. What had happened was that that very type of abstruse knowledge and wisdom that was being cultivated by these occult sciences was the thing that was utterly misleading the nation. Confidence was placed in the stars and their courses and not in the power of the Living God. Here is where the proud attitude of self-glorification is referred to again. For trust in the knowledge that a man can concoct leads man astray.

Verse 11. Now comes the threat of the inevitable disaster. It will be of such a sort that Babylon will not be able to control it. The futility of the devices she has been employing will become very evident on the day of judgment. Incantations and magic formulas, and the endless repetition of them is futile procedure. In fact it will all lead up to a catastrophe so overwhelming that the like will never even have occurred to Babylon. All this may be summed up in the one word: "God resisteth the proud."

4. Sorcery Is of No Avail in This Calamity (vv. 12-15)

47:12-15 12. Step forth now with your spells
and your many sorceries,
with which you have toiled from your youth;
perhaps you will terrify [me].
13. You have wearied yourself with your many consultations;
let them step forth and save you,
those that divide the heavens,
that gaze on the stars,
that at the new moon make known
something of what will come upon you.
14. They are nothing but so much chaff
which fire consumes.
They cannot deliver even themselves
from the power of the flame.

It is not a coal for warming oneself,
  no firelight to sit by.
15. Such have they become with whom you have labored,
  the men who have done business with you from your youth
    up.
  Each one strays about in his own random way;
    there is no one to save you.

Verse 12. There was a passing allusion already to sorcery
in the previous section. Now the prophet goes at this subject at some length, because he had to demolish completely
the confidence that men might put in such deceptions. The
nations esteemed sorcery as very important. Israel may sometimes have envied the nations the possession of such mysterious powers. But they were no powers; they were grand de-
lusions. The prophet strikes a devastating blow at the whole
structure of sorcery. He hurls a challenge at the Babylonians. They are to step forth on the scene for a show-down,
equipped with all the wealth of resources that sorcery has
devised in the course of the centuries. She had not trifled
with these factors. She had "toiled" with them from her
youth. Astronomy and occult arts had been drawn on
heavily. It took years of intense study to become a com-
petent exponent of magic, spells, and sorcery. When the
prophet adds, "perhaps you may yet succeed," he does not
vaguely anticipate that something will be achieved after all.
This is sarcasm, as is the following statement, "perhaps you
will terrify" says the Lord. At this point we have added
a "me" in parenthesis, because it seems to be implied. Nor is
sarcasm unexpected in a taunt song.

Verse 13. The many hours of study devoted to these arts
are represented as having already wearied the nation, who
through her men of learning, particularly the Chaldeans, has
engaged in "many consultations." Again and again it would
be attempted to unravel the skein of the future. The ones
with whom learned consultations were held are challenged
to "step forth and save." They will be given a fair chance
to do something helpful, if they can. The ones who are

particularly in the mind of the prophet are the "ones that divide the heavens." The reference would appear to be to the astrologers and classification of spheres of influence, as the signs of the zodiac. For they are also described as those "that gaze on the stars," or as those "that at the new moon make known something of what will come upon you." All this is not too precisely defined and may be a reference to things astrological that we are not in a position to describe. But interesting is the careful phrasing, "*something* of what will come upon you." These prognosticators will sometimes hit the right thing, but all they offer will be fragmentary, and unsatisfactory.

Verse 14. Now the verdict upon this pseudo-science, pretentious but hollow! The whole lot of the college of fortunetellers, maintained at great expense and devoting much effort to the project, in the last analysis is "nothing but so much chaff," stuff worthy only of being consumed by fire. The writer charges them with not even being able to deliver themselves, let alone others, "from the power of the flame." Here flame stands for the divine judgment, which is often likened to a flame. The flame-figure is at this point given another turn and developed more fully. A flame could serve the good purpose of warming a man when cold. Not so this fire. Or it might be thought of as a cheery fire, or "firelight to sit by." Not even that may be claimed for this fire. Astrology is in fact the epitome of futility.

Verse 15. When it is stated that these men had worked hand in hand with the Babylonians, this may be a reference to the well-known fact that these groups of purveyors of secret arts had been furnished private quarters at national expense and had enjoyed special privileges, like priests. Of course, they are men who have been so long in the picture that they seem to belong there. These men have done business with the nation from her youth up. They are something distinctively Babylonian. But when the great reckoning comes, which the prophet describes as being in the offing, these persons will stray about aimlessly and helplessly, unable to save themselves or any other man. On this note of the utter futility of astrology ends this "magnificent taunt song."

Notes

Luther begins the new section with 46:12. We fail to see good grounds for so doing.

Verse 1. On the idea of a nation personified as a woman see *KS* 248 f. On the unique way of expressing the idea of "no longer to do a thing," see *GK* 120 c and *KS* 361 h.

Verse 3. Some would claim that this verse is an inept expansion of the idea involved, at least 3a. That approach is purely a matter of subjective impression. The first half of the verse rounds out the thought quite effectively.

"Will yield to no man" is a defensible translation of *'ephga'*, which *BDB* translates as "entreat" and *KB*, as "yield to asking." No matter how it is translated the net result is about the same.

Verse 4. Following the lead of the Septuagint some feel that this verse should be introduced by *'amar* ("he says") and then have v. 5 as that which the Holy One says, a harmless emendation but unnecessary.

Verse 7. The initial verb *'amar* is generally admitted also to have the meaning not of "say" but of "suppose." See *BDB*, p. 56.

Verse 8. In *'aphsi* the final syllable may be the remnant of an old case ending (*GK* 90 m).

Verse 9. The verb *ba'u* is a prophetic perfect.

Verse 10. For "in your wickedness" the Dead Sea Scrolls substituted "in your knowledge" substituting an initial *r* for *d*. Though that would make good sense, so does the text as it stands.

Verse 11. For "which you shall not know how to control" *KJ* has: "thou shalt not know from whence it ariseth." The word involved is *shachar*, "dawn." The rendering involved in *KJ* is, as *BDB* indicates "improbable." The word is now usually traced back to a kindred Arabic root meaning "to charm" or "to bribe away."

The initial verb of this verse appears in the masculine with a feminine subject, as is often done in Hebrew. See *KS* 345 b.

Verse 12. Elaborate emendations on this verse are attempted, but when all is said and done it still seems best, with *North*, to keep the text as it stands.

For "that divide the heavens" the *Septuagint* actually uses the word "astrologers."

Chapter XLVIII

I. A SHARP REBUKE AND A GRACIOUS CHALLENGE (Chap. 48)

As our caption indicates we see two elements set forth in this chapter, the first element, rebuke, is preponderant; the second, grace, here plays a secondary role. So we are in sympathy with those who term the subject of the chapter to be a summary word of admonition to the unconverted, or, as some put it: "Once again an attempt had to be made to stir up a people who had their doubts about good prospects for the future" (*Koenig*).

Our chapter presents a number of unique problems. We shall not attempt to describe and evaluate the various solutions that have been offered. But we do draw attention to one of the latest, one that has been worked out with great care. We refer to *Westermann's* treatment of the case. He takes issue with the obvious fact that two kinds of material appear in the chapter: some words speak graciously to the nation Israel, some words prefer sharp indictments of the same group. *Westermann* believes to have gotten around the difficulty involved by attributing the second group of words to the class of secondary additions, leaving the question open whether these additions stem from the author or from some other writer. Secondary materials are: vv. 1e, 4, 5cd, 7c, 8cd, 9, 10, 11c. This would certainly result in a chapter that had been abundantly reworked. But the critic is positive that we have anything but a unit chapter. The writer is always wavering between two types of material.

It must be admitted that a sharp, clear-cut, logical progression of thought is not in evidence in the chapter. But the truth of the matter appears to be that there are two sides to the author's message. We have sought to cover this aspect of the case by the chapter-caption: "A sharp rebuke and a gracious challenge." Both aspects of the message clamor for a hearing. Hardly has the one side of the matter been presented when the prophet feels the need of emphasizing the other aspect of the case. This is a situation like so many in the prophetic writings of the Old Testament: they present a blend of law and gospel. Somewhat harshly *Westermann* refuses to allow the question of what is genuine and what is not even to be raised in this context.

We choose at this point to present a condensation of the contents of this chapter in a somewhat more detailed outline.

a. vv. 1-2. A solemn introduction of a sharp rebuke. God is about to make a pronouncement and describes the spiritual state of those to whom this rebuke is addressed.

b. vv. 3-5. The beginning of the pronouncement. God's *fore-knowledge of past history* is an index of his full control of history. Thereby he anticipates and cuts short Israel's willful misinterpretation.

c. vv. 6-8. The same control of history is displayed by God's *foretelling of a new set of events.* No one knew of these things save God alone. God had to operate thus to shame rebellious Israel.

d. vv. 9-11. God's sparing of the sinners is due solely to his grace.

e. vv. 12-13. All things take their beginning from the Lord, and he survives them all.

f. vv. 14-16. The sending of Cyrus and the foretelling of his success is further proof of God's absolute control.

g. vv. 17-19. If Israel had hearkened to God in the past, she would now be most abundantly blessed.

h. vv. 20-22. Israel is invited to go forth from Babylon rejoicing.

Though outlines of the chapter like *North's* (*Prophecy and History*) have some value, they are too brief to be of much help.

One thing that almost every writer comments on is the extreme sharpness of the rebuke administered by our prophet.

We feel that too much is being made of this type of approach. Sharpness? Yes. Extreme sharpness? That is a matter of opinion. Passages marked by some measure of sharp rebuke would be the following: 42:18-25; 43:22 ff.; 46:8 ff.; 50:1-3. It becomes very difficult to determine which of these is to be labelled as the sharpest of all.

Another somewhat striking thing is the fact that idolatry is ascribed to the nations, whereas the opposite observation has frequently been made that idolatry becomes a dead issue for Israel after the Captivity. This is no longer a dominant sin after the Return from Babylon. The relative truth of this chapter on the subject appears to be this, that, though by and large idolatry lost its hold on the nation, it still survived as a private sin on the part of some and still constituted at least some measure of a threat to her healthy spiritual life as a nation.

1. Solemn Introduction of a Sharp Rebuke (vv. 1-2)

48:1-2 1. Hearken, O house of Jacob,
who are called by the name of Israel,
and have come forth out of the waters of Judah,
who swear by the name of Yahweh,
who call to remembrance the God of Israel
but not in good faith and sincerity.
2. For they call themselves after the Holy City
and lean upon the God of Israel:
the Lord of hosts is his name.

Verse 1. The prophet is speaking. This solemn introduction savors more of the spirit of the prophet Ezekiel than of the comfort of Isaiah. In fact this harsh note prevails till v. 11. The "this" of "hear this" (*RSV*) refers to what is about to follow. The ones addressed as "house of Jacob" are simply the ancient people of God, here designated after their historical ancestor. They have in addition the more honorable title of "Israel" — the covenant nation. A third term is used to heighten the solemnity of the address — they have come forth "from the waters of Judah" (the tribal ancestor of the southern kingdom). This somewhat difficult expression, which has invited a number of textual emendations, perhaps has nothing more in mind than a tributary derived from the main stream. So the majority of the people, being Jews, stem at this post-exilic date which is envisioned, from the mainstream Judah. In the somewhat eloquent description that follows, certain spiritual prerogatives are set forth, prerogatives that are distinctly her own. The nation may use the name of Yahweh wherever solemn oaths are required. She calls upon him to witness what they say, and he hears. Furthermore, she may call to remembrance whatever God has done for her in the past, praising his holy name. Such adoration is a further privilege. But alas, these sacred usages have degenerated to the point where they are no longer done "in good faith and sincerity." The whole verse then speaks of rare privileges bestowed but abused and regarded lightly. The fact that the two verbs last used ("swear" and "all to remembrance" (frequently have liturgical connotation, by no means puts the stamp of a liturgical gathering upon the people mentioned in the text in question. For to use verbs that have liturgical connotation does not say that such usage immediately conjures up a liturgical act as such.

Verse 2. Further bad habits that have been developed by this favored nation indicate in what area the bad faith and lack of sincerity just referred to are to be found. These people are wont to associate themselves with "the Holy City," unholy though they themselves are (on "Holy City" compare 52:1 and Dan. 9:24). They also are in the habit of "leaning upon the God of Israel, Yahweh of hosts is his name." But here too the implication is that they put their trust in him on occasions where such confidence is unwarranted. For "Yahweh of hosts" is the God of all worlds and is not lightly to be used as a refuge in connection with unhallowed purposes. So ends the solemn, ominous-sounding introduction.

2. The Beginning of the Pronouncement (vv. 3-5)

48:3-5 3. "The earlier prophecies I have declared from of old; from my mouth they went forth and I made them known. Suddenly I acted and they happened.
4. Since I knew how stubborn you are, and that your neck is like a sinew of iron and your forehead is of bronze;
5. therefore did I declare things from of old. Before they happened I published them, lest you say: 'My idol did them, my carved image and my metal image have ordered it.' "

Now the Lord begins to speak.

Verse 3. The prophet represents the Lord as also operating with an argument that he has been using effectively, the argument about God's foreknowledge of things that happened in the past. Here the emphasis lies mainly on the effect that this fact should have had on Israel and how it should have influenced the nation's thinking. In times past — here the line of demarcation in point of time is drawn where the Babylonian Captivity comes to pass. The significant events of Israel's history were again and again declared before they happened: Abraham's destiny, Israel's Bondage in Egypt, Israel's Liberation from this Bondage, the Conquest of Canaan, the coming of the Babylonian Captivity. The references to these events are the "earlier prophecies" here mentioned. They reach far back ("from of old"). Either speaking directly to individuals when he appeared to them, or through the mouth of his holy prophets, "which have been since the world began," God made the coming of these events known. People often knew a long time in advance of the coming of these events. Then "suddenly [he] acted and they happened."

Verse 4. A unique motivation for the prediction and for bringing the predicted event to pass is now given. Among other reasons that may be advanced for God's doing this, God advances this new one: "I knew how stubborn you are ... therefore did I declare things from of old ... lest you say:

'My idol did them.' " God's course of action was calculated to forestall some unwholesome attitude on Israel's part. She, as nation, was so stubbornly addicted to idolatry that she would be inclined to attribute such unusual acts of God to her idols, whereas the glory belonged to God. This stubbornness is often referred to in the Scriptures (see Exod. 32:9; Deut. 9:6, 27; Jer. 3:3; Ezek. 3:7). Here there is attributed to Israel a "neck like a sinew of iron," and a "forehead of bronze" ("your effrontery is brazen" translates *North*). Yahweh would nip in the bud this inclination to give the idols credit for what Yahweh did.

Verse 5. One is taken aback a bit by this reference to idolatry on the part of the Israel of the Exile. It is usually claimed that the Babylonian Exile cured Israel of her proclivity to idolatry, which had to be scored so frequently by the prophets, especially Jeremiah. The explanation for this seeming discrepancy may lie in this that the public and open practice of idolatry did fall away with the heavy yoke of the Captivity coming as a punishment for Israel's unfaithfulness. But even so, evils like idolatry have deep root, and the secret worship of idols may have still gone on behind the scenes. Witness the stubbornness with which witchcraft is held fast and practiced in many areas, always in secret and in the dark of the night. It could well be that when two types of idol-figures are mentioned ("carved image" and "metal image") the intention is to show that various forms of this old sin were still in evidence. Although it is also possible that the figure of speech called "hendiadys" is involved, two terms used for a composite single term, both together amounting to "metal image."

3. The Same Control of History Displayed by God's Fortelling of a New Set of Events (vv. 6-8)

48:6-8 6. "You have heard all this; now regard it, and will not you yourself declare it? From now on I make you to hear new things and hidden things which you have not known. 7. They are being created now, not long ago;

and until now you had never heard of them;
lest you say: 'Of course I knew them.'
8. On the contrary, you neither heard nor knew;
and besides your ear has long been completely closed.
For I know how very treacherous you are,
and you have been rightly called: 'a rebel from birth.' "

Verse 6. It has just been indicated that God had in times past revealed things which were to come, things here referred to as "earlier prophecies" (v. 3). Now another manifestation of divine foreknowledge is put forth — "new things," a term which refers to events that still lie in the future. But before turning to these "new things" the Lord once more encourages his people to cast one more glance back at these "earlier prophecies," to "study them" or as we translated above "now regard them," i.e., scrutinize them with care and take note of the fact that they were in a very significant way foretold with a purpose. In fact so striking is their prediction that Israel, as a result of her scrutiny of them, is challenged. For she must feel impelled, she herself, the stubborn one, to "declare it," that God so often foretold and so regularly brought to pass what was foretold. The thought is cast in the form of a challenging question. But all this lies in the past. "From now on" God is going to declare some "new things" to his people with a similar purpose in mind as when in times past he told them of impending events. Until now, not a one of the things he will declare has been disclosed; they are "hidden things," undisclosed for the present. Though not mentioned here, events like the overthrow of Babylon might be thought of. Though Isaiah had prophesied this (13:19) the fact as such was as good as unknown, for Israel had as yet not taken it to heart. Or perhaps it would be better to leave it undetermined what events the prophet had in mind, and so let the claim stand there in all its breadth. Or else, as *Delitzsch* expounds, the reference is to the New Testament era as such, the facts of which are abundantly set forth by God's prophets.

Verse 7. Working with this last assumption, as perhaps

the most reasonable one of them all, we can understand what the prophet now means when he says: "They are being created now, not long ago." Two thoughts blend into one: God creates these events; and, now first they are in the making. God's sovereign control of history for one thing is asserted. It may rightly be said that he "creates" the events that come to pass. But then the second thought, the details of what the Messianic age would bring in the days to come had never yet been revealed, "until now you had never heard of them." So the Lord delights to work in his control of history, that his overruling providence might prevail and that Israel might not say, "Of course, I knew them." For Israel was always sidestepping God's work in her behalf. She would not acknowledge freely what God had done and that the control of his acts was solely in his hands.

Verse 8. At this point the Lord resumes his sharp indictment of Israel. He charges the nation in its spiritual intractability, practically with never having learned her lessons in the past ("you neither knew nor heard"). She had degenerated in the course of time to the point where her ear has "long been completely closed." More than a measure of dullness or weakness is attributed to Israel. She has long been "very treacherous," a charge that God makes in a tone marked by some impatience. He seems to imply that the nation kept misconstruing what was told her. Sharpening the charge still more, the Lord advances to the point of asserting that if in times past it was claimed that Israel was "a rebel from birth" the accusation was correct. "Rebel" is the strongest term for sin and the sinner. One may well construe the whole charge as mounting to an ever higher pitch, until "rebel" is reached, as an almost thunderous close.

4. Sparing of Sinners Due to God's Grace (vv. 9-11)

48:9-11 9. "For my name's sake I will defer my anger, for the sake of my renown I will lay restraint upon myself,

that I may not cut you off.
10. I have assayed you — and not found you to be silver.
I tested you in the furnace of affliction.
11. For my sake, yea, for my sake I act thus —
for why should (my name) be profaned?
And my honor I will not give to another."

Verse 9. The tone changes abruptly. The sermon-call to repentance turns about and becomes a consolatory address (*Fischer*). In a truly evangelical spirit these words flatly reject any human merit or achievement as the possible basis for this radical change of attitude. God has a "name" or, we could say, a reputation for deferring anger. This attribute of his is called "mercy." That it is that motivates his dealing kindly with the sinner. The "renown" that he gets for dealing thus with the unworthy could also be designated as the "praise" that is given to him. The word involved could be translated either way. The description is rather colorful. The restraint that he lays upon himself, according to the root-meaning of the verb used, could be said to be a muzzle, preventing him from speaking the word of condemnation that is so richly deserved. For if he acted otherwise, the evidence of the case demands that he "cut off" his people.

Verse 10. This verse may be thought of as having been spoken with a sigh, a deep sigh. It underlines the lack of worth on the part of God's people still more strongly. To determine if there be not some good in them, he played the part of the assayer, he tested them in the "furnace of affliction," which is known to bring out hidden qualities in men. But the results were disappointing: (I have) "not found you to be silver." On the verse as a whole it is interesting to observe that the two verbs employed (assayed and tested) appear together many times (see Zech. 13:9; Jer. 9:7; Ps. 17:3, 26; 66:10; Prov. 17:3, etc.).

Verse 11. God's sole initiative and sovereignty could hardly be emphasized more than they are here — twice over "for my sake." The thought of v. 9 is being recapitulated. When a causal clause is added, "for why should my name be profaned?" the thought is that if God were minded to deal with his people as sternly as they deserve, then the affliction brought on his people might lead their heathen neighbors to make statements to the effect that God had left his own in the lurch, and so the honor of which he was deserving might wrongfully be attributed to other gods. Ezekiel 36:19-23 might serve as a sort of commentary on these verses.

5. All Things Take Their Beginning from the Lord (vv. 12-13)

In this half of the book, Isaiah is preoccupied with God and not with man, as has been often remarked. The passage about to follow is a good illustration of this.

48:12-13 12. "Listen to me, O Jacob, and Israel whom I called. I, I am the first, also I am the last.
13. Yea, my hand laid the foundation of the earth, and my right hand spread out the skies. When I call them [into being] there they stand!"

Verses 12, 13. First Israel is reminded of how she stands related to the Lord: she became his people as a result of his call addressed to her. He is "the absolute Originator" (*von Orelli*). He is on the scene before all things else. He calls all being into existence. But also when all things temporal shall have had their day and pass off the scene, he will still be there. To state the case a bit more concretely, His "hand laid the foundation of the earth," not only the earth as such but also the "foundation" (whatever that may be) on which the earth rests. This does not necessarily demand that there be concrete foundations as such for the earth to rest on. Whatever holds her in place, he put it there. Even more impressive is the next work mentioned, his "right hand spread out the skies." When he called earth and skies and all other created things into being at once, there they stood (cf. Ps. 33:9; Gen. 1:1 ff.; Rom. 4:17). That is the kind of God that called Israel to be his own people. That is the one with whom they are now dealing. He is the one who is now as-

serting his right to maintain them and not cast them off. The
tone of the passage is one of consolation. The ground has
been prepared for the great works of his that are yet to follow and that Israel might think him incapable of doing. For
the prophet is about to come back again to the subject of
Cyrus and his successful overthrow of Babylon.

6. The Sending of Cyrus Further Proof of God's Control (vv. 14-16)

48:14-16 14. "Assemble all of you and hear:
　　　　　　　who among them foretold these things?
He whom Yahweh loves will achieve his purpose against Babylon,
and his arm will be against the Chaldeans.
15. It is I, and I only who have spoken and have called him;
I have brought him on the scene and his purpose will prosper.
16. Draw near to me; hear this:
　　　'Indeed I did not speak from the beginning in secrecy;
Ever since things came to pass, there am I.'
　　And now the Lord has sent me endowed with his Spirit."

Verse 14. If God's sovereignty and absolute control in
general were under consideration in vv. 12-13, now comes a
specific instance of such control, to which the Lord pointedly
draws attention. Here everything centers around the work
and mission of Cyrus again (cf. 44:28).

Apparently these words address themselves to the people
of Israel, who are invited to assemble; for important disclosures are about to be transmitted to them. They are invited to listen closely to what is said. It is really an old argument that is again being submitted: the impotence of the
idols to disclose the future (see 41:21-24; 45:21 f.). In
"Who among them . . ." the "them" refers to the idols. They
knew nothing and could disclose nothing about what and
who were about to appear on the scene and do significant
work. At once the Lord assures his people that there is a
man whom he is about to send, and for him he has particular
affection because he will successfully achieve a work committed to him by the Lord; and this work is directed "against
Babylon" involving her overthrow in fact. "His arm will be

against the Chaldeans" signifies that his power will be in evidence against this mighty nation with headquarters in Babylon. It is now quite obvious that the thing implied is the total conquest of Babylon by Cyrus and his armies.

Verse 15. The Lord insists on it that he brought Cyrus on the scene, having himself spoken and called him. Others may not be aware of this. Cyrus himself may have sensed it but dimly. But the Lord actually brought this his instrument on the scene and prospered his efforts.

Verse 16. This verse is in the same vein as the preceding. Israel is still the one being addressed. The nation is invited to draw near and give heed both to the claim that the Lord is the revealer of things and is the one who exists prior to all things. The former claim appears to the effect that when God did reveal things that were about to happen, he spoke plainly and openly so that men had a clear prediction of what was to come to pass. Everything was done openly and above board. The proof for God's ability to predict is strong and irrefutable.

But now comes the last line, a crux for interpreters if ever there was one. *Muilenburg* despairs of a solution. Most commentators resort either to the claim of corruption of the text or the other claim of editorial addition. We freely admit that the difficulty is great, great already in this that suddenly the speech changes from the word of the Lord to the comment of the prophet. We offer an interpretation with some diffidence. The prophet speaks of his own mission as being one of the acts of that God who ordains and controls all things; and he adds that he comes "endowed with his Spirit," the Spirit whose coming to the nations would come like a copious outpouring of power on his own (see 44:3). This, we admit, is an unexpected turn of the thought but not an impossible or an unreasonable one. The prophet comes, sent as a herald of the victorious mission of Cyrus.

7. If Israel Had Hearkened in the Past (vv. 17-19)

48:17-19 17. Thus says the Lord, your Redeemer,
the Holy One of Israel:
"I am the Lord your God, who teaches you for your own good.
and directs you in the path you should go.
18. O that you had listened to my commandments!
Then your peace would have been like a river,
and your righteousness [prosperity] like the waves of the Sea.
19. Then your descendants would have been as numerous as the
sand,
and your offspring like its grains;
their name would never be cut off,
nor destroyed from before me."

Verse 17. All this (vv. 17-19) seems to be spoken to offset the possible criticism: If God is as kindly disposed toward his people as he is now asserting since v. 9, why his harshness in dealing with them in even allowing a captivity? He replies to this implied criticism by reassuring them that in all this he is still their "Redeemer, the Holy One of Israel." He is still "the Lord [their] God." In times past he had made it possible for them to fare well. He had taught them for their own good, and had even gone so far as to map out their path for them, the path in which they should go.

Verse 18. Had Israel listened to his commandments, which were the substance of his guiding directions, a number of very substantial blessings would have fallen to their lot. These commandments seem to be thought of as sufficiently well known by the children of Israel, for they were, with more or less regularity, read in assemblies of public worship. The resultant blessings that God would have been pleased to bestow would, first of all, be "peace," a general state of well being, extending over the whole of their existence. This peace would have been abundant and rich like a strongly flowing stream (a figure appearing also in Amos 5:24; Isa. 11:9; 44:4). This stream is in contrast to the shallow, flash-flood streamlets, or wadis, which are so much more common in the land of Palestine than are perennial streams. The Lord would bestow his gift copiously. Similar is the figure of abundance with regard to the "righteousness" bestowed, which here too implies the idea of abundance. For "waves of the sea" are certainly not to be numbered over the surface of the vast ocean. The whole verse bears a striking similarity to the passage in Ps. 81:13-16.

Verse 19. In addition numerous offspring would be granted to the nation by the Lord. The ancient promise of Gen. 15:5 would then have been realized to the full, descendants like the sand by the seashore. Such a nation would never be cut off or destroyed.

8. Israel Invited to Go Forth from Babylon (vv. 20-22)

48:20-22 20. Go forth from Babylon,
haste away from Chaldea.
Declare it with a shout of jubilation;
let this be heard.
Tell it out to the end of the earth;
say: "The Lord has redeemed his servant Jacob!"
21. And not did they thirst in the deserts
through which he led them;
he made water to flow forth from the rock for them;
he cleft the rock and the water ran out.
22. "There is no peace," says the Lord, "for the wicked."

Verse 20. The meter had been mostly 3:3 up to this point in the chapter. It now changes mostly to 2:2. *Muilenburg* calls the form "staccato imperatives."

Instead of announcing formally that the method of achieving his gracious purpose will be a glorious deliverance from the prison of Babylon, the prophet dramatically challenges his people to go forth, as it were, on their own initiative (cf. Gen. 19:15-22). As the people then answer the challenge and go forth they are to proclaim with jubilation that this deliverance is the Lord's work. So vociferously are they to make their proclamation that it will resound to the end of the earth. When the one redeemed is described as "his servant Jacob," this implies that after his deliverance Jacob will have work to do in the service of his God. Tasks yet to be done lie before him.

Verse 21. As the prophet visualizes what is to happen in this deliverance, it may be best to regard this verse as a kind of reflection upon the past of Israel's glorious history. Particularly, since a vast desert lay in the space intervening between Babylon and Palestine, an area where they who pass through might perish from thirst, the prophet lets Israel reflect upon the past as though it were a guaranty for the future. When God even gave water from the rock to his people Israel on two occasions (see Exod. 17:6; Num. 20:11), faith may well draw the conclusion that he will not fail his people in the present emergency. It is not said that a repetition of that miracle will again take place, but faith is allowed to draw inspiring hope from the events of the past.

Verse 22. This brings us to what is usually esteemed a later editorial addition that stands utterly unrelated to what has been presented in this chapter. Besides this same statement, word for word, appears in 57:21, closing off the second major section in the second half of the book of Isaiah. Is this then merely to be regarded as a somewhat artificial device for marking off sections one from the other? We believe there is more to it than that. The unique "peace" that they enjoy who listened to the Lord's commandments (v. 18) stands in sharp contrast to the lack of peace on the part of the wicked. Is that sharp reminder out of place in a chapter which on the whole bears the stamp of a sharp rebuke? Even though the tone in the second half of the chapter had turned to one of consolation, is it entirely inappropriate to let an undertone of rebuke sound forth once more before the close? The approach then would be the very opposite of that used by Paul in Gal. 6:16.

Notes

Verse 1. The construction goes from the finite verb (hear) to the participle ("the ones called"). Cf. *KS* 413 k. Then it goes over into the third person ("have come forth"). For "waters" some conjecture "from the loins" (*RSV*) by a slight vowel change; others go to an entirely different word with the Septuagint "from the seed"). The Hebrew is plausible as construed above.

Verse 4. The infinitive is used to express the equivalent of a causal clause (*KS* 403 d).

Verse 6. "Will not you yourself declare it" is a statement labelled by *Volz* as not making any sense whatever. We believe we have shown above that it does make sense, especially if it be noted that the insertion of the personal pronoun makes it emphatic that *they themselves* declare what is so very obvious. By the use of the personal pronoun a transition is made from the singular to the plural.

Verse 8. Instead of *pittechah* (a *Piel* form) we read the passive, *puttechah* (a *Pual* form), making the statement a case of litotes (denying the negative to obtain a stronger positive).

Verse 9. The compound preposition (*lema'an*) extends over into the second stich, and so takes a second object (*GK* 119 hh).

Verse 10. The expression "but not found you to be silver" is very much condensed in Hebrew — "but not as silver." It must surely be meant in a sense somewhat like our version.

Verse 14. "Who among *them*" involves a somewhat harsh change of person from the second to the third. Transitions like this are not uncommon. Some forty manuscripts retain the second person form (*bakhem* for *bahem*). Let the reader take his choice. "Against the Chaldeans" is another case where the preposition is not repeated (see *KS* 319 m and l).

Verse 16. Where the Hebrew merely says (he) "has sent me and his Spirit" it seems to catch the intended force of the statement if the word "endowed" be inserted, thus: "endowed me with his Spirit," as some commentators do.

Verse 21. The Hebrew form *holikham* represents a relative clause with the relative pronoun, so-called — omitted. Cf. *KS* 380 c.

Chapter XLIX

J. THE SERVANT'S ASSIGNMENT REDEFINED AND ISRAEL REASSURED OF RECOVERY (Chap. 49)

It has been observed by some that the subject under consideration now for the next seven chapters is the redemption of Israel. Again there are those who hold that the major theme of these chapters is The Servant of the Lord. The difference between these two approaches is not as striking as it might seem. Our above caption indicates that we incline more toward the second approach, all the more so since in Chap. 53 the Servant towers above every other consideration.

That we have actually come to a new section of the second half of the book is made obvious by the fact that a new series of subjects stand in the foreground, or, better, certain subjects that stood out in Chaps. 40-48 have retreated into the background. Among these themes that are absent is Babylon; also Cyrus; then, polemics against idols; court trials are lacking — a favorite theme for some time; and lastly Jacob and Israel have receded backstage to be replaced by Zion-Jerusalem.

We do well to take issue with a major problem which must be settled sooner or later: Who is the Servant of the Lord who appears speaking in the first seven verses of the chapter and is prominent through the rest of the chapter? The literature on the subject is voluminous. The problem is perennial. The difficulties involved in the problem are not simple or easy of solution. Even if some one solution is accepted, a relative validity of other approaches has to be conceded. The name "the servant of the Lord" is rich in connotation.

In addition to what has been said on the subject in Chap.

42, we should like to submit the following considerations. Though in this chapter in v. 3 the person under consideration is plainly called "Israel" that does not settle the question, because Israel may be taken in the nationalistic sense or as descriptive of the idea that God held up before his people in a spiritual sense. We reject the term as referring to the corporate Israel — the nation — for the following reasons: There is something a bit unnatural to have the *nation* have as object of its efforts the restoration of the *nation*. A nation cannot well restore itself. We speak soberly on the subject: this seems too much like exhorting a nation to draw itself up out of trouble by its own bootstraps. *North* contends that this is no more inappropriate than to say "that the first mission of the church is to the church." But this observation does not eliminate the fact that such a task could hardly be called a "mission," for mission means "sending": a group cannot be sent to itself.

Furthermore, it would be quite unnatural for a nation to say of itself that it was named (v. 1) "from the body of (its) mother." Such imagery may well apply to an individual, not to a nation.

For the present we add only one more consideration. Throughout the chapter the mission and the achievements of the Servant are described in such glowing terms as to be entirely beside the point as far as Israel's achievement of its mission could be concerned. Israel's achievements always fell so far short of the ideal, were so incomplete and inadequate that to describe them as is done in this chapter savors of a certain idle rhetoric, or a failure to face facts squarely.

Aside from this, there is the problem of the state of the text. Too many writers allow themselves too much freedom in the treatment of the text as though it were in a very sad state of confusion. Problems are involved, but it can hardly be claimed that there are many additions, many inversions, many omissions, much need of correction. By way of offering a sampling at the very beginning of the chapter, one writer would rearrange the verses as follows: 3, 5b, 4, 5a,

6, 7. Just because the prophet did not let his thought appear in the sequence we might have chosen hardly warrants a rearrangement according to our preference.

1. The Servant Disappointed but Recommissioned (vv. 1-6)

49:1-6 1. Listen to me, O coastlands;
give attention, O peoples from afar.
The Lord has called me from birth,
  while I was yet in the womb
  he gave me a name to be remembered.
2. He made my mouth like a sharp sword,
  in the shadow of his hand he hid me.
He made me a polished arrow,
  he hid me away in his quiver.
3. And he said to me: "You are my servant, Israel,
  in whom I will be glorified."
4. But I said: "In vain have I toiled;
  I have spent my strength in vain and to no purpose.
But yet my right is with the Lord,
  and my reward is with my God."
5. And now the Lord says,
  he that formed me from birth to be his servant,
to bring back Jacob to him,
  and that Israel might be gathered to him.
(So I was honored in the eyes of the Lord,
  and my God became my strength).
6. He says: "It is too light a thing that you should be a servant
    of mine,
  to raise up the tribes of Jacob,
and to restore the preserved of Jacob.
  I will also give you as a light to the Gentiles,
and to be my salvation to the end of the earth."

Verse 1. Some have suggested that the Servant, whoever he may be, is in reality telling the story of his life (*Volz*). Our approach to the problem of the identity of the Servant is that he is in the last analysis none less than the Messiah. By the Spirit of prophecy, the prophet is given the privilege of seeing the Messiah and is initiated into the problems of his (the Messiah's) ministry. It is more clearly apparent than in Chap. 42 that in some mysterious way it is to be the lot of the Messiah to achieve his purpose by suffering. He is the

Suffering Servant of the Lord. The full measure of his suffering will be indicated presently. For a short time his ministry is marked by the suffering that disappointment brings. But the experience is of world-wide significance.

And so he begins by inviting the distant shores of the West ("the coastlands"), representative of all remote areas of the then-known world, to give close attention ("listen"). Note the same approach in 46:3, 12; 51:1, 7; 55:3. The parallel statement invites "peoples from afar" to give attention also. The big issues of the history of mankind are to be weighed. What men should become aware of first is that the unique person who is under consideration has been destined by the Lord himself, even before birth, to a task of incomparable magnitude and importance. God's plans are not improvised as he goes along. They are distinctly made long in advance. The speaker is a man of destiny in the highest sense of the word. This fact is in line with the magnitude of his mission. One might say that in this respect he is a counterpart, even of higher standing than Cyrus, whom God also prepared beforehand for his unusual task. Besides, one thinks almost at once of the similarity of this case with that of Jeremiah, called before his birth (Jer. 1:5). The speaker has a sense of divine mission analogous to that of the great prophets of Israel, who were deeply imbued with a sense of divine commission.

But not only was this person divinely appointed before his birth to perform an unusually high task, he was also equipped with the requisite gifts to achieve his destined purpose.

Verse 2. The instrument with which he works is the word, spoken by his "mouth," which spoke words that were to be startlingly effective ("sword"), which is kept in such a way that its sharp edge will not be blunted, but be ready for effective use. "Shadow of his hand" signifies protection, or careful preservation. A number of parallel Scriptures come to mind in this connection: Heb. 4:12; Rev. 1:16; cf. also Jer. 23:29; and Eph. 6:17. A second telling figure clinches the point: the speaker is to be like "a polished arrow," kept in reserve in its proper quiver, to be fully effective when circumstances require it. The ministry of the man in question apparently is calculated to wound men for their own good. His ministry to men may involve pain and suffering on their part; it will have deep-going effects.

Verse 3. But the ministry of the man in question is summed up more comprehensively in the definition of it that the Lord himself gives: he is to be the Lord's "servant," a person totally committed to execute the commission that the Lord has laid upon him. This assignment is more fully covered by the fact that he is to be a new "Israel," the man who in a strange way carried on the Lord's work and fulfilled the destiny that was assigned to the nation Israel at large, to be the bearer of the message of divine truth to the nations, a task which the Israel after the flesh executed but poorly, but which awaits accomplishment. He is to be the true spiritual Israel, doing God's work, achieving the Lord's objectives in such a manner that it will redound to the great glory of God.

Verse 4. But this aspect of positive achievement of the Lord's work is for the moment pushed into the background. In spite of marvelous equipment for the task, the Servant's work will be marked by disappointing results. None will feel that more keenly than the Lord's Servant himself. He is represented as voicing his inner pain over his apparent lack of success. He says: "In vain have I toiled; I have spent my strength in vain and to no purpose." More clearly even than the New Testament Gospels the disappointing aspect of Christ's earthly ministry is here indicated at least for his three years ministry on earth. The fruits of this ministry were startlingly meager. The servant would put his best efforts into his labors, toiling and spending his strength. Visible results would not be in evidence. But still he knows that his efforts will not be totally fruitless, to state the case mildly. He has the "right" to expect some fruitage from the Lord, and he can safely leave the outcome in God's hands. The same ground is covered by the parallel statement: "My reward is with my God," i.e., the reward of my faithful work, for God will give success.

Verse 5. The Lord has an answer to the complaint of his servant. As the servant reports what God said, he brings into the picture a fuller statement of the Lord's plans for his servant. He recalls first the fact already emphasized, that he has been destined for his office before birth. Then he sets forth more fully that Israel's restoration was his assignment, and indicates that this assignment involved the spiritual revival, that is to say, nothing less than bringing the nation back into fellowship with the Lord. He adds to this parenthetically that he was aware of the fact that such a commission reflected an unusual honor upon him and that for the fulfillment of his task God "became his strength." So richly did God equip his servant and honor him. It is as though the servant were recalling the tremendous issues involved in his task.

Verse 6. Now the new form of his commission stands out the more distinctly. But once again in giving the fresh statement, the Lord recalls how comprehensive the original assignment was — for the issues involved were of a most tremendous scope — but the Lord does not withdraw from the obligations assigned, nor does he lighten the burden of responsibility laid upon the shoulders of his servant. Rather God adds much weightier burden to the one already being carried. Two terms indicate the new area of assignment. The first is that the servant is to be a light to the Gentiles. His person is to be such a light, or as it is often rephrased: the servant is to be the bearer of light or the instrument of light to them. No human agent's assignment ever involved such responsibility. For this reason in part, as indicated above, we consider this to be a definition of the work laid upon the Messiah himself. Of practically equal force is the definition of duty, that he is to be (God's) "salvation to the end of the earth." He is not only to be the bearer of salvation, but in his own person is to be the Savior. This is the second statement of the servant's new commission. The word of Jesus

(John 8:12) "I am the light of the world" agrees well with the first half of this commission. How true it is that men walk in darkness till Christ has come into their life! How true it is that he is "salvation" wherever men are to be found!

2. The Servant's Reassignment in Terms of a Glorious Restoration of Israel (vv. 7-13)

49:7-13　7. Thus has the Lord spoken;
　　　　　　the Redeemer of Israel, his Holy One,
to a one deeply despised, to one abhorred by the nations,
　　to a servant of tyrant-rulers:
"Kings will see [what is happening] and respectfully rise;
　　princes will prostrate themselves;
because of the Lord who is faithful,
　　and because of the Holy One of Israel, who has chosen you."
8. Thus has the Lord spoken:
　　"At a favorable time I have answered you,
in a day of salvation I have helped you;
　　and I will protect you
and give you to be a covenant to the people,
　　in order to establish the land,
and in order to reallot the desolate heritages;
9. saying to the prisoners: 'Step forth!'
　　and to those in darkness: 'Show yourselves!'
They shall feed along the roads,
　　and even on all sand-dunes shall be their pasture.
10. They shall not suffer hunger nor thirst,
　　neither parching heat nor the sun shall smite them.
For he that has compassion on them shall lead them,
　　by the springs of water he shall let them rest.
11. And I will make all my mountains to be pathways,
　　and my highways shall be set in order.
12. See! Some come from afar,
　　and see! Some from the north and some from the west,
and some from the land of Syene."
13. Rejoice, O heavens and exult, O earth;
　　break out, O mountains, in jubilant shouts!
For the Lord has comforted his people;
　　he will have compassion on his afflicted.

Verse 7. According to our above caption for this section, now first of all what the Servant's reassignment means in terms of Israel's experience is given in detail. Various phases of what the Servant can and will do for Israel are explored.

This means that the Restoration from Captivity in particular will be brought about by the Messiah. Strangely, *before* his Incarnation he brings blessings to his people. People of the Old Covenant may sometimes have dimly sensed this fact. He is represented as addressing his people by a prophetic word of reassurance (*Heilsorakel*), which he transmitted to the prophet, who asserts that this word comes from him who is both the "Redeemer of Israel" and the "Holy One." The first of these titles lays emphasis on the work of salvation which he achieves; the second on the work of judgment which he performs. His own are rescued; the oppressors will be severely dealt with. But now comes the startling aspect of the case: the Redeemer is anything but an impressive figure, for he is the one "deeply despised" and even "abhorred by the [outside] nations." As to rank and station among persons of authority, it must further be admitted that he ranks no higher than "a servant of tyrant rulers." They who judge by what the eye sees find no glamor in this deliverer at all. But though that may be the first unfavorable impression on the outsider, that shall all be changed. At this point the word of the Lord begins. Upon *his* authority we have it that men of highest ranks — "kings" and "princes" — will rise from their throne, surprised and impressed, and will go the limit, as far as showing honor is concerned and prostrate themselves before him. Something will have happened to elicit this act of adoration; he had said that he would restore his people and he proved himself "faithful" to his word. All honor is due to this Servant. It was not that the nation Israel possessed so much toughness and resiliency to stage a political comeback. It was a case of God's faithfulness. He who had once chosen Israel would not invalidate his choice (cf. Hos. 11:9; Isa. 5:16). He was "the Holy One of Israel."

Verse 8. We are taken behind the scenes and are allowed to hear another word, directly addressed to the Servant. The word is a promissory declaration of impending salvation. The Servant had cried out in despair. God heard him. The "favorable time" for answering had come. It was a "time of salvation," so God gave his help for Israel's deliverance. For the work that still remains to be done the Lord promises protection and fulfills the high destiny that he has in mind for this elect Servant. For his Servant is to be by divine appointment "a covenant of the people" that is: the mediator through whom he will bring his salvation of Israel to pass, as he had promised. In the course of realizing this objective the achievements of God through his Servant will include the rehabilitation of the land, and, so to speak, the ancient heritages which had lain waste during the Captivity would be reallotted to the families to which they traditionally belonged.

Verse 9. Still more is included among the achievements of this Servant: Of course, all this is cast in terms of an ideal and it is not to be expected that literal fulfillment will necessarily come to pass. But among the blessings listed are also these: they that were, so to speak, in the prison-house of the Captivity will receive the command to step out and show themselves. Prison walls can no longer hold them. Shackles fall from their limbs. At this point the figure undergoes a great change.

Verse 10. Israel is likened to a flock with its shepherd, the Servant. The figure is familiar since 40:11. Israel is being led from Babylon. New aspects of the case are that ample pasturage will be, as it were, provided along the sides of the road. Even, for that matter, the utterly unproductive sand-dunes shall produce sufficient pasturage as the flock passes by. Physical hardships (v. 10a) will be alleviated. Hunger and thirst, a seemingly unavoidable difficulty under such circumstances, will offer no obstacle. The parching heat of the sun shall be no problem. All these blessings are traceable to the deep compassion of the shepherd for his sheep. He shall, as it were, know how to find springs of water and suitable places for rest.

Verse 11. Now the prophet comes back, in the word of the Lord to the familiar concept of nature transformed for the convenience of the returnees. The rough and difficult mountains shall present no obstacle. For he who can call them *"my* mountains" because he made them, can also transform them to be mere pathways. Even, for that matter, "highways" will be readied for convenient passage.

Verse 12. The word of the Lord invites readers and hearers of his promise to look with the eyes of faith and they will see the flock coming in great numbers from all points of the compass, even from so far distant a land as Syene, which most likely was the modern Aswan, to the extreme south of the land of Egypt.

Verse 13. Such gracious deeds of the Almighty, done for his covenant people, demand a response. They are deeds done on so grand a scale that the whole of God's creation is pictured as taking note and they are here invited, by a bold personification to make their praises vocal. The heavens, the earth and the mountains are bidden to bear their part in the joyful task. For, to sum it all up: "the Lord has comforted (effectively comforted) his people." By changing the tense at this point, so to speak, the prophet seems to indicate that there are several stages in which the Lord's task will be performed: He *has* comforted; "he *will have* compassion" on his afflicted ones. This summons to praise rounds off this section masterfully.

3. Misgivings of Zion Alleviated (vv. 14-26)

a. The Lord Has Abandoned Us (vv. 14-18)

49:14-18 14. But Zion said: "The Lord has abandoned me; my Lord has forgotten me."
15. Can a mother forget the child she suckled,
    so as not to have compassion on the son she bore?
Even these may forget,
    but I for my part will never forget you.
16. See, I have engraved you on the palms of my hands;
    your [new] walls are before my eyes continually.
17. Your children are already making haste;
    those who destroyed and desolated you are going out from you.
18. Lift up your eyes, look all around,
    all of them have gathered and are coming to you.

As I live, says the Lord,
  you shall put them on as ornaments,
    You will fasten them as a bride does.

Verse 14, 15. Though the prophet speaks very confidently of a glorious future, it is by no means easy under the circumstances to accept the message as true. Zion has several misgivings. Experience had proved in the past that nations led into captivity failed to return. Could Israel really return? Her Captivity had gone on for decades. So voices were being heard here and there to the effect: the Lord has written us off — "abandoned," "forgotten" (cf. Lam. 5:22). By way of reassurance comes one of the loveliest words of the entire Old Testament. The Lord's concern for Zion is likened to what may be the most selfless love that mankind knows, mother's love. As impossible as it is for a normal mother to forget a child that she nursed at her breast, in rare cases an exception will be found, but the Lord's love for Zion is indestructible.

Verse 16. To change the figure, it is as though the Lord had deeply engraved the name, or picture, of Israel on the palms of his hands, that his eyes might lovingly dwell on her features and be continually reminded of the one whom he so deeply loved. Before his mind's eye he sees the city as she shall be, strong and well protected by walls that the enemy shall never demolish.

Verse 17. To this the Lord adds a vision of the future as he sees it from the divine perspective. Zion's children, the captives in Babylon, are already making haste to come back home. While they draw nearer and nearer, others are leaving the site to which her children are coming. Those leaving are "those who destroyed and desolated" the Israelites. Since the land and the city are therefore to be thought of as ready to be occupied, the whole body of the captive nation is thought of as responding to the invitation. In reality these words sketch what could have happened had Israel had a responsive and believing heart. The reality did not quite conform to the ideal visualized. In another charming figure the prophet describes what will happen. As a bride puts on her ornaments on her wedding-day and so enhances her beauty, so shall those who return enhance the nation's attractiveness. From the nature of the figures used it appears how dear to the Lord's heart and the prophet's heart the whole matter is.

b. The Land Is Waste and Its Inhabitants Few (vv. 19-23)

49:19-23 19. But as for your wastes and desolations
and your devastated areas,
you will be cramped for space to live in
and those who swallowed you up will be far away.
20. The children of you, the bereaved one, shall yet say within
your hearing:
"The place is too narrow for me,
make room for me to live in."
21. And you will say to yourself;
"Who has borne me these?
I was childless and barren, exiled and turned away;
and who has brought up these?
I was quite alone;
where have these come from?"
22. Thus has the Lord God spoken:
"See, I will lift up my hand to the nations
and raise my signal to the peoples.
And they shall bring your sons in their bosom,
and your daughters shall be carried on their shoulders.
23. Kings shall be your foster fathers
and their queens your nursing mothers.
With their faces to the ground shall they do reverence to you;
and they shall lick the dust on your feet.
And you will know that I am the Lord;
they who wait for me will not be disappointed."

Verse 19. There is another strong misgiving that many in Israel felt in those days: The land lay waste and its inhabitants were few in number. This factor is not couched in so many words, labelled as a misgiving, but from the manner in which the Lord makes mention of it, it clearly appears that he was putting into words what they felt and had no doubt often said. At once the reassurance is given that the evil will be completely remedied. The people will be so many that

they "will be cramped for space to live in" (cf. Zech. 2:5).
At the same time those that afflicted Israel will be off the
scene. They can no longer engage in their oppressive acts,
nor can they afflict Israel. The very opposite situation will
prevail (v. 21). Mother Israel watching over her children
shall overhear them saying in effect that the land is over-
crowded with inhabitants. The words that will now be used
are: "The place is too narrow for me; make room for me to
live in."

Verse 21. Mother Israel is further pictured as saying:
"Who has born [*KJ*: "begotten"] me these?" Something
must be added to the mother-children figure. Those that
she brought forth herself and those that others bore for her
count as her family. During the Exile, Mother Israel was
not having children: Israel's numbers were not increasing.
She was "childless and barren." She views her offspring at
this point (purposely left vague) with great astonishment.
They are numerous, or, they will be at some still undefined
future. So Israel keeps saying over and over again with
amazement: "What happened? How did all this come to
pass?"

Verse 22. In this verse the Lord himself answers Israel's
question. He represents himself as having given the signal to
nations the world over that harbored captives from Israel to
gather and bring these unfortunate ones home. The captives
are thought of as young children that are to be carried in
the bosom or on the shoulder. In fact so radically will the
situation have changed (v. 23) that they whom Israel served
(kings and queens) will serve *Israel*, and will count it an
honor, as it were, to tend her children. In token of reverence, not for Israel but for the God that dwells in the midst
of Israel, these dignitaries will fall with their faces to the
ground, and in a somewhat exaggerated figure, when they
have their faces bent so low, they will practically lick the
dust on the feet of those to whom they pay homage. At this
point it would seem that the figure before whom they do
reverence shifts to Zion. When these things come to pass,

discouraged Zion shall take fresh courage, for they will again have been offered a proof that the Lord is God, keeping the promises which he has made to his ancient people. Or as it is often stated in the Old Testament: "They who wait for the Lord will not be disappointed." "Waiting" in such situation implies that the soul has been fixed on the Lord and on his gracious promises.

c. Captives Cannot Be Liberated (vv. 24-26)

49:24-26 24. Can the prey be taken from the mighty man, or the captives of a tyrant be rescued?
25. Surely this is the word of the Lord:
"Even the captives of a mighty man may be taken, and the prey of the tyrant may be rescued.
Whoever contends with you, I myself will contend with him, and I myself will rescue your children.
26. And I will make those that maltreat you devour their own flesh,
And they shall be drunk with their own blood as with new wine.
And all mankind shall know that I am the Lord, your Savior, and your Redeemer, the Mighty One of Jacob."

Verse 24. Now comes the third misgiving that would plague the nation Israel in Captivity: Captives, especially captives of a weak nation like Israel in the hands of a mighty nation like Babylon, are irretrievably lost. Note here how Babylon is actually called "the mighty man" and "a tyrant."

Verse 25. Over against such misgivings the prophet pits a clear and promissory word of God, "Surely this is the word of the Lord." At first this word of the Lord merely sets the Lord's word over against doubts and misgivings. In this word that the Lord pronounces in Hebrew a very emphatic "I" stands as subject: "Whoever contends with you, *I* myself will contend with him" and "*I* myself will rescue your children." Who can contend with the Almighty? Therefore Israel will be rescued as surely as God is God.

Verse 26. A somewhat revolting picture is presented of the fate of the Babylonian conquerors: As they maltreated Israel so shall they be given over to internecine strife, civil war. For the expression "to devour their own flesh" involves a meaning of "own flesh" as in 58:7, namely their next of kin. The same thought is contained in the following line, being in strict parallelism with the one preceding. With this half of the verse Ezek. 38:21 and Zech. 14:13 may be compared. It should however be noted, that though the resurrection, the political resurrection of Israel, is indicated and promised, there is no thought here of Israel dominating the world and gaining world-wide victories; nor of Israel taking revenge on her conqueror. But it is indicated that what the Lord does by way of restoring Israel will attract the attention of nations over the wide world. They will recognize that Israel has a Lord and Savior. To this are added a few more glorious titles in the exuberance of joy that the passage breathes. It should be noted that all these are titles that the Lord gives himself.

Notes

Verses 1-7. Some would rearrange the verses of this section as follows: 3, 5b, 4, 5a, 6, 7. We believe the regular sequence which the text presents makes as good a sequence, if not a better, than the rearrangement propounded. Perhaps "named my name" (v. 1) may be rendered "gave me a name to be remembered" which gives a more colorful translation.

Verse 5. "To bring back Jacob to him." In Hebrew the "to him" reads "not," both forms being pronounced the same. It has been conjectured that a pessimistic view of history led the scribes to read the negative, though the other reading is given in the margin. The marginal reading is quite commonly accepted.

Verse 7. For "tyrant rulers" the Hebrew has a mere "rulers." However the word seems to be meant in the sense of tyrants as is also the case in 14:5.

Verse 15. In *merachchem* the initial *min* is a *min* separative (*KS* 406 n). The *gam* following shortly thereafter is used in a concessive sense (*KS* 394 d).

Verse 18. The article in *kakkalah* is used generically.

Verse 20. *Geshah* — is imperative feminine from *nagash*, "to draw near." Very strangely from meaning "to move closer" it comes to mean "move farther away," or "to make room."

Verse 24. If v. 24 is read in the light of the answer given in v. 25, then *tsaddiq* must be replaced by *'arits* ("tyrant") as the *Septuagint*, the *Syriac* and the *Vulgate* do.

Chapter L

K. ISRAEL SELF-REJECTED, THE SERVANT STEADFAST (Chap. 50)

As for a general approach, we are still going on the assumption that Chaps. 49-55 center around the Servant of the Lord. Opinions are rather widely divided as to the exact nature of the material in this chapter. Is it a lament? Is it a psalm? a prayer of complaint? a royal psalm of confidence? Or is it perhaps a prophetic confession? The wide variety of form of the material of this chapter shows that form criticism does not always stand on firm ground. A person who seems to fill a prophetic office seems to be making a confession of the difficulties he experienced in the performance of the duties of his office. Though this applies to vv. 4-11, how does the section vv. 1-3 fit into the picture? We expect to demonstrate as we move into the chapter that its thoughts are coherently developed. The chapter is unified.

Delitzsch has a simple outline on which ours is based; but by labeling vv. 1-3 as another "misgiving," we have also indicated how our chapter reaches back into the one that precedes.

Perhaps, as far as the metrical structure of the lines of the chapter is concerned, *Skinner's* approach may still hold true: "The scheme is obscure."

1. Another Misgiving Alleviated: Is the Covenant Abrogated? (vv. 1-3)

50:1-3 1. Thus has the Lord spoken:
"Where is the certificate of your mother's divorce
with which I put her away?
Or which of my creditors is it
to whom I sold you?
Nay, it was for your iniquities that you were sold,

and it was for your transgressions that your mother was
put away.
2. Why, then, when I came, was no one there to meet me?
why when I called, no one to answer?
Is my hand really inadequate to redeem?
Or have I no strength to deliver?
Nay, by my rebuke I dry up the sea,
I turn its ocean currents into a desert;
their fish would stink for lack of water and die for thirst.
3. I clothe heavens with blackness,
and make sackcloth their covering."

Verse 1. A court hearing is being conducted by the Lord,
similar to 42:18-25 and 43:22-28. Israel is guilty of misconduct but is not ready to admit it. She is behaving as though
the Lord had put her aside and cancelled the covenant that
he had made with the nation at Sinai. The Lord follows
through on this situation treating Israel as though she were
the wife and he her husband. The analogy leads to a striking refutation of the claim that he might have cast off his people. For according to basic Mosaic law (cf. Deut. 24:1) if a
man did divorce his wife he was legally bound to give her a
certificate to make the transaction legal. There is no such
certificate in existence. Therefore no divorce has taken place.
A separation? Yes, a temporary separation. But not a divorce.

Then in this hearing a second analogy is drawn upon:
Did the Lord sell his own into slavery? Here again, as Exod.
21:7; II Kings 4:1; Neh. 5:5, indicate, a man might sell his
own children into slavery to pay off a debt that he might owe
to a creditor. Is it thinkable that some one has a financial
claim upon the Lord because of which he must sell his own
people into slavery? Preposterous! Israel is in slavery and
she is separated from God, but that is not the Lord's fault.
Israel is guilty. She has brought this calamity upon herself,
by her iniquities and her transgressions. At this point we may
well suppose that a stunned silence pervades the court room.
Being charged with guilt she had to admit her guilt.

Now to sum up this somewhat difficult first verse —

looking at Israel's present plight in her Captivity, is it thinkable that this all came about because the Lord, as a hot-tempered husband, cast off his wife and finalized the transaction by a writ of divorcement? Of course not. Or is it possible the the Lord was in debt to some one and unable to pay and had to resort to the sale of the very members of his family to meet his obligations? Such an assumption is equally out of place. Israel brought all its misery upon itself. She has not been overtaken by some heavy doom. She misconstrued the Lord's share in what had transpired.

Verses 2, 3. Why then should the nation behave as though the Lord had been the cause of their doom? She was obviously taking such an attitude. When the Lord came, speaking by the mouth of his prophets, nobody responded. Any gracious overtures that he made were ignored. When he called by the prophets that Israel should come back, why this dead silence on the nation's part? Or to consider another possibility — had the Lord grown weak so that he was no longer capable of redeeming his people as he was wont to do in times past? To prove the contrary, the Lord cites a few instances of works of power that he can perform. It is true that the works cited are of a *destructive* nature to clinch the point that he can work *constructively*. But the point at issue is that the Lord has power unlimited. A sharp word of command from his lips, and the sea dries up, as happened at the Red Sea passage in the days of Moses. Similar rebukes are noted in 17:13; Job 38:11; Ps. 104:7; 106:9. With equal ease he can control the currents, or tides, of the ocean, reducing the area to the dry land of the desert. Adding a bit of color, as striking evidence of what his power can do would be the mass of fish, wriggling about, squirming and dying and stinking. To add a third example of works of power of which he is capable (v. 3), he is even able to work mighty signs on the face of the heavens covering them with blackness. Has this word anything in particular in mind? Is there here an allusion to the darkness that engulfed Egypt in the Exodus days? Or perhaps to some heathen creation epic? Or may this word be pointing to the future, when the great judgment of God shall overtake the earth? The last mentioned possibility has as much likelihood as any. There is a certain grandeur and sweep to the style which magnifies the great Creator God. Sackcloth as covering for the heavens is merely another colorful way of saying that the very heavens must suffer when the Lord displays his power as the final Judge of all things.

2. The Servant, an Example of Trust in Adversity (vv. 4-6)

50:4-6   4. The Lord God has given me an expert tongue,
      to know how to sustain the weary with a word.
Morning for morning he wakens, he wakens my ear,
    to hear as those who are taught.
5. The Lord God has opened my ear
    and I was not rebellious, I did not turn backward.
6. I gave my back to the smiters
    and my cheeks to those who tore at my beard.
    My face I hid not from shame and spitting.

Verse 4. The Servant, whom we already met with in Chaps. 42 and 49 appears, one might say, unexpectedly, speaking a monologue. He tells what he suffered for his people's sake, and without saying so, sets an example for God's people, showing them how they should steadfastly trust in the Lord. As to form, his words are *kinah*-like, i.e., in the customary lament patterns, for there is something of a tragic tone in this recital. It is really the so-called "lament of an individual" that appears here, something like the laments of Moses, Elijah, and Jeremiah, telling the burden of the prophetic office which these men bore heroically. These words also have rightly been said to describe the Servant's "Gethsemane." Four times from vv. 4-11, a double name of God is used, introducing vv. 4, 5, 7, 9. Literally translated the title is "the Lord Yahweh." We have been translating Yahweh as "Lord." So to avoid the troublesome "Lord, Lord," we resorted as did *RSV*, to the somewhat inaccurate "Lord, God."

This, being one of the Servant-passages, so-called, is often regarded as a later insertion into the text by some later writer. But if the four Servant-passages are set side by side it becomes apparent that, as *Skinner* remarks, this passage is an "indispensable link" in the chain, letting the measure of suffering that the Servant must endure come increasingly obvious.

The Servant begins by pointing out what unusual gift had been given him for the fulfillment of the duties of his office, primarily the gift of an "expert tongue." The Hebrew describes it as the "tongue of learners," i.e., a tongue adapted to deliver effectively the message that is given him to communicate. This is one of the distinguishing marks of the Servant. This gift enables him in particular "to sustain the weary with a word." Who are these weary ones? Since, according to Chap. 49, the Servant's mission has to do both with Israel and the Gentiles, the "weary" apparently are to be sought in both groups, Israelites laboring under the burden of the law and finding no peace, and Gentiles laboring under the oppressive burden of idol-religions that afforded no peace to the burdened conscience of the sinner. We regard the "word" employed by the Servant in the fulfillment of his tasks as being nothing less than the gracious gospel (cf. Matt. 11:27). In addition to the expert tongue, the Servant has the gift of a listening ear. That gift enabled him always to be able to give because he was always receiving from God what he needed to give. God is described as supplying every day, as a necessary gift, an alert ear, keeping it sensitive to the divine teaching. As true man he had to receive continually the message of life. As a result he remained a "learner" all his days. For the Hebrew has it: "to hear as learners," the same word used in the beginning of the verse. So the servant had the "tongue of learners" and the "ear of learners."

Verses 5, 6. Once again the Servant alludes to the fine care with which he was taught to listen indicating that the Lord had virtually opened his ear. But if a man has this double equipment — ability to hear well and to speak well, the mes-

sage being what it is, often in the spirit of sharp reproof
where the nation's sin was involved, it was bound to happen
that dangerous opposition would be encountered. The Servant knows this. He could have refused the obligation that
these gifts imposed, claiming that too much was at stake.
But as the Servant emphatically claims, he on his part was not
rebellious. He did not turn away from this assignment. Here
the propriety of the use of the adjective comes obviously
into the picture, the adjective "suffering" — the Suffering
Servant of the Lord. That Israel would be rebellious, even
to the point of cruel treatment of the Lord's Servant, was
intimated already in Jer. 7:13, 25. It is true, no further details that were to be involved in this situation are given. But
the nature of the types of painful suffering that would be
encountered is foreseen very accurately. For one thing he
would be smitten painfully upon the back; scourged, in fact.
Men would tear at the beard that covered his cheeks. They
would spit upon his face. But he, consistent in his behavior
would so readily accept it all, that he even offers himself to
his tormentors. That these were traditional forms of treatment of criminals in the Orient in days of old appears from
passages such as Neh. 13:25; Num. 12:14; Deut. 25:9;
Matt. 26:67; 27:30.

Special mention should be made in this connection that
the case in hand was the first instance, as *Westermann* rightly
remarks, where the suffering involved in a prophetic mission
was willingly incurred, because the person in question recognized that the suffering involved was God's will. These
thoughts come to a climax in Chap. 53. Such suffering undertaken with complete willingness marks the highest and
most fruitful type of suffering.

3. The Servant Also an Example of Steadfastness (vv. 7-9)

50:7-9 7. But the Lord God helps me;
    therefore I have not been disappointed;
therefore I have set my face like flint;
   and I know I will not be put to shame.

8. My Vindicator is near:
   who will start a lawsuit with me?
Who is my adversary?
   Let him come near to me.
9. Behold, the Lord God helps me;
   who will pronounce a verdict against me?
Nay, they will all wear out as a garment,
   and the moth will eat them up,

Verse 7. There is something triumphant about the tone of this part of the chapter. The suffering involved may be very heavy. The victory will be all the more glorious. The passage soars on the same level as Rom. 8:33, which passage grounds on this one. The certainty of divine help makes all the difference; "The Lord God helps me." If the preceding section laid emphasis on the "trust in adversity" that the Servant manifested, the present section seems to make a point of the "steadfastness" that he displays. The key-note is sounded first — "The Lord will help me." In the past he has not been disappointed when he fell back upon the Lord. That certainty of help has made such an impression on him that he has "set [his] face as a flint." He will not give his adversaries the satisfaction of seeing him flinch when mal-treated. He is certain that in the future he "will not be put to shame." There are at least two parallels in prophetic literature: Jer. 1:18, Ezek. 3:8-9. But in no instance was this word fulfilled more marvelously than in the case of Christ.

Verse 8. But this steadfastness is based on nothing other than the nearness of his Vindicator, not on any capacity of his own to absorb punishment. Therefore with this Helper always accessible he challenges any and every opponent to "start a lawsuit" with him or be his opponent in a public trial. In the steadfastness begotten in rich experience he knows he can meet any challengers and come through vic-torious.

Verse 9. The same certainty of ultimate success, in what-ever task he was engaged by divine assignment, that was ex-pressed in v. 7, is reiterated in v. 9. On the ground of the Lord's help the Servant stands as upon a firm rock. Charges

may be hurled at him. They fall to the ground, repelled by
the shield of divine protection. In fact, in the end not he but
they will wear out and come to ruin, as the expressive figure
now used indicates: "they will all wear out as a garment"
eaten by moths. A rare measure of confidence and steadfastness are displayed here, a steadfastness not based on in-
flated opinions of self but upon a divinely wrought certainty
necessary for the fulfillment of the task assigned by the Servant's Lord. It must be admitted that the Servant depicted
is a very striking figure, whose potential is met fully only
in Jesus Christ.

4. There Is Light for the Faithful, Judgment for the Adversaries (vv. 10-11)

50:10-11 10. Is there any one among you that fears the Lord,
obeying the voice of his Servant, who walks in deep
darkness,
    not even a glimmer of light guides him?
Let him trust in the name of the Lord
    and firmly rely upon his God.
11. Lo, all of you who strike fire
    and surround yourselves with a girdle of sparks;
by all means walk in the flames of your fire,
    and among the sparks you have kindled!
This is destined for you from my hands;
    you shall lie down to suffer torments.

Verse 10. The Lord is obviously speaking in these two
verses, indicating that two possible outcomes are involved as
an outgrowth of the attitude that men take to the Servant of
the Lord, for he is a personage of such tremendous importance. In the first three lines he describes the attitude of a
God-fearing man, who finds difficulty arising for him from
the fact that he takes the right attitude toward the Lord's
Servant and obeys his voice. They who follow the Lord
without reservations, may frequently find themselves in situations of "deep darkness," even to the point where "not
even a glimmer of light guides [them]." Such persons are
counselled by the Lord to "trust in the name of the Lord and
firmly rely upon God." This counsel carries with its echoes

from the preceding verses. They in reality describe the attitude of the Servant of the Lord. He should serve as example for such. That is the connection of v. 10 with what precedes. The Servant may be a man of mystery. But the time will come when his example will serve as a welcome guide.

Verse 11. Now the other side of the matter, the judgment of the adversaries. One expanded figure is set forth. The wicked machinations that they are guilty of over against the godly are like sparks with which the wicked try to hurt and harm those who fear God. The wicked are like a man who is striking a flint that the sparks may be used to kindle the fire. These sparks fly in every direction. They encircle or engirdle the man. Those who kindle the fire are half-sarcastically bidden to go right on in their course. For in the destiny that God controls for all such, they shall find the sparks falling on themselves, kindling their own garments, kindling a fire that they cannot extinguish. They shall lie down in torment and perish miserably. On this ominous note the passage closes. It is a part of the work of the Servant to make the wrath of man praise him.

Notes

Verse 2. In *mippedhuth* the initial *min* serves to introduce a negative clause of result. Cf. *KS* 406 h. Again in *me'ayin* the *min* involved is the *min* causal.

Verse 4 To understand the structure of this verse we do well to note that *nathan* is a perfect, speaking of what God had already given, whereas *ya'ir* is an imperfect, indicating what he continues to do.

Verse 9. The *hu'* after *mi*, though it is the personal pronoun only serves to add a certain livelier tone to the question (see *KS* 353 r).

Verse 10. We have kept the pointing of *shome'a* as the *MT* has it, a *kal* participle. This makes good sense, though the *kal*, imperfect, according to the *Septuagint*, could have been used. *Chashekhim*, being also a plural, marking a kind of superlative, is construed adverbially as a *beth* of sphere.

Verse 11. It would seem that *North* has done more than any commentator to clear up this somewhat difficult verse.

Chapter LI

L. COMFORT ABUNDANTLY ADMINISTERED
(Chaps. 51:1-52:12)

Chapter 48 had addressed itself to the unfaithful in Israel. Chapter 49 had introduced something of the same sort. A different approach now lets the word of the Lord address itself to the faithful, as v. 1 shows. However the thought-sequence of the chapters would seem to call for the first part of 52 as still continuing the preceding chapter. Besides in a rather natural progression of thought ten units present themselves, apparently planned by the writer and all falling naturally into place under a title like "Comfort abundantly administered." All of which shows that the initial message, whose keynote was sounded in 40:1 is merely being developed more thoroughly. Various captions might be used to advantage, for the material here as usual in the second half of Isaiah is extremely rich. Some would use a caption like "Salvation" and find added to this note certain eschatological overtones. Besides one can easily detect a high level of sanctified emotion very especially in this section. The meter again is mostly 3+ 3 with occasional 3 + 2.

1. The Lord Can and Will Establish His People (vv. 1-3)

51:1-3   1. O listen, you who eagerly pursue righteousness,
   you who seek the Lord.
Look to the rock from which you were hewn,
   and to the quarry from which you were digged.
2. Look to Abraham, your father,
   and to Sarah who bore you.
For he was but one when I called him,
   and I blessed him and made him many.
3. For [even so] the Lord will comfort Zion,
   he will comfort all her waste places.

He will make her wilderness like Eden
 and her desert like the garden of the Lord.
Joy and gladness will be found in her,
 thanksgiving and sounds of praise.

Verse 1. Men find it hard to agree on the translation of
the word that is most commonly rendered "righteousness."
"Deliverance" (*RSV*) has a measure of propriety. So has
"integrity" and the German *Heil*. But here it seems proper to
think in terms of several concepts. The word may mean
imputed righteousness in the sense of being put right with
God. But one need not stop short with that concept. For
such imputed righteousness, if sincere, always brings with it
the desire to produce ethical conduct worthy of a justified
man. So we take the entire phrase "pursue righteousness" as
a description of sincere godliness, and the mark of a faithful
member of God's chosen people. An apt parallel expression
is to "seek the Lord," that is to say to reach out eagerly and
sincerely for true fellowship with God. Such true Israelites
are invited to "look to the rock from which [they] were
hewn, and to the quarry from which [they] were digged."
We are not left to vague guesses as to what the call has in
mind, for v. 2 gives the official interpretation.

Verse 2. The rock is Abraham; the quarry is Sarah. The
propriety of the figure in regard to Abraham is rather obvious: from the one column of rock the individual rocks were
hewn. What was first a unit rock is the one from whom many
came. Exactly how Sarah is to be construed in the figure
"quarry" seems a bit puzzling, since this is the only instance
of the use of this particular word in the Old Testament.
Perhaps the figure means about the same in both cases. Besides, the fact that Abraham may rightly be regarded as the
father of the nation is clear enough. In the second instance
to say that Sarah "bore" the nation must not be pressed too
strongly. But the point in both instances is distinctly made
when the text goes on to point out that Abraham was called
when he was "but one," and the prospects of developing into
a nation were most unlikely. But it pleased God to "bless

him and make him many." As he once did in days of old he can surely do again. The *Jerusalem Bible* uses an apt translation in this connection when it says: he "was all alone." We should remind ourselves here that increase in population was regarded as one of the prime blessings for the Lord to bestow (cf. Hos. 1:10; Jer. 3:16; Ezek. 36:10, 11; Zech. 8:5) and a prominent feature in eschatology.

Verse 3. Other modes of establishing Israel are indicated. First the whole process is comprehended in the one term "comfort," which includes feeling sorry for the one in need and also administering help, as *Westermann* especially loves to point out. Echoes of 40:1 ring out rather clearly at this point. A colorful figure is resorted to. Israel in Captivity is thought of as a waste land, whose desolation is to be brought to an end, so that what was like a waste now will be like the famous paradise of days of old before he calamitous fall into sin. This one far-reaching change in the land is indicative of many similar ones that shall stand out. Four more items are listed as being in evidence throughout the nation. "Joy and gladness" will again be found because of the transformation that is to take place. And the response on Israel's part will be "thanksgiving and sounds of praise." This last part could be reminiscent of Jer. 30:19.

2. The Lord's Salvation Will Endure (vv. 4-6)

51:4-6
4. Hearken to me, you my people,
    and give ear to me, my nation.
For instruction will go forth from me,
    and my norm of judgment will I appoint
        as a light for people.
5. My victory is near, my salvation has gone forth,
    the coastlands wait for me
    and for my arm they hope.
6. Lift up your eyes to the heavens,
    and look to the earth beneath.
For the heavens will disintegrate like smoke,
    the earth will wear out like a garment;
        and they that dwell in it will die like swarms of gnats.
But my salvation will be forever,
    and my victory will never be annulled.

Verse 4. The Lord is about to make a solemn pronouncement to which he wants his people to give strict attention. What is about to take place in Israel is not a mere passing phase of history. For God builds solidly; he promises an enduring future for them. Heaven and earth may pass away but the Lord's kingdom will endure forever. God is deeply concerned for the future of his own. Israel is the basis of all development, but what is developed there is for the people generally. All this growth and development is to begin with "instruction" that Israel gets as to the big issues involved. Besides he will appoint a lasting "norm of judgment" for Israel's use in estimating values. But the light kindled in Israel will throw its kindly beams "for people" the world over.

Verse 5. The same prominent word occurs here as in v. 1, but it is now to be translated as "victory," a possibility that cannot be reproduced in English. In fact all the keywords used here are practically synonymous: instruction (law), judgment, righteousness, victory. All point to the achievement of the Lord's glorious objectives. This has led some to translate "victory" as the "fulfillment of my promise." All this is spoken of in the perfect tense, for it all refers to things that have as good as happened. God's successful overall rule could hardly be described more simply and clearly than in the words, "my arm will rule the people." All the issues of history lie in the hollow of God's hand. Ultimately these benefits will accrue to all nations. The nations themselves in the secrets of their heart wait for the time when they will have a share in these blessings. And so it may rightly be said by the Lord: "The coastlands [the shorelands of the Mediterranean] wait for me, and for my arm [i.e., the proper display of divine power] they do hope."

Verse 6. By way of contrast, the Lord invites his people to consider things that seem unalterably fixed and sure — the heavens above and the earth beneath. Nothing appears to be more stable than these works of the Lord's hands. But they are not among the things that endure to all eternity. And when they go off the scene, the "heavens will disintegrate like smoke," vanishing as though they had no substance. But the old earth will gradually wear out and be cast off like an old garment. The dwellers upon the earth will share in the same lot in the great judgment, perishing like swarms of gnats, in a merciless and total judgment, many though they may be at the time the judgment takes place. Those seemingly durable things shall all vanish away. All that last will be God's "salvation," the deliverance from all evil, for which we have been taught to pray. Or to state the case differently, "my victory shall never be annulled."

It may yet be remarked that this section (vv. 4-6) contains a number of expressions that are clearly echoes of the Servant passages, a matter which we cannot now pause to trace down.

3. Slanderous Attacks by Enemies Cannot Harm Israel (vv. 7-8)

51:7-8 7. Listen to me, you who know righteousness,
you people in whose heart is my instruction.
Fear not the reproach of men;
do not be alarmed at their revilings.
8. For the moth will eat them up as a garment,
and the clothes-moth will eat them as wool.
But my victory shall last forever,
and my deliverance to the last generations.

Verse 7. The voice of authority that speaks is that of the Lord himself. He deals with what may have been a painful issue in those days. Men, especially the Babylonians who were Israel's captors, had heard what claims this little nation had made about its relations to the Lord and about the glorious future that lay in store for her. Since everything seemed to be going amiss with Israel, they readily became the objects of scorn of their powerful captors. Reproach, scoffing, and reviling, Israel had to endure aplenty. No doubt, this all became a painful experience for Israel. For insults may be very difficult to bear, especially when they are unwarranted. So the Lord now proceeds to speak a reassur-

ing word to his true people, those who in v. 1 were described
as "eagerly pursuing righteousness." Here they are said to
"know righteousness," where "know" implies a deeper and
earnest acquaintance with (cf. Josh. 23:14; Jer. 31:33 f.).
That the ones addressed have more than an externalistic
knowledge of the Lord appears from the fact that they are
said to have God's instruction in their hearts. The Lord here
exhorts his faithful ones not to let themselves be intimidated
by reproach and revilings.

Verse 8. This summons to go on bravely is supported by
an argument like that found in v. 6. For the Lord points out
that they who revile his chosen ones will vanish as even the
heavens and the earth shall. The familiar figure again appears,
the garment devoured by moths. But among the things that
endure are God's victory and deliverance, which he shall
work for his people. So the emphasis up to this point has
been on the enduring things that the Lord is building.

4. Display Your Power, Arm of the Lord (vv. 9-11)

51:9-11 9. Awake, awake, display your strength,
                   O arm of the Lord;
awake as in days of old,
    in generations long past.
Were you not the arm that hewed Rahab in pieces,
    that pierced the sea-monster?
10. Was it not you that dried up the sea,
    the waters of the great deep?
you that converted the depths of the sea into a way
    for the redeemed to pass over?
11. And the ransomed of the Lord shall return
    and shall come to Zion with shouts of joy;
everlasting joy shall be their crown,
    and sorrow and sighing shall flee away.

Verse 9. Verses 9-11 are an answer in the form of a prayer
to all the assurance that the chapter has offered till now. For
till now the chapter has been a challenge to have confidence
in the cause of Israel that the Lord espouses. Emboldened by
his word the prophet, in the name of the people, prays that

God may bring all these things to pass. At the same time these three verses apostrophize the arm of the Lord (cf. 52: 10; Luke 1:51), challenging it as though it were a responsible agent ready to go into action. The arm of the Lord *is* powerful. Now let it furnish proof of it. God's arm has been known historically to achieve great things "in days of old." One outstanding victory that it achieved was the mighty act wrought in the crossing of the Red Sea. This event is referred to when "Rahab" is mentioned. For the name Rahab means the one that "acts stormily or boisterously." It is a name used several times for Egypt (see 30:7; Ps. 87:4). At the same time Egypt (or her ruler) is referred to as the "sea monster" (see 27:1; Ezek. 29:3; 32:2). When the proud and boisterous Egypt acted defiantly over against God's demand to let his people go, then the arm of the Lord went into action and "hewed into pieces" the wild beast, or to use a parallel expression, it "pierced the sea monster," or overcame Egypt. The slaughter of the wild beast is proof of the power of God. The arm of the Lord did such a mighty work once. He can do it again. Whether there is a reference here to a mythical sea-monster of the Babylonian Creation Epic, will be examined in an Excursus at the end of this chapter.

Verse 10. The prophet brings in a direct historical allusion to the Exodus when in bold terms he describes what happened as a drying of the sea and the waters of the great deep. What was depth of water was converted into a path for the children of Israel to pass over. Mighty works like this should be pondered. They furnish excellent groundwork for faith to build upon.

Verse 11. Now comes the well-grounded conclusion relating to the situation involved. The big question that kept troubling Israel was, Can the Lord actually bring back his people from Captivity? He both can, and is able to do it with a unique display of power and glory. Those whom God will free, "the redeemed of the Lord" — they will not break their own shackles — they will return, not merely making a feeble attempt to do so, and "shall come to Zion with shouts of joy." The description of the experience is one of the most gladsome scenes of all that the Scriptures present. A joy that cannot be quenched will take possession of the returnees: "everlasting joy shall be their crown." They are virtually likened to kings and royalty. A joy, not self-induced, but overpowering, shall irresistibly take possession of them ("overtake them") "and sorrow and sighing shall flee away."

This verse is identical with 35:10. The prophet appears to be quoting himself. Why not? The sentiment well bears repeating.

5. A Reassuring Answer from God (vv. 12-16)

51:12-16 12. I, I am he that comforts you.
Why should you be afraid of man who dies,
of the children of men who fade away like grass?
13. and forget the Lord, your Maker,
who stretched out the heavens
and laid the foundation of the earth —
and be continually afraid all the day —
of the oppressor, when he sets himself to destroy?
And where is now the wrath of the oppressor?
14. The crouching captive already makes haste to throw off his shackles, and he shall not die in the deep dungeon nor shall he lack bread. 15. For I am the Lord your God, who stirs up the sea so that its waves roar. 16. And I have laid my words in your mouth; with the shadow of my hand I covered you, planting the heavens and founding the earth, and saying to Zion: "You are my people."

Verse 12, 13. Man prays; God answers (v. 12-16). We are not dealing with a superficial optimism, nor with unfounded promises, but with divine assurances deeply grounded. Therefore with a doubly emphatic "I" the Lord points out that he is condescending to speak "comfortably" (!) to Jerusalem. To get the right measure of this divine comfort we must estimate who it is that might inspire fear. It is "man who dies," vs. the living God. It is "the children of men who fade away like grass." To be intimidated by these opponents amounts to "forgetting the Lord [their] Maker."

The prophet never tires of stressing that the Lord is the omnipotent Creator. With never-ceasing wonder he recalls that the mighty heavens were stretched out by him, and the foundations of the earth were laid by him. Whatever may have given solidity and firmness to the earth, there can be no question about it that on God's part it was solid building. Can he who engages in such mighty and enduring works find the control of the children of men to be a problem? Only by overlooking tremendous works of God such as these can men lapse into fear of men when they oppose God. In fact at this point it appears how silly man's misgivings in reality are, when the work of the Lord is considered.

Here the sentence structure grows a bit complicated — not unclear just complex — for the writer is packing away big thoughts within a narrow compass of lines. But we are reminded that there is an "oppressor" — no doubt the strong Babylonian world-power. This oppressor, we are reminded, "sets himself to destroy." The ancient animosity of the world over against the kingdom of God is involved. But already the enemy is as good as defeated, for that is what the question implies, "Where is now the wrath of the oppressor?" As antagonist God must view the strength of the destroyer as ridiculously small.

Verse 14. The next three verses may be prose (not according to the *RSV*). But that has no further bearing on the interpretation, in fact it may be purely accidental.

Verse 14 as such is fraught with much difficulty, which we shall not endeavor to explore, giving, if possible, merely a feasible exposition. "The crouching captive" is the nation Israel. He crouches because the prison envisioned is small, low, and cramped. Since God wills it so, the freedom he is about to enjoy lies within his grasp, if in faith he will lay hold of it. All he needs to do is to throw off his shackles. For the next clause we take our cue from the Jerusalem Bible translation. This clause merely restates from another point of view what, by the grace of God, is actually happening: "He shall not die in the deep dungeon." He seemed destined to death. His case seemed hopeless. It is far from that. Rounding out the picture, one minor but colorful item is added, the force of which we may catch by the insertion of the adverb "ever," viz., "nor shall he [ever] lack bread." After his captivity is ended, all his wants will be so adequately supplied that he shall never suffer hunger again. This interpretation of the verse is not forced or unreasonable, and vindicates the verse against those who magnify the difficulties, claiming among other things that everything in the verse is "clumsily patched together" (*zusammengestoppelt*).

Verse 15. Another reference by the good Lord himself to his successful control of the forces of nature ("stir up the sea so that the waves roar") shows how well founded all his claims of control are.

Verse 16. In this verse the Lord concludes his comforting reassurance. Having just described what enormous resources are at his disposal, he now indicates how he purposes to use them. In a word, he works through men, enabling them to achieve results. But again he works through men first of all by laying his words in their mouth. Resorting for a moment to New Testament terminology: the Lord enables his faithful servants to speak his powerful gospel message, that "power of God unto salvation." They speak and God remakes men through the word spoken. And where this work involves dangers, it pleases the Lord to cover them with the shadow (protection) of his hand. The three participles — infinitives in Hebrew (*KS* 402 z) — that follow are a bit difficult to construe: "planting . . . founding . . . saying. . . ." All three describe divine forms of activity. It seems best to regard them as describing those works that God will do as the grand climax of his saving work, when he establishes the new heavens and the new earth, where all things are right.

6. No Ground for Israel's Despair and Inaction (vv. 17-20)

51:17-20   17. Bestir yourself, bestir yourself, up on your feet, O Jerusalem!

You who have drunk at the hand of the Lord
   the cup of his wrath.
Yea, the beaker of reeling
   you have completely drained.
18. Of all the children which she brought forth
   there was not a one that acted as her guide,
not a one that took her by the hand
   of all the children she had raised.
19. These two things have befallen you —
— and who shall be sorry for you?
devastation and destruction, famine and the sword;
   who will comfort you?
20. Your sons have fainted;
   they lie at the head of every street
      like an antelope caught in the net.
they have experienced the wrath of the Lord to the full,
   the rebuke of your God.

Verse 17. Apparently the calamity of the Captivity was so heavy that the nation practically lay there utterly prostrate, unable to even think of any constructive enterprise. In this section the pitiful state of the nation is pictured. The prophet seems to be addressing the nation. But in spite of all that has befallen, the nation does not need to take a defeatist attitude. In view of all that has been said, despair and inaction are not called for. Rather she is to be active about her assigned task. Still the prophet does not press the point of action; in deep sympathy he pictures her misery in all its depth. The figure that dominates this description is that of the cup of divine wrath that the nation has been obliged to drain. The Lord thrust this cup at her. The contents was God's righteous wrath at the people's sin. The nation had no choice. She had to drain it completely. She then fell to the ground. None could help her. The hour of God's judgment was upon her. There she lay prostrate till the divine anger had spent itself. How common this figure in its various aspects is, appears from the following passages: Jer. 25:15-31; Hab. 2:16; Ezek. 23:13-15; Lam. 4:21; Zech. 12: 2; Ps. 60:3; 75:8; Mark 10:38 f.; John 18:11.

Verse 18. A pathetic touch is added when it is noted that none of her children, figuratively speaking, could lend her any assistance. The Lord appoints and no man can say him nay. He appoints the times of judgment.

Verses 19, 20. In a word, clearly patterned after 47:9, the misery of the unhappy nation is summed up, first in terms of what befell the city — "devastation and destruction" — and then in terms of what befell her inhabitants — "famine and sword." One aspect of a siege-scene is developed a little more at length (v. 20). The siege of the city is in progress. Men are falling in the streets, perishing with hunger, or cut down by the weapons of the enemy. They are hopelessly entangled in death, "like an antelope caught in the net," as the apt comparison has it. The force at work behind it all was the "wrath of the Lord" which dare never be trifled with.

7. The Cup of God's Wrath Is Being Transferred from Israel's Hands to Those of Her Enemies (vv. 21-23)

51:21-23 21. Therefore hear this, you afflicted one,
   drunk but not with wine.
22. Thus says the Lord, Yahweh;
   and your God, who defends the cause of his people:
"Lo, I have removed from your hand the beaker of reeling,
   the cup of my wrath you shall not have to drink any more.
23. And I will put it into the hand of your tormentors,
   who say to you, 'Lie down flat
      that we may trample over you,'
and you have made your back like the ground,
   like the street for men to pass over."

Verse 21. The cup-of-wrath-idea is to be developed a bit more fully. A second term has appeared, parallel to the "cup of wrath," an expression that we have translated "the beaker of reeling," which second name suggests one possibility that is also connected with drinking of this cup, namely staggering blindly and helplessly under the impact of the drink. The nation is being invited by the Lord to give particular heed to the announcement about to be made. These are not two separate cups, but two names for the one cup, the term "beaker" being used only here. This verse may be patterned after 47:8, the taunt song on Babylon.

Verses 22, 23. It now appears that he who had dealt with Israel in wrath, still, strange to say, will deal with them in mercy and champion their cause publicly, a course that has repeatedly been taken (cf. 41:1; 42:4; 43:8-13; 50:8-9). A beautiful name is coined by the prophet for the Lord, faithful in all his dealings with his people, the name "the Defender of the cause of his people." He it is who alone can determine how long the cup of wrath shall be in a nation's hands. He has decreed in the present instance that the day of affliction is over. This cup will still be in the picture, but now it will be given into the hand of the tormentors (v. 23). From this it appears, from the fact that they are called tormentors, that the victors (the Babylonians) had practiced the usual cruelties on the vanquished. Not only had they used a gesture of conquest (like Josh. 10:24; cf. also Ps. 110:1) but had trampled over the backs of the captives, yea, had made a street of them for "men to pass over." They who practiced cruelty will suffer cruelty in return.

Notes

Verse 1. "From which you were hewn" — in this clause the "from" and the "which" have been omitted. See *KS* 380 c and *GK* 155 k.

Verse 4. The possessive "*my* people" . . . and "*my* nation" should be retained as *RSV* has it. The chapter is concerned with the nation Israel, not with the nations. The last word of this verse may be retained and rendered "I will appoint." No need of emending the text to obtain the adverb "suddenly." The words that appear in this area — *torah, mishpat, tsedheq, yesha‘* are practically synonymns for the Lord's help which he will reveal in due time.

Verse 6. We have followed the prevailing trend to translate *ken* as "gnats," even though no case occurs where the singular is thus used. To translate it "so" makes it difficult to extract a plausible sense.

Verse 11. It would appear that a conjunction (*waw* conversive) has fallen out before *nasu.* In 35:10 the *waw* stands.

Verse 12. In "comforts you" we prefer to read the singular suffix with the *Septuagint* and *Symmachus.*

Verse 13. "Sets himself" (*konen*) involves a verb which is used in the figure of setting the bow on the string.

Verse 15. "Stirs" (*roga'*) is a participial form. See *GK* 65 d.

Verse 17. In "beaker of reeling" a genetive construction is involved where the genetive expresses the result: a beaker that causes reeling (*GK* 128 q).

Verse 19. In the last word, *y* should be substituted for *aleph*, which latter expresses the first person, which is intolerably harsh.

Verse 22. "I have removed" is a perfect of certainty, often translated as a positive future.

EXCURSUS ON "Rahab."

Verse 9. At this point it is customary to refer to a Babylonian myth, which is supposed to be in the background of the prophet's mind, the battle of Marduk with Tiamat, the monster of the great deep. Six (or seven?) passages are referred to in this connection. They are: Isa. 30:7; 51:9 f.; Ps. 89:10 f.; 87:4; Job 26:2 f.; 9:13; Ps. 40:5 (?). The name Rahab appears in all these passages and is supposed to be this monster. A careful examination of the passages, one by one (as made by Eduard Hertlein, ZATW, 1919/20) does not support this approach. For in every case "Rahab" which means the "boisterous one" is a standing designation of Egypt, without any mythological undertones. For Egypt as world power in her day was "noisy, proud, boisterous." No passage of those commonly referred to in this connection contains a reference to some mythological creature. Our passage, in particular, interprets itself. For v. 10 describes, without figure, what is being thought of, namely the overcoming of the waters of the arm of the Red Sea, which was the obstacle in Israel's way in the Exodus days. Verse 9 describes the allusion in terms of a figure. God overcame Egypt that stood in the way of the Exodus. Verse 10 abandons the figure and makes an obvious reference to the dissipating of the waters of the Red Sea. So it is consistently: Egypt is always the entity thought of when the word Rahab is used in these passages.

We concede that there may be mythological language used in Scripture, because there just is a mythological flavor in certain current expressions in familiar usage. Nothing indicates that "Rahab" has such a flavor.

Chapter LII:1-12

L. COMFORT ABUNDANTLY ADMINISTERED (cont.) (Chap. 52:1-12)

We consider Chap. 52 as being the continuation of Chap. 51, as our outline at the beginning of the book indicates.

In approaching this chapter a number of major difficulties stare us in the face. They may be summed up about as follows: vv. 1-2 is said to begin a certain thought which is not brought to a conclusion; after v. 2 some lines dropped out; then a glossator added vv. 3-6 in prose; but no one quite seems to be able to make a consistent thought out of these verses. We hope to be able to indicate in a measure that logic and coherence mark the opening of this chapter.

The thoughts move on a high level of joy and exultation; these are some of the grandest passages of the great prophet. In vv. 1-2 the prophet addresses first the city, then its inhabitants to take an aggressive, hopeful attitude. Verses 3-6 the Lord is speaking showing what justification he has to set his people free and help them.

8. Zion Awake! (vv. 1-6)

52:1-6 1. Wake up! Wake up!
Put on your strength, O Zion;
put on your glorious garments,
    O Jerusalem, the holy city.
For no more shall there come into you
    the uncircumcised and the unclean.
2. Shake yourself from the dust,
    rise and sit on your throne, O Jerusalem.
Loose the bonds off your neck,
    you captives, you people of Zion,
3. For thus says the Lord:
    You were sold for nothing, and you shall be redeemed without money.
4. For thus says the Lord, Yahweh: "My people at the first went down to Egypt to sojourn there. Also Assyria oppressed them for

no reason at all. 5. Now therefore what do I find here?" — this is the word of the Lord — for my people have been taken away for nothing. They that rule over them shriek out [harsh orders] — this is the word of the Lord: "continually all the day long my name is blasphemed. 6. Therefore my people shall know my name; yea, therefore shall they know on that day that it is I that am saying, Here I am."

Verse 1. This summons to Zion obviously constitutes a contrast to the taunt-song on the daughter of Babylon (47: 1 ff.), who is bidden to go down into the dust and take on the role of a slave. Zion is to come up from the slave-status and become a queen. She is to awake from the stupor of captivity, bestir herself and take on her regal functions, for the day of her deliverance has come. She *was* clothed in the habiliments of a slave. She had put aside, among other things, even her strength. All she felt was weakness. Now she is to resume her former strength and engage in her tasks assigned to her by her God. Rich, glorious, sumptuous garments befit the state in which she now finds herself. For she will again be the "holy city." This includes, among other things, that the "uncircumcised and the unclean" shall no more appear as attackers within the city. Obviously the prophet is not speaking of the political entity called Jerusalem, but of the ideal city of God as she shall appear in the consummation of all things.

Verse 2. The figure just used (the queen putting on strength) is developed a bit more in detail. She is pictured as rising up from the dust in which she had lain, shaking off the dust, standing up and walking with queenly dignity to her throne; as she goes she looses the bonds from her neck, as captives are often represented in monumental inscriptions as bound together to one another by ropes around their necks.

Verse 3. The basis on which this deliverance rests is now set forth by an unusual argument. The Lord is represented as advancing the justification for his deliverance of Zion — "for thus says the Lord." In one simple statement this justification is set forth; "You were sold for nothing." Ap-

parently this is a figurative way of describing the Babylonian Captivity. This can be likened to a sale, a one-sided
sale. Babylon acquired Judah but paid nothing for it. Therefore the people of God can be freed for nothing, without the
payment of a special price, simply on the strength of a divine
order. Judah can be redeemed without money. Apparently
the issue is not redemption from sin, nor a question of whether
Jerusalem was guilty and deserving of punishment. The
Lord appears as champion of his people. Babylon, from one
point of view, was guilty in her treatment of Judah. Judah,
from one point of view, was innocent over against Babylon.
The Lord, without setting any further forces into play,
could call for the freedom of his people. Without further
ado, the nations would have to liberate them at his call.

Verse 4. In fact a kind of historic pattern is disclosed by
the prophet as prevailing during the entire period of Israel's
existence. In Egypt Israel appeared as guest. Egypt had no
claim upon her, when Moses demanded that she be released.
But her rights were violated by Pharaoh. Then centuries
later Assyria appeared on the scene of history. Though from
one point of view, the prophet viewed Assyria as a tool in
God's hands (10:5 ff.) to punish Israel's apostasy, still from
the point of view of Assyria as a nation, she had no rightful
claims on Israel. This is implied in the brief statement in reference to Assyria. Assyria oppressed Israel "for no reason at
all." This approach shows what broad insight the prophets
in their day displayed in their evaluation of current events.
They could appreciate both sides of an issue.

Verse 5. The seemingly vague statement, "Now therefore
what do I find here?" in context clearly refers to the Lord
looking at the Babylonian situation, particularly in so far as
the Captivity of Judah was concerned. The answer to the
question that the Lord poses to himself must run somewhat
as follows: In the case of Babylon we have a matter like
that of Egypt and Assyria. Here, too, Israel was taken in
without her conqueror's having paid an adequate price, without Babylon's having due right and title to what she held.

Too much of selfish imperialistic designs were mixed up in Babylon's claims. God was entitled to the privilege of demanding that his people be set free. Babylon's rulers in the meantime were "shrieking out harsh orders" in typical tyrant-style. Some oppression of captive Israel had definitely been practiced. God's verdict in the matter is contained in the claim that by thus riding rough-shod over Israel Babylon was dishonoring the Lord. For no doubt many a time the conqueror said to the conquered: "Where is now your God?" (cf. Ps. 42:10; 115:2; Joel 2:17). So the holy name of the Lord was being blasphemed all the day long.

Verse 6. All that has just been said amply justifies the deliverance from Captivity. When the Lord thus vindicates himself and what he is doing, Israel will have a truer and deeper knowledge of the Lord ("My people shall know my name"). In this deliverance it will be as though they would see their God standing in their midst, identifying himself and saying: "Here am I." It is in this spirit that Zion is to awake and put on her strength and become a true queenly personage.

9. How Beautiful upon the Mountains Are the Messenger's Feet (vv. 7-10)

A different meter prevails in this section; it is in a tripping 2:2 pattern. Besides the imagery is drawn from the battle field. The battle is over, the victory won.

52:7-10
7. How attractive upon the mountains are the feet of the messenger,
announcing, "All is well!"
bringing good news, proclaiming deliverance;
saying to Zion: "Your God has proved himself king."
8. Hark, your watchmen, they have raised their voice!
together they shout for joy.
For eye to eye they see
the return of the Lord to Zion.
9. Break forth into joy, sing together,
you waste places of Jerusalem;
for the Lord has comforted his people,
he has freed Jerusalem.

10. The Lord has made bare his holy arm,
    before the eyes of all the Gentiles.
All the ends of the earth
    shall see the salvation of our God.

Verse 7. Practically each line is a jubilant note of victory. As indicated above the scene is cast in military terms — just after the battle. People and officials are gathered anxiously waiting for a report on the outcome of the battle. Strictly speaking this however was not a battle. The question pending is, How is it with the captives in Babylon? Is their liberation achieved? Suddenly they spy a runner. He must be the messenger with a report on the outcome. All can tell even at a distance from the eager attitude of his running that good news is speeding his course. Oh, how "attractive" those feet appear! The whole scene is laid in Palestine; the mountains are those of the Holy Land. The Babylonian country is a flat plain. As the messenger comes near, his first cry is "All is well!" The announcements tumble over his lips: "good news," "deliverance." He finally manages to sum it all up effectively: "Your God has proved himself king." Of course, Yahweh has been king right along. But now, by liberating his people he has demonstrated conclusively that the reins of world-government are firmly in his hands. He can achieve whatever he pleases. This special meaning of the verb "rule" appears elsewhere (cf. Exod. 15:18; Ps. 93:1; 97: 1; 99:1; Isa. 24:25).

Verse 8. Now the whole group of those who had been anxiously awaiting the messenger's report break out simultaneously into a loud shout of joy. Shouts of joy fall pell-mell from their lips. For one thing is now perfectly clear to them: The Lord has again turned to his people with favor, he has come back and deigns to dwell in their midst as in days of old. Where his glory had departed from his holy city with the coming of the Captivity, this glory again enters in to take up its dwelling there. Or, as some have stated it: Israel has again become the center of the Lord's manifestation (cf. 40:9).

Verse 9. Verses 9 and 10 are a typical feature of Isaiah, a jubilant hymn bringing to a triumphant conclusion a line of thought that depicts what the Lord has done. Other hymnic conclusions of a similar sort are to be found: 42:10-13; 44: 23; 48:20 f.; 49:13. It is as though the prophet offers for the use of the congregation a hymn suitable for the occasion. At the same time he exhorts the people to be sure to offer sacrifices of thanksgiving. But very strangely and quite poetically he addresses himself to the "waste places of Jerusalem" in what some have called "an exuberant paradox" to "sing together" in harmonious chorus. It is as though all along even the ruins had felt the unhappy state of the nation. There could be no greater comfort for the holy city than to have her freedom restored.

Verse 10. The Lord's munificent blessing for his people is further described as a case of his "making bare his holy arm before the eyes of all Gentiles." During the Captivity the Lord's arm had, as it were, been swathed in the folds of his garments, preventing him from using it freely. In 51:9 the nation had appealed to the arm of the Almighty to manifest its saving strength. This prayer has been answered. Even the dimmed eye of the Gentiles cannot help but see that the Lord has gone into action. In fact, "All the ends of the earth have seen the salvation of our God." Israel's return from Captivity was an event that challenged world-wide attention.

10. Leave Babylon (vv. 11-12)

52:11-12 11. Depart, depart. Go out from there
Touch nothing unclean.
Go out from the midst of her.
    Purify yourselves, you who bear the vessels of the Lord.
12. For you shall not go forth in haste;
    you shall not leave as men who flee.
For the one who leads the way is the Lord;
    the God of Israel is your rearguard.

Verse 11. In a sense Babylon is the epitome of wickedness as well as the prisonhouse of Israel's captivity. From both points of view she is to be left behind by the people of God. For the expression "Go out from there" the Jerusalem Bible has translated rather aptly: "Leave that place"; and for "Go out from the midst of her" it offers the translation: "Get out of her." Both translations help us understand more clearly by their very abruptness that we have a call for immediate action. Babylon is not mentioned by name in this verse but no one can doubt that she is the place that is to be left behind. The added summons, "touch nothing unclean" indicate the whole attitude that the prophet aims to cultivate. The stain of sin, worldly pride and idolatry is upon the city and upon everything in it in spite of the splendor and glory of the empire. She is the very spirit of worldliness. Therefore she and all that she stands for must be disavowed. Here the prophet somehow realizes that in the Return the holy vessels, once taken from Jerusalem's temple, will be given back to Israel, and though it may appear a very external thing, so completely shall the people regard their Return not as a nationalistic achievement but as a Holy enterprise. Ritual cleanness is a proper counterpart to true sanctification. One cannot be indifferent to ceremonial uncleanness with impunity. They who are entrusted with the vessels of the Lord (perhaps the priests and Levites) are to be mindful of this injunction.

Verse 12. The Return of Israel is now described in terms of a great deliverance of days of old, the Exodus from Egypt, only there will be certain notable differences. For one thing, in days of old Israel had to flee posthaste. Now it shall be a leisurely and dignified procedure (cf. Deut. 16:3; Exod. 12: 39). But the last point made is one of similarity. As the Lord went before and followed after Israel so shall he on this occasion "lead the way" and also "be the rearguard" (Exod. 13:21 f.).

So Israel is exhorted to take part in a glorious experience. So the prophet administered comfort.

Notes

Verse 2. Because the Hebrew text, as it reads, seems to say: "Rise up, sit down" many feel impelled to make a slight emendation, which results in the rendering: "Arise, O *captive* Jerusalem"; but even that minor emendation is not necessary. For the word *shebhi*, "sit down," may be taken in the rather common sense of that verb: "sit on your throne," a translation offered already by the *Septuagint*.

Verse 3. The statement, "You were sold for nothing" seems to clash with other statements of the prophet, such as 50:1; 42:24; 43:22-24, where the thought is expressed that Israel's Captivity-experience was the result of her many and great sins, a fact which cannot be denied. But at this point the prophet is not attempting to give an all-sided treatment of the causes of the Captivity. It simply is true that if the Captivity is viewed as a financial transaction God gained nothing by selling his people into captivity. But if it be claimed that he did not sell them for a price, for no cause of guilt at all, then the statement applies to the godly remnant in Israel. For that remnant was not being punished, as *Koenig* in his commentary, rightly points out. But the simpler rendering still is: The Lord gained nothing by the transaction when he sold his people to Babylon.

Verse 5. We are, of course, reading the last word of the verse as *meno'ats*, not *minno'ats*.

Verse 6. When it is pointed out that the expression "in that day" appears only here in the second half of the book, it should be pointed out that they that accept the unit-authorship of the book can also point to 7:18, 20, 21, 23. And it should be remarked that an author's earlier style must not always correspond to the style employed later in life.

Verse 8. The phrase "eye to eye" has an utterly different meaning in English than in Hebrew. In English it means something like agreeing completely in one's approach and outlook with another. In Hebrew the meaning is "close at hand," something like being so near that you can see the whites of the eye of the person approaching. See *KS* 402 i.

Chapter LII:13—LIII:12

M. THE SUFFERING SERVANT SUCCESSFUL IN HIS REDEMPTIVE WORK (Chaps. 52: 13—53:12)

We come to the fourth and greatest of the songs of the Suffering Servant. Unfortunately it is often overlooked that the Song begins with the last three verses of Chap. 52. This complete section quite obviously divides itself into five strophes, each significantly marked by one (or two) initial keyword. As this poem progresses, or gathers momentum, the verses grow in weight and length. But it should be indicated from the outset that we have here a kind of song of triumph, as the opening line already suggests.

This Servant Song presupposes the previous three (cf. chaps. 42, 49, and 50). It can hardly be understood without those that precede it. It prepares for Chap. 54:1 ff.

Yet there is a plaintive and even sorrowful note in the poem. As *G. A. Smith* has indicated, the style is "broken, sobbing and recurrent." The light in the poem is very bright, and the shadows are exceedingly dark. We may safely brush aside the suggestion that some one other than the prophet wrote this chapter. To catch the full flavor of this Song we must not overlook the fact that nowhere in the course of it does the Servant himself speak, nor does he appear. He is the object of discussion. He "haunts" the poem.

Textual problems stare us in the face. There are some difficult lines in the poem. *Volz* speaks of the text as sadly corrupted, *schwerverderbt*. Each commentator almost attempts generous corrections. A few, like *Muilenburg*, dare to make the assertion that there are good grounds for maintaining the text as it traditionally appears in the form accepted by the Hebrews. The *RSV* showed admirable restraint when they accepted only two variants in the chapter. When numerous changes are made, conjectures for the most part, the distinctive features of the chapter are largely lost. It is also true that, as some have counted, twenty-six words appear that are found in this chapter only (*hapax lego-mena*). Some seem to be trying desperately to rob the chapter of both its uniqueness and its originality, when, for example, they stress what they believe to be kinship with Babylonian Tammuz legend, his dying and recurrent rising. But the differences between the two are far more striking than the points of similarity. All that needs to be conceded in this area is that the Hebrew prophet may have had some knowledge of the Babylonian material, but hardly used it in this poem.

And who was its author? Two major schools of thought stand out. One school says it was Deutero-Isaiah, the Great Unknown, the writer of the rest of the material of this second half of the book. The second school says it was a totally unknown stranger. There is still a third group, larger than is usually supposed, who attribute this, as well as the rest of the book, on good evidence, to Isaiah, the son of Amoz (1:1).

As to the title to be set at the head of this section we have chosen "The Suffering Servant Successful in His Redemptive Work." It is almost impossible to find a title comprehensive enough to do justice to the chapter. "The Fourth Servant Song" is a bit prosy as title. Our own title lacks a reference to the big theme that underlies the whole, vicarious atonement.

As to the form in which this material appears, some have noted the similarity with laments. But that is a merely superficial similarity. Some, with better justification, label its character as a praise psalm, (*Lobpsalm*). But to stop short with that approach, proper as it is in part, overlooks the somber minor key in which it is written. But it still comes closer to the triumph-note that marks the psalm as a whole.

One unique feature that stands out most prominently is

the fact that the author delights to devise certain basic themes which he stresses when he first presents them. But as the poem progresses, he keeps recurring to these major themes (the vicarious suffering, total obedience, utter willingness to suffer, the guilt of the people of God, divine approval). These keep reappearing as themes or sub-themes in this grand symphonic poem.

A marked feature that is quite significant is that it is being recognized more and more that the poem bears no traces of the environment from which it sprang. It is virtually impossible to assign any period of Israel's history as the age in which it originated. Intimately connected with this feature is the question, How did the unique insight (vicarious atonement) originate and find expression? The only tenable answer we seem to be able to find is, it was a divinely imparted spiritual insight that did not spring from the prophet's mind, or result from meditation over great theological issues, nor did the native genius of the writer arrive at these conclusions. But still for all that it develops with unique emphasis the deep possibilities of vicarious sufferings, develops it in a measure not outdone even by the New Testament writers.

Before we examine the text as such, it may prove helpful to point to a problem the full answer to which we are not able to offer. We refer to the *time* factor in the poem. At times the point of approach seems to be that a certain feature of the prophet's message lies in the present; it is discussed as happening. Then the issues seem to lie in the past; they are an accomplished fact. Then again all the good things envisioned seem to lie somewhere in the future, even the remote future. We offer a very partial solution to the problem. There appears to be a certain timelessness about the issues discussed. In the counsels of God they are as good as realized. They are in one sense also in process of realization. Certain factors are still to be accomplished. A disregard of the time-factor enshrouds the whole picture.

Yet for all the difficulties that the chapter offers it is and will forever remain one of the grandest and most dearly beloved passages of Sacred Writ. Faith grasps these verities, gratitude feeds on them; hope is nourished by them.

What this chapter meant in the early life of the Christian church has been shown in a striking booklet by Hans Walter Wolff, *Jesaia 53 im Urchristentum.* He shows that from the earliest days it was regarded as a prophecy of eschatological-messianic character. He, however, also defends the approach that Deutero-Isaiah, the supposed author of Chaps. 40-66, experienced in a measure the things foretold in this chapter and so Deutero-Isaiah becomes a type of the Messiah. But the main point of his treatment of the subject is that the church always construed the passage in a Messianic sense. *Wolff* shows that the New Testament stands on this ground, as well as early fathers like Clement, Barnabas, so too the Didache, and other New Testament Apocrypha. Special importance is attached to Justin the Martyr. Wolff greets with delight the fact that the exponents of the theory that the Servant in Israel is losing ground.

1. Greatly Exalted after Being Deeply Humiliated (52:13-15)

52:13-15 13. Lo, my Servant shall be successful;
he shall be high and lifted up and greatly exalted.
14. Just as many were awestruck at you —
his appearance was so distorted from that of a man,
and his form scarcely seemed human —
15. so again shall he startle many nations.
At the sight of him kings shall hold their mouth shut;
because they have seen what had never been told them;
they have taken note of something the like of which they had never heard.

These three verses contain in capsule-form what is unfolded at greater length in Chap. 53, only the thought is in reverse order: In these three verses success is stressed first, then the lack of it. In Chap. 53 humiliation comes first, exaltation second.

Verse 13. The Lord is speaking. He is asserting that, appearances to the contrary, his Servant will achieve what he sets out to do. The verb could be translated "he will deal prudently" (*KJ*) but the stress lies rather on the results of prudent dealing-success, (or *RSV*): "he shall prosper." The same verb is used in the Lord's promise to Joshua (Josh. 1: 7, 8) and with reference to David (I Sam. 18:14). It is also used specifically with reference to the Messiah (Jer. 23: 5). In the latter connection it fits most admirably. For who ever achieved greater success than the Lord's Christ? That a superlative degree of success is being thought of appears from the three verbs heaped up in the rest of the verse ("be high and lifted up and greatly exalted"). So God grades the work of his Son. Success of every sort and description shall be rightly attributed to the Servant. He did his work very well.

Verse 14. At this point the sentence structure, though clear, becomes somewhat involved. The first line of v. 14 is to be followed up by the first line of v. 15, the two intervening lines constitute a kind of parenthesis. As men were awestruck at his extreme disfigurement, so will nations be startled at the totally unexpected development that things will ultimately take in the further turn from humiliation to exaltation. The parenthesis indicates that when the Servant was brought low this was something also physical. It actually involved bodily disfigurement. He was to be thought of as badly mutilated, more than man could bear; it was suffering that borders on the unthinkable. This being poetry, it does not require that every item specified was of necessity carried out to the letter. But still the striking correspondence between the thing prophesied and the fulfillment again and again fills us with wonder. Little wonder that many of the fathers of the church of days of old claim that the account reads as though Isaiah had sat at the foot of the cross.

Verse 15. So the amazement of the nations will be over the happy turn for the better that the lot of the Servant will take. He who had been brought so low will be so greatly exalted that, for example, kings, who are entitled and are

wont to speak up on all manner of important occasions, will
feel themselves to be so inadequate to even construe rightly
what is happening that in embarrassment will hold their
mouth shut. For what is happening will be quite beyond
them. The like of what they here see and hear was never
encountered by them before. Never was man brought so
low; never was anyone raised so high. This situation is, as
it were, a divine conundrum which calls for further elucida-
tion, which is now about to follow.

The Suffering Servant is

2. Totally Misunderstood because of His Seeming Insignificance (53:1-3)

53:1-3 1. Who believed what we heard?
       and to whom was the arm of the Lord revealed?
2. And so he grew up before him as a shoot,
   as a root coming up from arid soil.
He had neither form nor dignity
   that we should regard him;
   and no beauty that we should delight in him.
3. He was despised and shunned by men;
   a man weighted down by sorrow and acquainted with grief.
He was like a thing from which a man turns away his face;
   so we despised him and deemed him insignificant.

Verse 1. A different speaker is heard from this point on.
Some would say he is the prophet and those who are spreading the message of comfort of 40:1. Others claim it is the
nation Israel. We suggest a different approach. In these verses
we seem to overhear the believing portion of the nation as
they discuss the tragic death that occurred in their midst, the
death of the Servant of the Lord. Luke's account (24:13 ff.)
where the two disciples on the way to Emmaus discuss recent events would be a good parallel to what our chapter offers. So to speak, here we seem to hear two disciples standing on a street-corner in Jerusalem reviewing the things that
happened on Good Friday in the light of the better insight
that came after Pentecost. They express especially their
amazement at the complete misunderstanding they were

guilty of in regard to the remarkable figure that appeared as the great Sufferer in their midst. Who believed what reliable witnesses told about him, especially his claims to divine sonship? The nation's first reaction was total unbelief. The believing, penitent Jews after their baptism still marvel that they could have been so obtuse. What they here say is almost a penitent confession, at least it grows out of a penitent spirit. The second question drives home the point more strongly. That the Lord was at work and employing his divine strength of arm in what was happening on Golgotha never entered any one's mind. They still marvel as they reflect on this blindness.

Verse 2. It has been rightly remarked about the following verses that they tell the life's story of the Servant from the cradle to the grave. The humble beginnings of his life seemed so inauspicious. When he grew up as a lad in the streets of Nazareth, who took any particular note of him? He could be likened to an insignificant "shoot," a bit of vegetation that is scarcely noticed. Yet this term points to the Messiah (cf. 11:1, 10). So no one attaches particular importance to "a root coming up from arid soil." It seems doomed to wither away early. From this point onward it almost seems that the person described is Jesus of Nazareth hanging on the cross, or standing in the judgment hall of Pilate. At that particular juncture of life there was nothing attractive about this person. He may even be said to have been the epitome of repulsiveness. What beauty of form he may have had, had been virtually beaten out of him by his tormentors. Since with significant assignment there usually goes corresponding "dignity" it is rather striking that in this case such dignity of bearing seemed to be totally absent. Not only among the Greeks in days of old but practically among all people, beauty was regarded as a kind of prerequisite of greatness. At this juncture of his life the Servant did not meet this requirement. When the Servant was on trial no one considered him worthy of defense. No one would have thought of choosing him as a deliverer. The language at this point is like that of the psalms of lament, because the lot of the person in question was a lamentable one.

Verse 3. The impression made by the Servant at one point in his career was not only a case of being unimpressed by him but even a matter of being repelled by him: "he was despised and shunned by men." This reaction was not that of a special few but it was universal. The nation rejected him. This impression is now cast in terms that have become proverbial: he was "a man weighted down by sorrow and acquainted with grief." The first expression is usually rendered "a man of sorrows." This again translated literally would run "a man of pains." An abject and pitiful figure comes to mind. Not that he was such in reality. This expression seeks to cover the most extreme form of misunderstanding that prevailed. He was in reality everything but that. Add one further factor to all this and the impression of wretchedness is complete: "He was like a thing from which a man turns away his face" (cf. 49:7). By this time the lowest point is reached in what becomes almost a dreary repetition : "So we despised him and deemed him insignificant."

In reality the Suffering Servant was

3. A Willing Substitute for the Guilty Ones (vv. 4-6)

53:4-6 4. Surely, ours were the ailments that he bore;
   ours were the sorrows that he loaded upon himself.
  But we on our part esteemed him a marked man,
   smitten by God and afflicted [by God].
5. Yet he was pierced through by our transgressions,
  crushed because of our guilt.
   The punishment producing our welfare was upon him;
   and by his wounds healing came to us.
6. We had all gone astray like sheep;
  each of us had turned his own way.
 But it was the Lord who made the guilt of all of us
  fall upon him.

Verse 4. Verses 1-3 were a record of a pitiful misunderstanding. Verses 4-6 reveal the real facts of the case. Therefore the initial "surely" marks a strong adversative to what went before. It could also have been translated: "but in fact" (*BDB*). By a kind of rhyme — an unusual feature in Hebrew — a feature that we attempt to capture by moving "ours" forward, the adversative character of the verse is made all the more evident. Nothing was wrong with him; all was wrong with us. He on his part became the substitute for us. The more familiar translation has it: "Surely he hath born our griefs." The word really means "sicknesses," but is used for a wide variety of ailments. The verb following allows for taking the burden and carrying it for us as well as for bearing the evil consequences that should have fallen to our lot. While he was doing all this, we on our part were still laboring (say these converted Jews) under the misapprehension that, because so heavy burdens lay on the Servant's shoulders, he must be "a marked man," whom God had singled out for unusual punishment because of unusual guilt on his part. Yes, God had both "smitten" and "afflicted" him.

Verse 5. Nothing could be farther from the truth. It was *our* transgressions that had pierced this Servant of God through. They had "crushed" him. Strong verbs are used because the effects falling on this man were so extremely painful. It will be noted that at this point the figure changed from that of a sick man to that of a wounded one. It would, however, be undue pressing of the letter to insist on it that the Servant actually was also afflicted by sickness. The next line probes still deeper into these divine, saving mysteries. The very familiar *KJ* version says little to the average reader: "The chastisement of our peace was upon him." This is an entirely un-English mode of speaking. *RSV* has clarified the issue a lot by rendering: "Upon him was the chastisement that made us whole." None have rendered this line better than *Luther*: "The punishment was laid on him that we might have peace." Though the word used in almost every case bears the thought of *corrective* suffering, i.e., "chastisement," we hold with those who take the word in the sense of "punishment" (*Strafe*), because otherwise the sin-bearer himself would stand in need of correction. And, oh, the marvel of it all: "by his wounds healing came to us!" "Wounds" is actually "stripes," the welt left by the lash on the back of the man scourged. On "punishment" cf. also von Rad, *Theologie des A.T. des Alten Testaments, II, p.* 267.

Verse 6. It yet remains to point out the fact that there was no hope for rescue anywhere in the human race. They who speak are still the Jews, but the reader cannot help but feel that if even none of *God's people* could achieve deliverance, there would be none in the wide, wide world able to help. But here it is pointed out that all had "gone astray." How could they show others the way? Self-willed, men were going the way of their own sinful choosing. So the Lord had to take the man of his own choosing and lay the burden of the task on him. In this area — and it all again and again adds up to vicarious atonement, stated and restated, defined and redefined — in this area, we say, lies the explanation of the unparalleled suffering that the Servant had to undergo.

4. Utterly Innocent, Totally Submissive (vv. 7-9)

53:7-9 7. He was harrassed, though he humbled himself,
    and did not open his mouth.
As a sheep that is led to the slaughter
    and as a ewe before its shearers is dumb,
    so he did not open his mouth.
8. By oppression and an unjust sentence he was taken away;
    and as to his fate, who gave it any thought?
        For he was cut off from the land of the living,
    because of the transgression of my people was he stricken.
9. Men gave him a grave with wicked persons,
    and with a rich man in his death;
        although he had done no violence;
        and there was no deceit in his mouth.

Verse 7. It is no longer the Lord who is speaking. Perhaps it is the prophet. The unique degree of suffering that the Servant endured is a matter of constant wonderment for the prophet. Equally striking is the fact that all suffering was borne without a word of protest or complaint. This latter fact is an indication that the Servant endured willingly whatever was laid upon him. Had he suffered under protest and reluctantly, his suffering would have been impaired as to its effectiveness. In this respect the Servant stands in sharp contrast to men of the Old Testament who had a large measure of suffering to endure, like Job and Jeremiah. They were very vocal in their cry of anguish and in their protestations of innocence. So the comparison with a sheep, or a sheep-mother (a "ewe") is very much in place. The last line of the verse is not an idle repetition, or a clumsy copyist's mistake. It stresses an important point that should stand out. Here also lies the basis for the very choice name that John the Baptist used for Jesus, "the Lamb of God" (John 1:29, 36).

Verse 8. This has been rightly labelled "a notoriously difficult verse." What we offer as interpretation is merely what appears to us as feasible and in agreement with the context. The first line could well be a summary description of how judgment was passed on the Servant as a result of his trial. The verdict rendered was a glaring instance of oppression and at the same time a flagrant example of an unjust sentence. "Fate" in the line that follows is not what the Greeks and Romans meant by that term (an inscrutable power working ruthlessly) but merely *what befell him* in the course of the trial just mentioned. Men witnessed a grave miscarriage of justice and did nothing about it: they gave it no further thought. The next line implies a cruel and unjust termination of a human life: "he was cut off from the land of the living." The speaker, overwhelmed by the importance of the substitutionary atonement involved, falls back once more upon it as the only explanation of an outcome so strange. A momentary personal note enters the picture when the prophet observes the fact that it was his own people ("*my* people") that were the beneficiaries of this strange transaction.

Verse 9. As the Servant's suffering was strange and perplexing so there was a significant series of happenings associated with his *burial*. For one thing, the totally innocent one was given a kind of treatment that would have been more in agreement with the career of a "wicked person." "He was reckoned with the transgressors." To be very exact about it all, the classification with wicked persons applies to the company in which he suffered and died. Not to his burial. But who would quibble about such trifles. In the line that follows usually the difficulty is removed by a textual change which eliminates the term "rich man." We prefer to let the text stand as it is and to see one of the strange marvels of predictive prophecy which however was well worthy of record. For by an unusual and entirely unexpected turn of events, Jesus (i.e., the "Servant") was given a decent and honorable burial (Matt. 27:57 ff.). The concessive clause "although he had done . . ." reaches back to the second line preceding: he was given unseemly treatment though he had been guilty of no major crime deserving dishonorable treatment. In fact, not only of no heinous misdeed, but not even of an improper *word* was this Servant guilty: "no deceit was in his mouth."

5. Amazingly Successful in His Life's Work (vv. 10-12)

53:10-12   10. Yet it was the Lord's will to crush him.
He put him to grief.
When he shall make a trespass-offering,
   he shall see offspring — he shall prolong his days;
And that which pleases the Lord [his plan of salvation]
   will prosper in his hands.
11. And so after the toil of his soul he shall see satisfaction.
   By his experience he, my righteous Servant,
      shall make many to be accounted righteous.
   He, namely, will take their guilt upon himself.
12. Therefore I will allot to him the spoils of victory among the
      great,
   and he will divide the booty with the mighty.
   For that he poured out his soul unto death,

and was counted with the transgressors;
when in reality he bore the sins of many,
and intervened for the evildoers.

Verse 10. This Song began (52:13) on a victory-note. It comes to a conclusion on the same note. Though it dwelled extensively on suffering, for the Lord's Servant's sufferings were many, yet pain in God's service leads to glory, as *G. A. Smith* remarks. This suffering was not accidental. It was a part of a great divine plan. "It was the Lord's will to crush him," though "crush" in this case surely implies no hostile purpose. Even so *KJ* may be misunderstood when it says: "Yet it pleased the Lord to bruise him," if one insists on introducing sadistic thoughts at this point. In these words the emphasis lies on divine causality, also in the statement "he put him to grief." Suddenly the tense of the verbs changes; all is now viewed as future, perhaps with the intent of showing that what is viewed as accomplished still remains to be done: "When he *shall* make a trespass offering." The language of the Old Testament sacrificial system is at this point employed, not with the intent of indicating detailed specifications but perhaps only because in the trespass offering "all the blood was scattered over the altar" (Lev. 5:14 ff.). Intricacies of types of sacrifices might be explored here in the spirit of the Letter to the Hebrews. But perhaps no more is intended than stress on the fact that the Servant's anguish was in every way the fulfilment of a great divine plan. It had been foreshadowed by sacrifices. Nothing about it was accidental. But the main point seems to be indicated in the line that follows: "he shall see offspring — he shall prolong his days." This certainly involves a strange paradox — he has died, yet he prolongs his days. We cannot avoid the conviction that this points forward to the death and resurrection of Christ. The "offspring" mentioned, it would appear, are spiritual, although in view of the fact that the Old Testament deems it a great blessing to live long and have many descendants, one might rightly think of this aspect of the case. In any event he that died lives on and carries on the work that God has entrusted to his care — the work of salvation. Translated into New Testament language, the work of governing and guiding the church in its task of saving souls "will prosper in his hands."

Verse 11. The pronouncements of this verse are weighty. The success the Servant achieved is being spelled out at greater length, for his achievements are many and without a parallel in the annals of mankind. So that in the second line the Lord himself again begins to speak. For only he himself can do full justice to an adequate description of this phenomenal success. But echoes of the great suffering keep recurring — "the toil of his soul." When that is ended "he shall see satisfaction," that is, he shall look back upon a task well and brilliantly done. For the salvation of many a soul is involved. It might well be expected that when the Lord himself sums up the work of his Servant that he would begin with a statement of the work that is the most momentous of all. He does just that when he ascribes to him the work of "making many to be accounted righteous." In other words what he achieves is justification by faith. This then is briefly and simply redefined: "He, namely, will take their guilt upon himself," again an echo of vicarious atonement.

Verse 12. It has been rightly claimed that no passage of the Old Testament presents more problems than this. Yet it is quite obvious that a note of triumph prevails throughout and echoes of the great issues that have been dealt with in this chapter keep ringing throughout. In post-battle language the scene is first of all one of distribution of spoils after a decisive victory has been won. "The great" and "the mighty" are on the scene and the Servant among them receiving his well-deserved share, in fact, receiving the lion's share, to use a slightly incongruous figure. The Lord indicates why he, the Servant, is so strikingly deserving of the major share of booty; "He poured out his soul unto death," a more expressive way of saying that he gave his all in the great conflict in which he was engaged. This calls to mind that he even went the limit of being "counted with the transgressors," as set forth at great length in v. 9. Fact of the matter is, as the Lord keeps reiterating, in reality "he bore the sins of many," as vv. 4-6 had so clearly set forth. All these encomiums come to an end in a most effective summary in the words: "He intervened for the evil-doers." The verb here used really says more than "made intercession." It means to go all out in acting in behalf of another person. For this reason we claim that the statement is so apt a conclusion.

Notes

It is utterly impossible within the narrow compass of this exposition to give exhaustive treatment of all the issues that clamor for attention — word studies, grammatical niceties, textual problems, etc. We are able only to furnish an elementary approach and give in summary fashion the findings that grew for us out of a somewhat detailed study of the issues involved. We contend that a careful cursory reading of the fourth Servant Song impresses the reader with the rare merits of this singular Scripture. This impression keeps growing, the deeper one probes.

In our *Notes* we shall attempt to touch at least upon the major critical problems involved.

52:14. The third word of the verse (*'alekhah*) ("at thee") is usually changed to "at him" (so *RSV*), a reasonable emendation, following the lead of the Targum and the Syriac. But the text may be allowed to stand as the Masoretes have transmitted it. Then it will be interpreted as a sudden address of the Servant, whom the Lord regards as standing in his presence. Then the discourse turns to the third person from the first. In Hebrew such a change of person is far less disturbing than in English.

52:15. "Startle." This verb has long been a bone of contention. *Luther* and *KJ* represents the tradition that the verb means "sprinkle." In more recent times an Arabic root has been found which allows for the meaning "startle," an approach followed already by the *Septuagint* translation (*thaumasontai*). Men like *Hengstenberg, Edward J. Young* (*Westminster Theol. Journal*, May, 1941) and *von Rad* have ably defended the traditional meaning "sprinkle" in the sense of ceremonial purification. Perhaps the majority of scholars prefer "startle." The latter approach has as its major support the fact that an obvious contrast is demanded by the verse between "were awestruck" and our verb *nazah* ("to sprinkle"). But *to be awestruck* and to *sprinkle* do not constitute a contrast. Therefore we incline slightly in the direction of the majority in this instance, although even *BDB* admits that the second meaning is a bit "dubious." *North* suggests a rather far-fetched translation: "So shall many nations guard against contagion by him."

53:1. For "who believed," *Westermann* suggests the translation, "Who could have believed?" — a translaton which suggests that the contemporary unbelief was but natural and lifts the responsibility for unbelief off the shoulders of the nation.

On the use of a question to obtain a negative conclusion see *GK* 151 a.

Verse 2. Striking instances where national deliverers were also men of striking attractiveness would be Joseph (Gen. 39:6) and David (I Sam. 16:18).

Verse 3. For "weighted down by sorrow" many still use the *KJ* translation "man of sorrows." It should be noted, however, that "sorrows" is an intensive plural, constituting a kind of superlative, a fact which our translation seeks to capture.

Verse 5. Rather striking instances where the idea of substitution appears are the following: Gen. 18:23 ff.; 19:29; I Kings 11:13, 32, 34; II Kings 19:34; 20:6; Ps. 89:4.

Verse 7. The repetition in this verse of the words, he "did not open his mouth," is not relieved by glibly describing this as a gloss.

The difficult word in this verse is *dor*, the simplest meaning of which is "generation" i.e., "men living at a particular time" (*BDB*). *RSV* apparently takes the word in this sense. *Volz* suggests "descendants." "Fate" seems to fit most readily into the picture. See *KB*, p. 206.

Verse 9. Strangly for "in his death" the Hebrew has a plural "deaths." The simplest explanation may lie in the fact that the word for "life" (*chayyim*) also is a plural noun, which in the plural form indicates life in its many-sidedness; in its complexity. So "death" in the plural indicates the many things involved in dying.

Verse 10. We have translated the third line: "when he shall make a trespass offering." For this *KJ*, for example, offers: "when thou shalt make his soul an offering for sin." Fact of the matter is that the Hebrew word "his soul" may be an emphatic subject for "he." In this instance this is the simplest rendering of all, and relieves us of the need of textual emendations.

Verse 11. The *min* in *me'amal* is a *min* temporal (*KS* 401 f.). The second line of the verse is described by *North* as "grammatically execrable." It is true that it does not flow too smoothly. But it still is a glorious and comforting word.

Verse 12. The last word of the verse is an imperfect, *waw* consecutive separated from its *waw* by a phrase, a fairly common construction in Hebrew. Cf. *KS* 368, h, i, k.

Chapter LIV

N. AN EXAMPLE OF THE SERVANT'S SUCCESS (Chap. 54)

The preceding chapter, though not usually regarded from this point of view, had a deep undertone of success running through it. It began with the statement, "Behold, my Servant shall prosper" (52:13) and ended with a comprehensive description of the Servant's manifold success (53:10-12). We may therefore well regard Chap. 54 as being set forth in the same vein. It presents a significant example of this success, and so the close connection of thought between Chaps. 53 and 54 is clearly indicated. We make a special point of this, because the tendency is still somewhat strong to regard the "fourth Servant Song" as a later insertion between 52:12 and 54:1. Aside from other points which indicate that Chap. 53 rightfully holds and held its present position apparently from the time of the first writing of the book, this is a significant point.

Still the title that we have given this chapter is far from exhausting all the rich possibilities that the wealth of material of this chapter offers. So, for example, *von Orelli* uses a title like "Zion's Blessed State of Grace." *Muilenburg* gives as heading "The Consolation of Israel."

As to form men are inclined to regard this as a salvation oracle. The summons with which the piece opens are reminiscent of hymns of praise (cf. 44:23; 49:13; 52:9). We may also take note of the fact that an obvious strain of deep pathos marks Chap. 53, whereas Chap. 54 is marked by a deep note of joy. *Calvin,* quoted by *G. A. Smith* makes a rather pertinent remark: "After having spoken of the death of Christ, the prophet passes on with good reason to the church that we may feel more deeply in ourselves the value and efficacy

236

of his death." This statement is surprisingly like *Luther's* opening remarks on this same chapter: "Even as in the preceding chapter the prophet had described Christ as the head of the kingdom, so here his body, that is the church, is described, as being oppressed, unfruitful, and forsaken. But he comforts her and promises her great offspring."

Some writers find six strophes, clearly outlined, within this chapter. Others find two. We incline to a tripartite division.

1. A Promise to Zion of Numerous Offspring (vv. 1-3)

54:1-3 1. Shout for joy, you barren woman, who have not born a child;
burst forth into shrill and joyous shouts,
you who have not been in labor.
For more numerous are the children of the forsaken one
than the children of the married woman.
2. Enlarge the area of your tent,
and spread out the curtains of your habitation;
make plenty of room;
lengthen your tent ropes and plant your stakes firmly.
3. For you will burst forth in every direction,
and your descendants will take possession of the Gentiles;
and they shall cause desolate cities to be populated.

Verse 1. The passage before us is one marked by strong emotion. Shouts and shrill cries are called for; there is great occasion for joy and jubilation. The one in whose life this great joy appeared is not mentioned by name, but no one doubts that it is Zion, the Old Testament church. During the Exile she had been greatly reduced in numbers. So to speak, the curse of sterility had descended upon her, a curse felt more keenly in Oriental countries than among us. This curse was to be taken from her. Her children were again to become numerous. From having been a Rachel she was to become a Leah. Rounding out the picture a bit more fully: Her husband, none less than the Lord himself, had forsaken her. She could have no children. But the promise here runs to the effect that her children will ultimately be more in numbers than those of a woman not forsaken. This is a familiar subject in the Scriptures (see 49:18 ff.; 51:1 ff.; Zech. 2:1-5; Hos. 1:10-12). To be a little more specific, the destruction of Jerusalem could be likened to the divorce from the husband; the period of the Exile was the season of barrenness. This was not however a promise that saw immediate fulfilment. There was indeed an appreciable increase in numbers on the part of the Jews after the Exile, but nothing that could come in any wise near to the situation here described. Here is a divine promise which is in process of being fulfilled but awaits total fulfilment in the ages to come. Lest man gain the impression that the Lord's promises are taken lightly by him, the closing reassurance, "thus says the Lord," is appended.

2. If the Lord spoke the preceding word, this verse may now be regarded as an amplification of the thoughts of v. 1 spelled out by the prophet himself. In anticipation of the increase of the number of the members of this family, the mother is bidden to take steps to accommodate the new additions to the family by marking out a larger space as tent-area, by spreading out larger tent-curtains, and by using longer ropes and firmer stakes. In fact she should make "plenty of room." Nothing is gained in the overall picture by using the term that Israel is likened to a "beduin-princess." An ordinary enlarged household is under consideration. The terminology is reminiscent of the sacred days of the wilderness wanderings of Israel, when the nation dwelt in tents, a harmless anachronism.

Verse 3. Now three figures are used to describe the experience. First from every side children burst forth from the tent — a "population explosion." So it becomes apparent why the enlargement of the tent just spoken of is necessary. One wonders that one tent could have held so many. Next follows a total change of the picture in terms of occupation of territory: the numerous nation, Israel, shall overflow into the territory of the Gentiles. This figure is followed by a

third one: deserted and abandoned cities are taken in hand
by Israel's overflow population. So a nation which had been
thinking in terms of possible extinction and of gradually
dying off is reassured that such is not the case.

2. This Promise Reinforced (vv. 4-10)

54:4-10 4. "Don't be afraid, for you will not be made ashamed;
be not confounded, for you will not be embarrassed.
For you will forget the shame of your youth;
   and will not remember the disgrace of your widowhood.
5. For your husband is your Maker,
   'Lord of hosts' is his name.
   and your Redeemer, the Holy One of Israel.
6. For you were a woman forsaken and deeply grieved,
   when the Lord called you.
Would the wife of one's youth indeed be disowned?
   says the Lord.
7. For a brief moment I left you,
   but with great compassion I will gather you again.
8. In a flash of anger
   I hid my face from you for a moment;
but with everlasting kindness,
   I have had pity upon you,"
     says your Redeemer, the Lord.
9. "This situation is to me like the days of Noah,
   when I swore that the waters of Noah's days
     should not again sweep over the earth.
   so now I swear that never again
     will I be angry with you or rebuke you.
10. For mountains may depart
   and hills fall away;
but my loving kindness shall not depart from you
   and my peace-pact shall not fall away,"
says the Lord who has compassion on you.

Verse 4. All the visible evidence pointed to the contrary
conclusion, namely that Israel would continue to lose ground;
and Israel may well have been most reluctant to believe the
promise just given. So a special word of the Lord is given,
bidding the nation to cast its fear and confusion aside. She
will not be in a position where she set her hopes high and
then found them all evaporating into thin air and so she
would be laughed at for having indulged in idle dreams. A

strong double assurance is given that this shall in no event happen. In the second (i.e., parallel) statement two verbs are used which are usually distinguished in the following way: "confounded" involves being actually in a state of utter confusion; "embarrassed" refers to personal embarrassment, being painfully aware that things have turned out disastrously. When the prophet adds, "for you will forget the shame of your youth" that might be a reference to the humiliating experience of the ancient bondage in the land of Egypt and might at the same time be thought of as including all disasters of old. For the humiliation of the Egyptian bondage burned deep into Israel's consciousness. Then the prophet adds: "and [you] will not remember the disgrace of your widowhood." Here the reference must manifestly be to the Babylonian Captivity. The blessing that the Lord is about to give will completely eradicate all remembrance of these painful experiences. So v. 4 summed up from a fresh point of view, the first three verses of the chapter. Now follow the words that reinforce all this.

Verse 5. Impossible as all that is promised may seem, it will yet come to pass. Now the statement comes back to the figure used above: God, the husband; the nation, the wife. And this husband is none other than the nation's "Maker." He could, and did create a nation. He can remake the same nation for he is also "the Lord of hosts," i.e., he has the whole host of created things always at his beck and call. He further rightly bears the title "Redeemer," a name which connotes responsibility for the well-being of another. At the same time he bears the name, "the Holy One of Israel," which title involves the fact that he is flawless in the performance of his obligations to his chosen people. To cap the climax, he "is rightly called the God of all the earth." All these descriptive names of the Lord reinforce his present promises to Israel. The Lord knows it will be a long while till these promises are fully realized. Therefore he strongly grounds them in eternal verities.

Verse 6. Using once again the figure of a woman abandoned by her husband, the prophet helps the nation recall how bitter her lot once was when he called her back into a state of divine approval. But that *unhappy* state now lies entirely in the past. For there is another angle to this case: This forsaken one once enjoyed the distinction of being, as it were, the "wife of [the] youth," when lovers love ardently, living through experiences which can never be completely forgotten (cf. Prov. 5:18; Mal. 2:14 f.). In the spirit of the Hebrew language the use of a pointed question ("Would the wife of one's youth indeed be disowned?") is the equivalent of a very positive assertion. God says in effect: I cannot give you up.

Verse 7. The Lord is still making "assurance doubly sure." He does this now by two clear and meaningful figures. The words "for a brief moment I left you" employ the figure used above, the figure of a wife abandoned by her husband. Though sometimes the Babylonian Captivity is regarded as having lasted quite a while, here, in retrospect, it is said to have been only "for a brief moment." The thought continues by blending into another figure, that of children that have been scattered by some disaster and are now being sought out again and gathered into one congenial group. This gathering is said to have been done "with great compassion."

Verse 8. The thought of v. 7 is restated in v. 8 under still another figure, that of a man in just anger flaring up for the moment. But pity gets the upper hand over anger. This turn of attitude is traced back to the Lord's "everlasting kindness." It may here be noted that the statement attributing all these mercies to the Lord grow in extent at the conclusion of v. 6 and v. 8 and v. 10. Here (v. 8) it takes the form "says your Redeemer, the Lord." The vv. 7-10 have rightly been labelled as the high point in the poem, v. 10 in particular, as a "corepassage" (*Kernstelle*) of the Old Testament (*Haller*). Certainly words of strong consolation could hardly be expressed more aptly.

Verse 9. More is to follow by way of reinforcing God's

gracious promises. A historical incident is referred to by way of fitting illustration. The writer knows the history prior to God's particular dealings with Israel; specifically the event of the great Deluge in the days of Noah. When the Flood had done its work, God gave solemn assurance to the human race in the person of Noah (Gen. 8:20-22) that flood waters should not again sweep over the earth, though strictly speaking no formal oath was pronounced. But we may well claim that a solemn promise under the sign of the rainbow is as much of a guaranty as any oath. As God promised then, he swears now that there will be no repetition of the disaster of the Captivity — "I will not be angry with you or rebuke you." If at this point a man recalls that there came a similar disaster nevertheless in the destruction of Jerusalem in A.D. 70 it should be remembered that in our statement the emphasis lies on the faithfulness of the Lord in keeping his promise, not on unconditional blessing. For all of God's promises are in a sense conditional.

Verse 10. Comforting reassurance could not be spoken more tenderly than in this verse, a favorite passage of the people of God through the centuries. The point is that God-wrought salvation endures. A favorite method of Biblical writers to express this thought is to use "cosmic comparisons" (*Muilenburg*); (cf. 51:6; Jer. 31:35; 33:20, 21). The hills and the mountains in particular are here referred to as symbols of that which endures (Ps. 36:6; 46:2 f.; Hab. 3:6). It might be conceded that these "eternal hills" could totter and collapse; but it cannot be conceded that the Lord's "loving kindness" (this seems the richer translation in this context) shall not depart. More precisely stated, "my peace-pact shall not fall away." This reference to the "covenant" (we used the word "pact" in our translation) seems to involve a subtle allusion to the work of the Servant of the Lord in passages such as 42:6 and 49:8. At this point the citation formula grows broadest of all: "Says the Lord who has compassion on you." This was certainly one of the grandest of Old Testament passages.

3. The Future Glory of Zion (vv. 11-17)

54:11-17 11. O you afflicted one, storm-tossed, disconsolate,
lo, I will lay your stones in mascara,
and set your foundations with sapphires.
12. And I will make your pinnacles of rubies,
your gates of carbuncles,
and all your boundary walls of precious stones.
13. And all your sons shall be taught by God,
and great shall be the prosperity of your sons.
14. You shall be established on a foundation of righteousness,
and you shall be so far from oppression
that you shall not fear.
And from terror, that it will not come near you.
15. If indeed you should be attacked
that will not be my doing;
whoever attacks you shall fall to ruin upon you.
16. I am the one who has created the smith
who blows upon the fire of charcoal,
and produces implements to work with;
and I have created the ravager to destroy.
17. Every weapon that is forged against you must fail;
every tongue that rises up against you in court
you shall prove guilty.
This is the inheritance of the servants of the Lord,
and their vindication coming from me,
says the Lord.

The future glory of Zion involves

a. Costly Building Materials (vv. 11-12)

Verse 11. As the address begins, the Lord has before him one who is "afflicted, storm-tossed, disconsolate." She is bidden to envision for herself a glorious future where everything will be enhanced "down to the very stones" used in construction. It is true that this describes a kind of architectural approach to the glories of the future. Yes, even that. In the somewhat detailed description now following we find ourselves to be a bit perplexed because the terms used appear to be technical building terminology. This is partly because we cannot quite tell whether the precious stones referred to constitute building material or describe their use as lending beauty to the stones that they encircle.

It is even possible that some mosaic-like pattern is involved. To add to our difficulty, no one quite knows exactly what stones are referred to. But perhaps strangest of all, these stones, common and precious, are not being used in the construction of a place of worship but seem to appear on buildings and city walls. This is a far cry from Ezekiel who, in Chaps. 40 ff., practically limits himself in his description of the temple buildings. But still the impression created by our passage is one of rare beauty and high glory. Passages like 26:1 ff.; Rev. 21:9 ff., 18-29 may be compared.

A few details: "antimony" seems to have been a kind of "mascara," though it strikes us a bit strange that the tuck-pointing of common stones with a sort of black border should lend beauty to the ordinary stone. Yet the effect could have been striking.

Verse 12. A hint as to what may be involved in this verse — The "pinnacle's" could refer to the upper fringe of the battlements, where the red, glowing rubies give a rare setting to the whole picture. It next appears that the gates themselves were made of one precious stone each. The "boundary walls" may be a reference to the encircling walls of the city. Sumptuous as it may seem, precious stones are used for plain city walls, for in this picture there is nothing plain.

b. Fear Vanquished (vv. 13-14)

Verse 13. Now some of the spiritual values of the new Jerusalem! The two verses, 13 and 14, constitute what may be called *Segenszusage* (a promise of a blessing). Such promises are usually given to an individual. Here they reach out over a glorified city. Passages in the same vein would be Ps. 91; 121; Job 5:17-26. The substance of our passage is "all your sons shall be taught by God." Superior, divinely-inspired knowledge shall be freely given to the children of God, knowledge which it shall be life eternal to have (cf. John 6:45). As a result of such knowledge or perhaps, in addition to it, shall be the great "prosperity" that these true children of God shall enjoy. In the Hebrew the word here rendered as "prosperity" is that rich, comprehensive term "peace," which in addition connotes victory and in general a state of total well-being.

Verse 14. By recasting the order of the words of this verse we seem to get closer to its import. The emphasis appears to lie on the stability of the new state of affairs ("you shall be established"). Then upon the good foundation which is requisite for such stability — "righteousness." At this point the question suggests itself: Is this the righteousness of good conduct or the righteousness imputed to faith? We incline to the opinion that both may be thought of, primarily the latter, which is the basis of all life acceptable to God. Here one result, growing out of this situation is especially pointed to — the absence of fear and terror. God's people will not be living in a state of continual apprehensiveness; this in contrast to their life during the Exile, where fears haunted them by day and by night.

But there was still the thought of being open to attack by the powerful enemy; for the enemy was strong and Israel was weak. The word here given offers separate treatment of the subject.

c. The Futility of Enemy Attack (vv. 15-17)

Verse 15. The first part of the verse could be paraphrased: Should it after all really happen that some one should venture to attack you . . . the estimate to be put upon such an attack is that it has no divine sanction: "it is not from me." (*RSV*) Or, as the *Jerusalem Bible* puts it "that will not be my doing." In fact, such unholy efforts will strike back on them that plot them: "Whoever attacks you shall fall to ruin upon you." The thought here leads us to recall Luke 20: 18. This last statement is difficult and may be translated in different ways. The situation is hardly so bad as to call for the verdict that the text is "badly corrupted." It fits well as it stands in the context in which it appears.

Verse 16. This situation calls for a further development

of the thought that all issues are continually under complete divine control. Rather unusual is the expression given to this thought. The point really is that even the smith who makes weapons and the weapons that he makes are possible only because God has also both of these under total control. That makes for the result that the smith who blows upon the coals at the smithy is enabled by God to function. The instruments he works with remain in the Lord's possession. They may sometimes be used by him as agents for destruction, for, as he says: "I have created the ravager to destroy." This "ravager" would seem to be a world-conqueror, like Sennacherib. God lets weapons be made, he creates him that wields them. He may let them loose as he once did against Israel, his people. But that is not the case now, as v. 17 indicates.

Verse 17. The illustration of the smith and the weapon is still under consideration. God's present attitude toward his people is: "Every weapon that is forged against you must fail." For that matter, any other attack that the tongue of man might direct against God's chosen ones shall also come to nought. In other words, Israel shall be publicly vindicated as enjoying the Lord's favor. The attackers shall be indicted. To this vindication of God's people as enjoying God's favor a few more pertinent thoughts are added. For one thing, Israel has not merited such favors from the Lord; they are a divinely bestowed "inheritance," freely granted upon his "servants." They, the nation, cannot merit such favor; but it surely will not fall to the lot of the unresponsive, who are not concerned about the doing of his will. God is the sole author and originator of his mercies. Isaiah always strikes the evangelical note — free grace, unmerited pardon.

Notes

Verse 1. In the first line of this verse there is a change from the second person to the third, a procedure followed rather frequently in Hebrew. Cf. *GK* 144 p.

Verse 5. The word for "Maker" is the plural form of the participle being a kind of plural of excellence. Cf. *GK* 124 k. The noun for "husband" is drawn into a similar plural.

Verse 6. The words "deeply grieved" in Hebrew are "grieved of spirit" — the last word being the well-known Hebrew *ru(a)ch*, which is sometimes used for an equivalent of a mood.

Verse 9. Two schools of thought prevail on the translation of the first word of this verse — *kimey*, which may involve either the plural of the word "days" in the construct, or it may involve the plural of "waters" in the construct. We have cast our vote in favor of the former. Strangely the meaning is hardly affected either way.

Verse 10. Grammatically the first clause of this verse may be translated as we have it, or it may be rendered by a concessive clause. See *KS* 394 b.

Verse 11. The second word "storm-tossed" is a *pual* participle with the initial *m* omitted. The situation is the same with the fourth word.

The verse is shorter than the rest. Has half a verse been lost? Who can tell?

Verse 14. What we translated as "shall be far," is really an imperative (*rachaqi*), but in Hebrew an imperative may be used as an imperfect to express assurance. Cf. *GK* 110 c.

Verse 15. The initial *hen* is distinctly an Aramaism and is to be treated as an "if," not as "lo."

The word *me'othi* is merely a variant form of *me'itti*, which is only a stronger form of "from" and means literally, "from with me."

Chapter LV

O. ZION CALLED TO APPROPRIATION OF SALVATION (Chap. 55)

Chapters 40-55 of Isaiah constitute a distinct phase with characteristic marks all its own. Our present chapter spells an appropriate close of the section. Or with a slightly different approach, Chap. 55 is the Epilogue of this piece even as Chap. 40 was a prologue.

As is usually the case with this prophet, such a wealth of material is offered that every commentator finds difficulty in trying to find an adequate caption for the chapter. *Muilenburg* suggests: "Grace Abounding." *Skinner* offers: "A Call to Individuals to Embrace Salvation." *The Oxford Annotated Bible* feels this is "A Hymn of Joy and Triumph." *North* follows an entirely different approach, suggesting: "Come for All Things Are Now Ready." The diversity of approach could hardly be more diversified.

But looking at the issue from a broader point of view, we may at least take note in passing that in the second half of this book, the first major subject was: The salvation God has prepared (chaps. 40-48). Then there was heavy emphasis on the agent who prepares this salvation — the Suffering Servant of the Lord (chaps. 49-55). This outline of the whole material makes it plausible to think at this point of the salvation prepared and the need of appropriation. This at least shows that there is some propriety about the caption we have suggested above.

First comes a gracious invitation, which has analogies elsewhere in the Scriptures, especially where wisdom is represented as calling men to the good things she has prepared (see Prov. 3:18; 9:5, 6; Matt. 11:28 f.). We said in the above heading that "Zion" is called upon to appropriate. Still this is less a corporate invitation. It addresses itself to individuals, to anyone who may be ready to take what is offered. It might be spoken of as an appeal made to a group of earnest-minded men assembled in a synagogue or in whatever meeting may have been customary in the prophet's day. In any case the prophet seems to be the speaker in the first seven verses. He addresses an appeal to his hearers which seems to be an Old Testament counterpart of the Parable of the Great Supper.

1. An Invitation to Accept God's Free Blessings (vv. 1-3)

55:1-3 1. Attention, every one that is thirsty, come for water; even if you have no money come!
Buy grain that you may eat, but come and buy grain;
without money and without price, wine and milk.
2. Why should you pay out money for what is not bread,
and your earning for what does not satisfy?
Just listen to me and eat choice food,
and have inmost delight in nourishing food.
3. Give close attention and come to me;
listen, that you may really live;
and I will make an enduring covenant with you,
namely the utterly reliable manifestations of mercy granted
to David.

Verse 1. Some writers have a feeling that things are somewhat in a state of confusion in this verse. It may be more to the point to think of some spots as being a bit rough grammatically because of the urgency of the appeal addressed to the prophet's hearers. Others find this verse a bit "unmetrical." But Hebrew poets were far less bound by the rigid rules of a metrical system than we are inclined to be. Being a call to action this verse is almost all imperatives. The speaker has gifts ready to distribute, primarily food — rich and tasty food — and drink — water and wine. These terms stand as symbols of impending salvation. This salvation is primarily thought of in terms of restoration from the prevailing Exile. The hunger and thirst plaguing the people are the weariness and discontent of the Exile (*Skinner*). Now the big point of this verse is that the food and drink offered to relieve the people's need is *free*. God has provided it. It is now ready. All that is required is an open hand, or an opened mouth, to take freely what is abundantly ready. Provision has apparently been made for every form of nourishment for every form of want of body and soul. We do well to think of the invitation as couched in terms of a ringing call proclaimed in stentorian tones. It may at the same time be said that the spiritual gifts hinted at by the terminology of food and drink are all incorporated in the one concept — the Word of God. The verse is a most urgent plea to accept freely all the good gifts that God has now in readiness for his own.

Verse 2. The plea grows more urgent. A contrast is pointed out. The nation with its many-talented people is devoting much effort to the acquisition of the lesser values. As has been suggested in this context, the Jews in Captivity in Babylon have put much effort into the pursuit of the lesser human values and had made themselves quite comfortable in the possession of material comforts. Why do that? cries the prophet, spending money for that which cannot satisfy, and is not the real bread of life. Here we hear echoes of the age-old truth: "Man shall not live by bread alone" (cf. Deut. 8:3; Isa. 44:3; Prov. 19:7 Matt. 4:4; John 4:10). If only this present plea be heeded there is available for all who will give heed, satisfying, nourishing, rich-tasting, soul-satisfying food.

Verse 3. When offers like this are made and God is ready to pour out of his super-abounding riches, then men should "give close attention." For men are then at the vital crises of life. It is an issue as simple as it can be. He is saying: "Come to me." All man needs to do is "come." Or stated differently: "listen." Then, from that point on, they may be said to "really live." At this point the prophet seems to feel that the offers of a present salvation can best be described in terms of the rich spiritual history of Israel's past, in the era of the stirring days of King David. In particular the truth now offered can be stated in terms of the covenant which God in his day freely gave to this great king. God promised to this man, once only an ordinary shepherd lad, great things, a dynasty and a kingdom. He had, to date, kept his promise in a striking manner. History was full of "reliable manifestations of mercy granted to David." As the Lord fulfilled the promises given to David, so he would now fulfill them for his ancient people, in the way in which the fourth verse more specifically indicates.

2. If Israel Accepts, Zion Will Become a Blessing to the Nations (vv. 4-5)

55:4-5   4. As I once made him a witness to the nations,
                 a leader and commander for nations,
5. so shall you call heathen whom you had not known,
    and nations you were not acquainted with shall come running
        to you,
because of the Lord your God
    and because of the Holy One of Israel;
        for he will have glorified you.

Verse 4. The reference to David is expanded at some length. The spiritual side of his call is spelled out. For in addition to making David's throne an everlasting throne, David was singled out to make the Lord known in a measure to the nations. For the many and unusual victories that David gained as king of Israel, he was making his Lord known to all the surrounding nations. David in this sense was a "witness." At the same time he was "a leader and commander for nations." The nations will not necessarily have arrived at a full and comprehensive knowledge of the Holy One of Israel. But that there was something unique about Israel's God will have begun to dawn on some. One may compare I Kings 5:7 in this connection. It is also a well-known fact that all the nations from the River of Egypt to the Euphrates acknowledged the sovereignty of David. Here, however, the "spiritual primacy" (*Fischer*) of David is under consideration (cf. also Ps. 18:43; and I Sam. 13:14). But the main point now being made in vv. 4-5 is: What the Lord once did for *David* that will he now do again for *Israel*, if she will but come and freely "buy" what he so freely offers.

Verse 5. The promises once made to David will now be laid with equal validity on David's people, a marvelous expansion of the scope of these promises. The first statement to this effect involves that Israel shall have power and authority to summon nations she had not known to help her carry out her mission. In fact nations are even represented as so filled with eagerness to share in the task that they "shall come running." What shall impel them to such eagerness of participation is covered by the phrase "because of the Lord your God and because of the Holy One of Israel." On this note this strophe comes to a "theocentric" conclusion, as Isaiah loves to do. This section then describes in a far-reaching prediction all that men did to witness for the Lord God in days of old and particularly what was done in New Testament times by way of sanctified proclamation. Every victory gained by the gospel is a fulfilment of this passage, and constitutes a part of the true glorification of Israel ("he will have glorified you.") For the Israel of old becomes "the Israel of God" with the coming of the days of the New Testament (cf. Gal. 6:16).

Is there then nothing Messianic about this passage? Not in the sense that we have here a direct reference to the Messiah. But he who is familiar with II Sam. 7:8-16, will not be content to leave the matter rest with such a remark. For in addition to promising to David an "everlasting throne" in the passage just referred to, the Lord promised to David one who would sit upon that throne. That factor is the greatest glory of this passage. So we shall have to say that though the prophet in this chapter does not dwell on the messianic content of the passage before us, the figure of the Messiah from David's line stands in the shadows and may not be ignored. Our passage is indirectly Messianic. Behind the

David referred to in these verses stands "great David's Greater Son."

3. But These Blessings Must Be Eagerly Sought with a Penitent Heart (vv. 6-7)

55:6-7 6. Seek the Lord while he may yet be found;
call upon him while he is near.
7. Let the wicked man give up his way of life;
and the worthless fellow his thoughts;
let him turn back to the Lord that he may have mercy upon him,
and unto our God, for he will abundantly pardon.

Verse 6. The Lord had been speaking in the fore part of this chapter. Now it appears that the prophet takes up the line of thought (vv. 6-7). What he says appears to be of a general character, applicable to men everywhere and at all times. But this word has a special relevance to the issue in hand and the situation just described (vv. 1-5). His words tie up with the initial summons to "come" and "buy." When gracious invitations are addressed to any body of men, the hour of grace has struck. It is a time for action. God is reaching out his hand; that hand must be grasped. God is seeking man; man must seek the Lord. Similar words spoken by the prophets are to be found in Amos 5:4; Jer. 29:12-14. Frequently the expression "Seek the Lord" is meant in the sense of offering a sacrifice. Here it would rather mean to seek him by prayer. But God is not always equally accessible. Sometimes he must withdraw his presence. Seasons of opportunity must be made the most of while they last. Sometimes he is "near," sometimes he removes himself. When he is near then he must be "called upon," that is, summoned to give his help.

Verse 7. But the other side of the coin is that sin must simultaneously with one's calling be laid aside, sloughed off and abandoned. Aside from this double action which holds good at all times, there seems to have been a special need at the time this appeal was made to break with sin. There seems to have been those who in Babylonian Captivity immersed themselves so deeply in the stream of life of that worldly capital that they became the prey of the corrupt mercantile procedures and were perhaps growing rich by devious devices. They were the "wicked man" and the "worthless fellow" who are being specifically summoned to break with their sinful way of life. That is the negative side of the summons. But the necessary positive aspect is contained in the words that follow: "Let him turn back to the Lord." That involves a complete right-about-face. As man backs away from sin he must draw consciously closer to God. Though the word penitence is not used in this context it is definitely implied. And he who penitently draws near to God will experience that he will by no means be cast out. God "will have mercy upon him" and "abundantly pardon." Pardon has to be abundant because apparently there was such an abundance of sin. One can hardly speak more comfortingly to the soul troubled by sin than is done in these words.

4. God Is Magnificent in Forgiveness (vv. 8-9)

55:8-9 8. For my thoughts are not your thoughts,
neither are my ways your ways, says the Lord.
9. For as the heavens are high above the earth,
so are my ways higher than your ways,
and my thoughts than your thoughts.

Verses 8, 9. Again we have what looks like a general truth, applicable to all manner of situations. But in this special context the statement describes God's method of dealing with sin. For when the word of the law strikes home with a man and the enormity of his guilt disturbs him, then it seems impossible that God's grace might cope with sin. The present text says that such misgivings are unfounded. There is something magnificent about the greatness of God's mercy. Far-reaching comparisons must be made to catch the full measure of God's pardon, comparisons like: "As the heavens are high above the earth. . . ." There is a beauty and

a measure of reassurance about such utterance that is overwhelming. The evangelist of the Old Testament is speaking. Here *Luther* remarks: "Thus far goes the admonition;
now he begins to raise up the weak." The prophet has offered proof for his previous claim about the magnificence of
God's forgiveness.

5. This Forgiveness Comes by Way of the Word of God (vv. 10-11)

55:10-11 10. For us the rain comes down and the snow from heaven,
   and does not return there but waters the earth,
and makes it bring forth and sprout,
   and gives new seed to him that sows
     and bread to him that eats;
11. so shall my word be that goes forth from my mouth.
  It shall not return to me empty.
But it shall achieve what I please,
   and be successful in the thing for which I commissioned it.

Verse 10. There is a tangible point of contact between
God, the merciful one and the sinner, the penitent one. That
point of contact is the word of God. Here God deigns to
explain how his word is as though it had a built-in quality of
"self-fulfilling energy." That divine word is dynamic. It is
sent forth by the Lord as a sort of messenger, who has a
specific commission. In a strikingly simple and telling comparison the Lord shows how he operates. His word is like
the rain and the snow that come down and stay in the earth
on which they fell; and they moisten and fructify the earth,
making things to stir with a hidden energy and to sprout,
so that the eternal cycle of seed-time and harvest fulfills itself, and new seed is provided for the man that sows and for
the man who needs bread to eat.

Verse 11. For God, who has again been speaking since
v. 8, now spells out in detail exactly how the word that
comes forth from his own mouth, and also after that from
the mouth of his prophet — how this word, we say, operates.
It comes forth like God's mighty creation word, omnipotent

and irresistible. Then it does its assigned task. At this point the figure of a messenger enters upon the scene: the word of God is such a messenger. He does not return with a mission unaccomplished. When he reappears he has finished what it pleased God to send him for. The task laid upon it has been successfully accomplished. Though this description always applies to the saving word of the gospel wherever it is sent forth, in this particular case the return from Babylonian Captivity seems to be specifically thought of. But the efficacy of the word of forgiveness, as outlined in vv. 8-10, is also not to be lost sight of.

6. The Great Joy Resulting from the Deliverance from Captivity (vv. 12-13)

55:12-13 12. For with joy shall you go forth,
and in peace shall you be led forth.
The mountains and the hills before you
shall break forth in jubilant shouts;
and all the trees of the forest shall clap their hands.
13. Instead of the thornbush shall come up the cypress;
instead of the nettle shall come up the myrtle.
And it shall be to the Lord for a memorial,
for an everlasting sign which shall not be effaced.

Verse 12. This section (chaps. 40-55) and Chap. 55 very appropriately come to a close on a note of joy, joy over the impending Return from Babylonian Captivity, a point of view that has been continually appearing and reappearing. The language discriptive of this great event is borrowed from the account of the Exodus from Egyptian bondage. As there was joy then, there shall be joy again. So also this Exodus shall be "in peace," not in panic or in haste but in the full assurance of faith in the God who has often redeemed his people. That figure of a band of men released and coming back free is replaced by the language of a festal procession, where men keep a feast and mark the occasion by jubilant shouts. To catch the exuberance of the festival spirit, we must note that the expressions of joy are so overwhelming that even "the trees of the field" are swept along into it and clap their hands for joy as a king of rhythmic accompaniment to the swelling chorus of joy. "The trees of the field" are the wild trees that grow promiscuously here and there; even they feel that they must join this happy chorus.

Verse 13. This new Exodus has been variously described and, as remarked above, is a favorite theme of the prophet (cf. 40:3-5; 41:17-20; 42:16; 43:1 f., 19-24; 48:20 f.). In highly figurative language that prophet now describes a marvelous transformation even of the vegetation along the road of the Return. Common, worthless desert plants, like the thornbush and nettle, will along the road of the Return be changed into trees of distinction and beauty, like the cypress and the myrtle. But all this shall serve not for the glorification of Israel, but for the enhancement of the glory of Israel's God. He shall thereby, as it were, erect a memorial (Hebrew: "name") for himself, and establish an everlasting sign for himself, which can never be effaced. The language seems reminiscent of the procedure of kings of the Orient, who were wont to record their achievements, especially those of a military sort, in the rocks, that they might be read by generations to come. But new conquerors often appeared on the scene and mutilated or destroyed inscriptions left by their predecessors. The memory of God's salvation-acts can never be destroyed.

Notes

Verse 2. "For that which does not satisfy" is an expression that uses the *be* of price and a compound negative noun, "not satisfaction." See *GK* 152 a.

Verse 5. "Because of" is twice used toward the end of the verse. The first time it reads *le ma'an*, the second time just plain *le*, which is merely an abbreviated form of the preposition. See *KS* 319 o.

Verse 6. The verb "may be found" is a good example of the so-called *Niphal tolerativum*.

Verse 7. "Abundantly" is a good case of the use of the *Hiphil* in place of an adverb. (*KS* 399 m). *North* has a simplified rendering of "he will abundantly forgive" in the words: "He is always ready to forgive."

Verse 10. We have translated the second half of the second line with an adversative "but" ("but waters the earth"). Some translate it "except." It all depends on what the writer's conception of things meteorological was. Did he know of evaporation, condensation, and super-saturation? If he did then it would be good to translate the *ki 'im* as "except."

Verse 11. If "the word" refers to the word by which the Lord appointed the Return from Captivity then it might be well to point *yetse'* as *yatsa'*, referring to a word already pronounced.

THE THIRD PART
OF ISAIAH

Chapter LVI

II. THE THIRD PART OF ISAIAH (Chaps. 56—66)

A. A SUPPLEMENT TO CHAPTER 55 (Chap. 56)

Since 1892 (*Duhm*) the rest of Isaiah's book (chaps. 56-66) has by the majority of Old Testament scholars been considered as belonging to a third author, who for want of a better name has been labelled as Trito-Isaiah, that is: Third Isaiah.

The reasons for giving him a separate entity are in brief the following. A vocabulary appears from this point onward, not entirely new, but one that brings in quite a few new features. Besides the theological position brings with it new emphases which had not appeared in Second Isaiah. With a new vocabulary and a new theological position goes, of course, new subject matter, which neither Isaiah himself, nor Second Isaiah dealt with. As to the general tone of the material offered in these chapters it is commonly asserted that Trito-Isaiah does not display quite as high a level of inspired fervor: he is not so often swept off his feet into truly inspired and inspiring utterance. Then, among other things, the words of this writer are said to stand out against a different historical background than that of all the material preceding.

We do not find these arguments very impressive. New vocabulary brings in new material. But one merely needs a simple additional assumption: As the years passed the prophet attained to new insights: he kept growing all his years. The more mature prophet presented his new insight gained by continuing inspiration. Similar is the matter of a different theological position. Old truths acquired new depths under the guidance of the Spirit. Must a man remain static in his theological position? Add to all this the fact that the prophet enjoyed a rather long ministry during which the historical situation may well have changed quite a bit. Add further the fact that it is quite reasonable to believe that as Isaiah prepared his people for the Captivity, so he also prepared them by material calculated to fit the nation for the era after the Return.

These are but a few of the considerations which induce us to discount the theory of a Trito-Isaiah.

We are not hostile to the idea that Chaps. 56-66 contain a core of material traceable to Isaiah, to which core relevant material may have been added by faithful disciples of Isaiah, writing at a later time in the spirit of the matter. But the idea should not be too repulsive and too unbelievable that the Lord let inspired men produce prophetic messages that in exceptional cases were calculated to serve for the guidance of God's people, being produced at some time prior to the development of this new situation. Compare also 41:12-14, where God challenges the gods of the heathen to match him in the power of being able to disclose the future. So we are quite content to hold to the view that the original prophet Isaiah is the author also of Chaps. 56-66.

At first glance 56:1-2 seems unrelated to what went before. Chapter 55 was concerned about having the nation appropriate to itself the free grace of God. But even then already free grace was not cheap grace. It meant not only to accept God's mercy, but also put men under obligation to live a life worthy of the calling wherewith they had been called. To such a position Isaiah calls his people. He says: Live lives that are in harmony with being saved by grace. Incidentally one of many indications that the author of the present chapter is familiar with what is commonly called Second Isaiah, we may note that 56:1 voices the same thought as 46:13.

Here may be the place to indicate that our chapter does not become guilty of an unhealthy emphasis on external things when it stresses the keeping of the Sabbath and the Law. Only by divorcing Chap. 55 from 56 can such a position be arrived at. Exposition must consider the context.

The state of the Hebrew text is on the whole good, in spite of *Duhm's* charge to the contrary.

1. The Importance of the Observance of the Law (vv. 1-2)

56:1-2 1. Thus says the Lord:
"Keep the Law and do what is right.
For my salvation is about to come;
 And my righteousness is about to be revealed.
2. Oh how very happy is he who does this
 and the son of man who holds fast to this;
keeping the Sabbath so as not to profane it;
 and restraining his hand from doing any evil."

Verse 1. The first two verses constitute a *Heilsorakel* (salvation oracle). They are introduced with a solemn, "Thus says the Lord." As indicated above, the word aims to inculcate faithful observance of the Law. It is therefore Torah-instruction. Our translation is a slight oversimplification. But "Keep justice" (*RSV*) ignores that which constitutes "justice," has been spelled out by Israel's codes. And "Do righteousness" is an un-English mode of speech. It has therefore been aptly rendered: "Do what is right." The *Jerusalem Bible* says, very much to the point: "Have a care for justice and act with integrity." The reason why the nation should be meticulous about the faithful observance of the Law is that the intervention of the Lord in the affairs of Israel is about to come. We could say that the case is like that of the New Testament writers, who reinforced the call to godly living by a reference to the impending coming of the Lord to the Final Judgment. And that is practically what the last line means: "My righteousness is about to be revealed." For "righteousness" may be construed (*Fischer*) to signify "righteous intervention." God is about to take a hand in the affairs of his people; let them live accordingly.

A sense of immediacy marks the word, even as did John the Baptist's preaching (Mark 1:15).

Verse 2. What was recommended in v. 1 is pleasant and brings blessings with it, as this beatitude ("Oh how very happy, . . .") indicates. The "this" of v. 2 refers to the attitude stressed in v. 1, viz., the blessedness of godly living. Only at this point the attitude of the *individual* is indicated. Personal religion as well as corporate piety gets its due emphasis, with a bit more of stress on the corporate aspect of the matter in the earlier days. An unexpected aspect of godly living seems to appear at this point, the observance of the Sabbath. This observance had apparently grown in importance during Israel's Captivity experience. For the keeping of the Sabbath was one area in which faithful adherence to the Lord could effectively demonstrate itself as an act of confession. In Mosaic times (Exod. 20:8 ff.) the Sabbath enjoyed distinction. This distinction was greatly enhanced in Exilic and post-Exilic times, as the following passages indicate: 58:13; 66:23; Ezek. 20:12 ff.; 22:18, 26. To this one item of importance, a reminder of general character, is added as an obvious expression of the good life: "restraining [one's] hand from doing evil." Some consider this a reference to social wrongs. But the word is broader. It covers all sins against one's neighbor. Both verses taken together show close affinity of spirit with Ps. 1.

2. Admission of Strangers and Eunuchs to the Congregation of Israel (vv. 3-8)

56:3-8 3. Let not the stranger [i.e., proselyte] who has joined himself to the Lord say:
"The Lord will utterly separate me from his people."
And let not the eunuch say:
"Lo, I am a withered tree."
4. For thus says the Lord:
"To the eunuchs who keep my Sabbaths,
and choose the things that I delight in,
and hold fast my covenant;
5. to them will I give in my house and on my walls
a monument and a name

better than sons or daughters.
I will give to such an everlasting name
which shall not be cut off.
6. And the strangers [proselytes] who join themselves to the Lord
to minister to him and to love the name of the Lord,
even to be his servant,
every one of them keeping the Sabbath so as not to profane it,
and holding fast to my covenant;
7. these I will bring to my holy mountain,
and make them glad in my house of prayer.
Their burnt offerings and their sacrifices
shall be accepted on my altar.
For my house shall be called a house of prayer for all people."
8. An oracle of the Lord God,
who gathers the scattered of Israel:
"I will gather others to him
besides those already gathered."

Verse 3. How this section (vv. 3-8) attaches itself to vv.
1-2 is difficult to ascertain. It could be that the importance of
observing the Law in those days was in danger of being over-
done in some respects. Important as it was to prevent persons not cleaving to the God of Israel from being allowed to·
hold membership with the true people of God, there were a
few areas where this caution could have been unduly rigor-
ous. These areas had to do with proselytes and eunuchs.
The proselytes are described as "strangers who have joined
themselves to the Lord." That is saying merely this: These
persons have been attracted to the One and True God and to
his pure and spiritual worship. That there were some worthy
Gentiles of whom this was true appears already from a word
in Solomon's dedicatory prayer (I Kings 8:41-43). Now
it is true that Deut. 23:3-6 forbade the admission of Moabites
and Ammonites into the congregation of Israel. It appears
now in these later days these prohibitions were about to be
expanded so as to cover the case of other innocent Gentiles,
especially since it almost appears that proselytes were becoming somewhat numerous. Some may have been overheard saying: "The Lord will utterly separate me from his
people." A note of sadness seems to have crept into such a
pronouncement, for Israel's religion had strongly attracted

them. In like manner a class of unfortunates, eunuchs, were in danger when considered as material for membership in Israel, of being shut out from the inner circle of true worshippers. This could even have included such outstanding personages as Nehemiah. And such too might have been overheard saying, with a note of sadness, "Lo, I am a withered tree." For Deut. 23:1 could have been made to apply to their case. Both classes of personages are advised not to take such a glum view of things. The Lord, in this verse virtually grants true-hearted men of this type the privilege of full membership among his people.

Verse 4. Taking the case of the eunuchs first — the Lord advises them that if their life gives evidence that they are sincere in their desire for membership, they will in no wise be barred from entrance with God's people. A few typical examples are cited of practices that they will follow in such a case. They will, for one thing, keep the Lord's Sabbaths by proper observance of the day. They will also manifest delight in the things that the Lord delights in, like the keeping of his commandments. They will hold fast God's covenant. This would include the rite of circumcision. But it would involve more than that: it would base the entire relationship with God on his covenant-word and promise, even as would any true-hearted son of Abraham.

Verse 5. The word of the Lord to the eunuchs continues. If they have done their part, he, on his part, will grant them certain rewards and emoluments to give evidence of his approval of their sincere quest of him. The first of these need not be taken literally. It guarantees to the eunuchs what we might call a memorial plaque, hung up on the walls of the Lord's house. In addition the Lord promises to such persons a "name," that is a reputation, among the people of Israel, which will indicate what these people are reputed to be, a reputation more outstanding than that of having left behind numerous offspring, a blessing which the Orientals even then already prized very highly. In fact the "name" will be such that it "shall not be cut off."

Verse 6. And now the proselytes — here called "strangers" or "foreigners" — of them it is also expected that they will give some positive evidence that it is a deep-seated concern for them to knock at Israel's door that they may be admitted. A few samples of such evidence are submitted. First, their quest is given a favorable appraisal in that they are said to be consciously joining themselves to the Lord, as was already said of them in v. 3. Their objectives and motives are set forth: they want to engage in "ministering" to the Lord, that is to say, participate in the meaningful worship at Jerusalem with God's people. They also want to give visible expressions to that impelling motive that urges them on in this quest, namely they "love the name of the Lord," to which must be added that fine objective that they want "to be his servants." That is, they want to be used up in doing the will of the Lord. Again (as in v. 2) the keeping of the Sabbath plays an important role. For he that walks carelessly can in short order "profane" this holy day. But they have learned how to sanctify it. Here we may inject that there are some indications in the Scriptures that proselytes were more numerous than we might have imagined. We are thinking of the passages where these possibilities are more fully spelled out, passages like Isa. 2:2-4; 60:1-14; 66:18 f.

Verse 7. Now a listing of the mercies that God has in store for earnest seekers after the truth. The "mountain" to which the Lord will bring them is the temple-mountain. They know that the truth of God is centered and preserved there. And when they are admitted to this sanctuary and what it stands for, the Lord will "make them glad in [his] house of prayer." The joy of worship, of which the Scriptures so frequently speak, will then be realized, and somehow it will involve "prayer." There prayer will be made and answered. Speaking in the language of those days, and especially of the Old Testament, there "their burnt offerings and their sacrifices shall be accepted on [his] altar." A man of those days, also in Israel, thought of worship primarily in terms of sacrifice. And that proselytes might have a strong desire to share in sacrifices to the true and living God is apparent from Lev. 15:14 ff.; 22:18 ff.; 17:8 ff. That a type of *universal* religion was contemplated for the future appears from the assertion here made: "My house shall be called a house of prayer for all people." The distinct emphasis of this promise lies on the last words, "for all people" (cf. also Mark 11:17).

Verse 8. This line of thought is rounded out by this verse, which for emphasis' sake is labelled as "an oracle of the Lord God." It states that not only will such unusual persons as proselytes and eunuchs be granted admission to the fellowship of Israel, but "others" — apparently a sizeable contingent — will be gathered to him "besides those already gathered." This promise is uttered in the spirit of the well-known passage (John 10:16) concerning the other sheep that the Lord has.

3. Israel's Degenerate Leaders (vv. 9-12)

56:9-12 9. All you beasts of the field, come to devour;
yea, all the beasts of the forest.
10. Her watchmen are blind;
the whole lot of them know nothing.
They are all dumb dogs that cannot bark.
They lie about dreaming,
they love to slumber.
11. And these dogs are voracious;
they can never get enough.
Such are shepherds who have no intelligence.
Each one has turned to his own way;
every man entirely to his own profit.
12. "Come, let me fetch wine,
let us guzzle strong drink;
and tomorrow shall be like today,
only much more so."

Verse 9. This section actually runs on to about 57:13, dealing with the degenerate leadership of Israel. But because of the chapter division, we are letting Chap. 57 appear almost like a separate entity. Verse 9 has been described as resisting every effort at interpretation. The situation is hardly as desperate as that. The verse does initiate a proclamation of judgment (*Westermann*). As the thought is further developed it becomes apparent that the unworthy leaders of the nation are under sharp scrutiny. They are utterly remiss in performing their official duties. It is assumed that the judgment of God has already befallen them. Beasts have overrun the land and slain many. These beasts are now invited to come and finish their bloody business by devouring the bodies of the slain. Perhaps the "beasts of the forest" are considered more ferocious than "the beasts of the field." Both together are serving the purpose of being agents of God's just judgment. Ezek. 34:1-10 has some analogy to this passage.

Verse 10. The leaders of the nation are called "watchmen" for the obvious reason that they are to keep on the alert to warn the nation of approaching dangers. The only question is then whether these watchmen are prophets or priests. Prophets seem to be assigned more commonly to this function as may appear from Jer. 6:17; Ezek. 3:17; 33:7. Occasionally priests seem to be appointed to this task (see Jer. 14:18). A sweeping indictment is pronounced: These watchmen are "blind." They fail to see that dangers, grave dangers, threaten the welfare of the nation. Not seeing what is obvious enough, they have grown entirely ignorant as to what the nation really lacks: "The whole lot of them know nothing." With almost insulting plainness of speech the prophet indicts the leadership by the charge: "They are all dumb dogs that cannot bark." Any cur might raise the alarm when a thief or a robber enters. These men have sunk beneath this level. They all have taken their responsibility so lightly that they spend their time dreaming and slumbering.

Verse 11. As suggested by the figure of the previous verse, these watchmen are for the moment classified as watchdogs. But about all they seem to do is to feed themselves greedily. They are voracious, of ravenous appetites. That is what the "shepherds" are like — another sudden turn of the figure. They have so little appreciation of the responsibility of their assignment that they may be said to have no intelligence at all. The only concern they seem to have is to go the way of their own choosing, each man looking out for his own profit.

Verse 12. Without introduction — the reader can readily discern who is talking and to what purpose — a word is suddenly flashed on the screen presenting a typical utterance of one of these degenerate leaders, setting forth another prevailing vice, drunkenness. They crave variety in their drinking-bouts, wine one day, strong drink the next. One leader volunteers to go out and get the drinks. "Guzzle" implies copious indulgence. The height of their ambition seems to be to have the morrow outdo today in the quantity consumed.

The indictment of these irresponsible leaders continues into the next chapter.

Notes

Verse 3. The word for "stranger" in Hebrew is "son of the foreigner" with no emphasis on the word "son." *Ben* is merely a relation word.

Verse 4. The verb "hold fast" is participial as to form, the progression being from finite verb to the participle — not an unusual construction in Hebrew. See *KS* 413 r.

Verse 5. The Hebrew word for "monument" is *yadh*, i.e., "hand." The same word appears in I Sam. 15:12.

Verse 6. "To profane it" — in Hebrew the construction is the infinitive with a *min* separative. Both together make a negative result clause. (See *KS*, 406 n.)

Verse 10. We prefer to follow the *keri* (Hebrew marginal reading) of the participle *tsophaw*, reading a *yod* before the *waw*, so making the suffix plural. The word for "dreaming" comes from a Hebrew root which may read in its initial letter either as a smooth *h* or as a rough *ch*. The former means "seeing a vision" the latter "dreaming." We prefer the latter.

Verse 12. The text reads, as we have rendered: "let *me* fetch," one man volunteering to go for the group. That fits the situation so well as to make textual emendation, based mostly on the versions, unnecessary.

Chapter LVII

B. THE TRIUMPH OF DIVINE GRACE OVER ISRAEL'S INFIDELITY (Chap. 57)

As we look back on Chap. 56 we recall that it ended on a note of lament over faithless shepherds, or rulers. This lament continues, now with the faithless *people* in mind. In other words the emphasis shifts from the shepherd to the flock. For the most part, commentators are of the opinion that this material was composed before the people left Palestine for the Babylonian Exile. There appears to be evidences of a background that is distinctively Palestinian — terebinths (possibly), wadis, clefts of the rock, etc. The lament which runs through both chapters turns into an indictment by the prophetic word. But where in our chapter a blistering denouncement opens the chapter, a kindly portrayal of divine grace comes strongly on the scene and so we arrive at the caption used above.

1. The Perishing of the Righteous — an Unheeded Warning (vv. 1-2)

57:1-2 1. Even the righteous have been wiped out,
  and there is no man that lays it to heart;
and loyal men have been taken away
  and no one took note of it.
For the righteous are [always] taken away from the evil to come.
2. He enters into peace,
  each one who has walked straightforward shall rest upon his bed.

Verse 1. To get some kind of setting for this chapter we may suppose, as some do, that this material may have been presented by some prophet (perhaps Isaiah himself) at a kind of synagogue meeting in the holy city. First of all an event that should have caused some alarm is drawn to the

271

attention of the hearers: Good men have been dying off in surprising numbers (cf. Ps. 12:1; Mic. 7:2). By this fact God is trying to say something to his people, but they have failed to take notice. So the prophet is telling them what it all means. Good people, the "salt of the earth," have been taken away, very likely by an unexpected death. Why does God allow that? That is the way things usually go before great calamities break in: "The righteous are alway taken away from the evil to come." This phenomenon has been observed so often that it may be laid down as a general rule. Thus the righteous man is spared, being off the scene before the calamity breaks. This does not seem to imply that their death is to be attributed to the violence which prevails on every hand, making life unsafe. But generally speaking, men are so dull-witted that they usually fail to see what God has in mind, and how he is sparing his saints much grief. Two passages from the apocryphal book of Wisdom may be compared (3:1-3; 4:7-17).

Verse 2. To present this truth in proper balance, two more thoughts need to be added. First of all, such a righteous man's death means for him that "he enters into peace." For him, "life's fitful fever" is over. To this thought the second one is a corollary, that they were truly righteous is evidenced by the fact that "they walked straightforward" and so their godly life testified to a right relation to God in faith. The "bed" upon which such are said to rest is their grave (cf. Job 17:13). It can rightly be asserted that this verse contains a certain measure of the hope of everlasting life, which was not much in evidence in the days of the Old Testament.

But the point toward which this thought moves forward is the fact that the numerous deaths of "loyal men" portended the breaking in of a major calamity, of which no man seemed even remotely concerned. This calamity could again be the Babylonian Captivity, which the prophet foretold abundantly but to which warning no man gave heed.

2. Rebuke of Sorcery and Idolatry (vv. 3-10)

57:3-10   3. But you there, come over here,
  you sons of the sorceress,
 you offspring of the adulterer and the harlot.
4. Whom are you ridiculing?
  against whom are you opening your mouth wide?
  and stretching your tongue far out?
 Aren't you a brood of transgressors, a pack of liars?
5. You who burn with lust over the idols
  under every green tree;
 and slaughter your children in the stream-beds
  among the clefts of the rocks.
6. And among the smooth stones of the streams in your portion,
  and to them you have poured out your drinkofferings,
7. Upon every high and lofty hill
  you have set up your bed,
  and you have gone to offer sacrifice even up there.
6. And among the smooth stones of the streams is your portion,
  you have set up your plaques;
 and having turned away from me, you have uncovered,
  and gone up to, and made spacious your bed;
 and you have made a bargain for yourself with them.
 You have loved their bed and gazed upon nakedness.
9. You have journeyed to Molech with oil;
  you have provided an abundance of perfumes.
 You have also sent your envoys far off,
  and made obeisance even to Sheol.
10. You wear yourself out with your many journeys,
  but you never admitted, "It's all in vain!"
 You found new life for your vitality;
  therefore you did not weaken.

Verse 3. This section (vv. 3-10) is a pronouncement of judgment (*Gerichtsrede*). It would fit into the days of Manasseh, under whose patronage every form of idolatry flourished. After the first two verses, which hinted at calamity that stood before the very door but was believed to be still far off, it is very proper to give an indication what the deep-seated cause of this calamity was: sorcery and idolatry, both in a highly developed degree. The passage carries echoes of Jer. 2:20 ff. and Ezek. 16:23ff. In Isa. 56: 10 the tone of rebuke was comparatively mild. In this chapter it is sharp and brusque. The opening address is a harsh imperative. A person authorized to rebuke bids the sinners before the divine judgment. They are called "sons of the sorceress," implying that they are strongly addicted to sorcery — magic arts, black magic, and all forms of witchcraft. The mother, so to speak, innoculated the children to practice such rites. The second choice title by which the sinners are addressed is "offspring of the adulterer." Apparently spiritual adultery, that is, idolatry, is meant. Though the difference between the two was often not clearly marked. Spiritual infidelity led to carnal adultery. So adultery here means defection, as in Hos. 7:4; Jer. 3:8 f.; Ezek. 23:37, etc. The first of the indicting titles, referring to the mother, would be keenly felt by those rebuked, because the Oriental felt deeply any slander against his mother. But the prophet is unsparing.

Verse 4. These persons now, the ones addicted to sorcery and adultery, adopted a superior attitude and looked down on those who faithfully held to the worship of the true God of Israel, and gave expression to their conceit by ridiculing the exponents of the ancestral faith. They gave coarse and insulting expression to their feeling of superiority by "opening their mouth wide" in a gesture of derision, and even far more so by "stretching [their] tongue far out." As a result, though the objects of their ridicule were in the first place fellow countrymen, in the last analysis, what they did was directed at the Lord Most High. For such who are so brazen in their rejection of the Lord, the prophet has two more very appropriate titles: "brood of transgressors" (i.e., rebels), and "a pack of liars." These are not merely harsh invectives but entirely fitting descriptions of what these unfaithful in Israel really were.

Verse 5. A multifarious variety and types of idolatrous cults was cultivated by the nation, whose God had done so many good things for them. These further classes of infidelity are treecults, child-sacrifice, and cult of stones. The description becomes a bit lurid. The idolaters are described as inflamed by unholy lust in pursuing this nature-cult and practicing it "under every green tree," an obvious hyperbole and a quite proper one to characterize the zeal with which these abominable practices were followed. This cult alone must have had adherents aplenty (cf. Deut. 12:2; Ezek. 6:13; II Kings 17:10; etc.). From the frequency with which child-sacrifices are alluded to, this specially horrible cult must have taken deeper root in Israel than we usually believe. See by way of illustration: Jer. 7:31; 19:5; Ezek. 20:31; 23:39; II Kings 23:10. Besides, apparently, a favorite place for performing such child-sacrifices was "in the stream-beds," or among "the clefts of the rocks," i.e., small caves in the wadi-beds which furnished a weird background for such practices.

Verse 6. Exactly what is meant by the "smooth stones of the streams" and what spiritual aberration is involved seems almost impossible to determine. But according to the context an idol-cult of some sort must be involved. Perhaps stones fantastically shaped by wind and sand (*Fischer*) were treated as particularly potent fetishes. In any case, the idols involved were regarded as Israel's "portion," that is, her prized inheritance, her most valuable possession (cf. Ps. 16: 5; 142:6; 119:57; Josh. 22:25). To objects such as these, drink-offerings and cereal offerings were dutifully brought. God has all this time been charging the nation with gross rebellion and transgression. He interrupts his indictment with the question: "Shall I be calm over these things?" For all such worship was also shot through with fertility-cult sexual extravagances.

Verse 7. A second description in even more vivid colors follows. We gather from the nature of the description that in this picture the Canaanite fertility-cult is largely being depicted, even as it is in Hosea and Ezekiel. Or it may be called the worship "in high places." Again with a measure of permissible hyperbole these things are said to take place upon "every high and lofty hill." Setting up the bed in these places implies preparations for the practice of the rites of the fertility-cult. Though all this involved some laborious hill-climbing, nevertheless "even up there" the sacrifices and what went with it were performed.

Verse 8. We cannot be entirely sure that we have rightly caught the details of the next act of infidelity that is described. We may have a fairly correct picture of what was practiced according to this description. Deuteronomy 6:9 and 11:20 had taught the people of Israel to write key-words of the Mosaic law on their doorposts and gates. These memory-verses (we called them "plaques") were, however, by this generation set back *"behind* the door" so as not to serve as uncomfortable reminders of the true God of Israel. Having thus turned away from him they are ready to practice the abominations which were characteristic of this cult. In fact the participants in these rites did not, as prostitutes were wont to do, make a bargain for money to be received, but instead made a bargain for themselves with them (i.e., the Canaanites), *paying them* to engage in such things. Nor was all this done with some measure of repugnance and reluctance. But those of Israel "had loved the bed" of lust and had even "gazed upon nakedness." In other words they delighted in indecent exposure, devoid by this time of all sense of shame.

Verse 9. The collection of prophetic oracles goes on, now in a kind of historic retrospect of things that are a matter of record of days gone by. The words are a bit difficult to interpret, but in these verses it seems to be a record of what troubles Israel went to, to engage in her nefarious conduct. Journeys were taken into other countries in order to take part in rites. So, for example, they sought participation in the rites which belonged to Molech, the chief divinity of the Ammonites (see I Kings 11:5, 7). To enhance the practice engaged in, even costly perfumes in abundance were procured. They sent "envoys far off" in order to make further contacts, even if sometimes humiliating obeisance had to be resorted to to get concessions. That is perhaps all that is involved in the phrase "made obeisance even to Sheol." We fail to see here an allusion to attempted contact with the deities of the nether regions, or to necromantic practices.

Verse 10. Yes, it might even be said of Israel that she "wore herself out" in the multiplicity of idolatrous practices. Especially in view of the journeys involved (see also II Kings 16:10 ff.; II Chron. 28:22 ff.). But she never tired of her pursuits. She was never ready to make the obvious admission, "It is all in vain," or as the *Jerusalem Bible* puts it, "I give up." The next sentence again is a bit puzzling. It may suffice to note a bit of the sexual connotation in the translation, "You found new life for your vitality." All these practices practically reinvigorated the idolaters. Therefore they "did not weaken." So ends the excursion into the area of the Canaanite fertility-cult.

Now comes, quite appropriately,

3. The Threat of Judgment (vv. 11-13)

57:11-13 11. Whom did you dread and fear
so that you behaved treacherously?
And me you did not remember,
nor take things to heart.
Did I not keep quiet at all this, even from way back?
But me you did not fear.
12. I for my part will expose this righteousness of yours;
these doings of yours, they shall avail you nothing.
13. When you cry out for help, let your loathsome idols save
you, —
yea, the wind will carry them away,
and a breath will take them away.
But he that takes refuge in me shall possess the land,
and inherit my holy mountain.

Verse 11. It would seem that some nameless fear impelled those idolaters on their course. Did the Canaanites themselves perhaps spread the rumor that, if their deities were not appeased, evil would befall those who were negligent? That may have been a major motive by which guilty Israel was driven. Of course, that involved that (they) "did not remember" the Lord, nor "take to heart" his gracious dealings with his people in times past. The Lord indicates that he had never made inordinate demands upon his people: he "kept quiet at all this," as far back as the memory of history reaches. He was patient and longsuffering. His self-restraint could have indicated to Israel what a gracious God the Lord was. But they were dull of perception. Him they "did not fear."

Verse 12. Now finally judgment is pronounced. God will now at last bring to light what it really is that has been going on and reveals how he himself will bring to light what has been happening. You feel secure in that you have kept the ordinances of idolatry. Such keeping was your "righteousness" — spoken ironically. If true righteousness was a worthy garb in which to appear before the throne on high, then Israel's righteousness, based on idolatrous practices surely was a garment of "filthy rags." God is going to make that very apparent. So he spells it out: "These doings of yours, they shall avail you nothing."

Verse 13. A threat of judgment is implied at this point, the nation will be driven into such extremities that they will "cry out for help." When the real test comes then it will become apparent how wretched deities the idols were. They are here called "loathsome idols" because their inability will, in such emergencies, be appalling. When the real test comes, they will be so helpless that any wind or breath will remove them off the scene. But grace triumphs over justice. The section comes to an end on a very positive note. All that the Lord requires, even of these guilty ones is that they "take refuge" in him. If they do this then the old covenant blessing made to Abraham will become a reality: they "shall possess the land" and enjoy all the blessings attendant upon such possession. When it is said that they will "inherit [his] holy mountain" this mountain is the mountainous territory of the land of Israel.

4. A Promise of Salvation (vv. 14-21)

57:14-21 14. And it shall be said:
"Build a road, build a road, prepare a way.
Remove every obstacle from the way of my people."

15. For thus says the high and exalted One,
    who sits enthroned forever, whose name is Holy:
"I dwell in the high and holy place,
    and also with him who is crushed and low in spirit,
to revive the spirit of the lowly,
    and to revive the heart of those who are crushed.
16. For I will not contend forever,
    neither will I always be angry.
For [every] spirit would faint before me,
    and the souls which I have made.
17. I was indeed angry because of the sin of covetousness,
    and I smote him, hiding my face in anger.
But he went on backsliding in the way of his heart.
18. I have seen his ways, yet I will heal him;
    and I will lead him and I will give him full consolations,
        and also to his mourners,
19. producing as the utterance of their lips:
    'Peace, peace to those afar off
        and to those who are near'
says the Lord: 'and I will heal him.'
20. But the wicked are like the stirred-up sea,
    for it cannot calm down;
        and its waters toss up mud and slime.
21. 'There is no peace, says my God,
    'for the wicked.' "

Verse 14. Logic or strict justice would at this point have launched into despair about Israel's future, or would have dictated harsh punishments. Grace is that quality which rises beyond logic and justice. It tells what God will do in spite of all that points to the contrary. Who it is that speaks and when and where is unimportant. Therefore these words are introduced by a mere: "And it shall be said." Thus the message as such is underscored. This word is *Heilsverheissung*, a promise of salvation. It demands constructive enterprise: "Build a road." The terms are reminiscent of 40:3. Only in the former passage the road was to be built for the Lord to travel on, and to come to his people. Here it is the road that leads to the achievement of God's purposes and is prepared for the people to travel on and thus come to their goal. That involves the removal of all obstacles that lie in the way of achieving what has been promised the nation. Littleness of faith, doubt, discouragement are to be pushed out of the way, for God is with his people. He is very near. He is at hand to help. Salvation in all its fulness is to be aimed at.

Verse 15. To strengthen them still more, a second word of encouragement is added. He is not too high and mighty to let himself be concerned about what is happening to his own. Indeed he is "high and exalted." He has always sat enthroned. His name "Holy" means here total dedication to his purposes. But exalted as he deservedly is, he is also pleased to take up residence with "him who is crushed and low in spirit." These words might seem to describe men who are deeply contrite over their sins, but in the whole context it rather applies to those who are deeply discouraged, who have lost heart, who are held down by discouragement. They have not utterly lost faith, but they badly need revitalization; and that is what the Lord promises to give them.

Verse 16. The thought that God is not too high to take note of lowly man in his misery is being developed further. When man goes astray God does not merely let him drift: he takes him to task. In Biblical language he "contends" with him (cf. 54:7-9; Gen. 6:3; Jer. 3:5, 12; Ps. 103:9). Or another way of stating the case is: he "will not always be angry. For the manifestation of his anger, unrestrained, would have as result that "every spirit would faint before [him]" for his anger is a consuming fire. Then all the souls which he had made would perish.

Verse 17. The thought of God's anger is not to be dismissed; it is a very real and stern concept. God here dwells on the fact that he had just grounds for being angry. There was one sin in particular which had provoked him, the sin of "covetousness." Apparently this sin played a larger role than we usually admit. It is doubly heinous because it usually gives birth to social injustices. Even after the Israelites came back from Exile they still nurtured this sin in their bosom. So the Lord hid (his) face in anger. He let them painfully feel his displeasure. Did that treatment move them to abandon this sin? Far from it. "He went on backsliding in the way of his heart." Now comes the surprising reaction of the Lord to all this.

Verse 18. The opening statement looks back for a moment, as much as to say: The Lord is fully aware of Israel's attitude. And "*yet* he will heal him." This form of presentation constitutes one of those surprising triumphs of grace over justice. The healing spoken of is one of a spiritual nature, being reminiscent of Exod. 15:26. This thought is quite appropriate here, for the sin spoken of in v. 17 was a serious malady. The Lord's gracious attitude is covered by a few more verbs showing his kindly attitude toward the undeserving: "I will lead him and I will give full consolations." Perhaps the last phrase is best interpreted by translating a bit differently than we have, namely: "and *especially* to his mourners." The more deeply they grieve, the more do they become the objects of the Lord's pity.

Verse 19. The structure of this rather long sentence becomes a bit difficult, though the thought is clear. When the Lord takes pity on his children that will now produce grateful acknowledgment in the form of thanksgiving and praise, which are here described as being the "utterance of their lips." The same thought is found in Heb. 13:15 and Hos. 14:2. How "Peace, peace" fits into the picture is perhaps best covered by *Muilenburg's* explanation: "One is tempted to view this as Yahweh's greeting (*shalom, shalom!*) to all who enter the city of Zion." These blessings are available to "those afar off and to those who are near," that is to the Hebrews gathered in their own land as well as to those who have not yet returned. Or, repeating the former thought of v. 18: God's blessing on his own may be adequately covered by the statement: "And I will heal him." Ephesians 2:14 may also be compared on the second line of the verse.

Verses 20, 21. Over against the fortunate lot of those who have let themselves be admonished by the Lord, stands as a proper conclusion a description of the situation of the wicked and impenitent. They have anything but peace. For they are like "the stirred-up sea" which cannot calm down, and who may be said "to toss up mud and slime." In a sense this statement is a warning; in another sense it is a stern conclusion. The earnest tone of the law comes into the picture over against the gospel tone, which had for a time come to the forefront. The same stern note is sounded in v. 21, which appeared already in 48:22 and marked the conclusion of a major section. When men advocate to excise this verse at this point they are overlooking how well the verse fits in after v. 20.

Notes

Verse 1. *Koenig* in his commentary classified the "taken away" (*ne'esaph*) as a gnomic aorist, which fact we sought to display by inserting "always" in the translation. For the translation of *mippeney* three possibilities are to be reckoned with: *min* separative, *min* temporal, and *min* causal. We believe that *min* separative agrees best with the context.

Verse 3. For *wattizneh* ("and she played the harlot") the *Septuagint*, the *Syriac*, and the *Vulgate* read *zonah* (*kal*, feminine participle) which makes for a smoother translation.

Verse 6. There is a play on words involved: *cheleq* from one root means "smooth" and from another means "portion." *von Orelli* has caught the point in his translation: Des Tales *Kiesel* hast du dir *erkiest*.

Verse 8. The word rendered "nakedness" in Hebrew is the word "hand." To render it "nakedness" seems at best a guess, but a fairly reasonable guess at that.

Verse 13. The word *qibbutzim* (with suffix) from the root *qabhatz* could mean "the collected ones" which has led to the translation "your collection of idols" (*RSV*), a translation which fits very well at this point. Our translation, "your loathsome idols," builds on the fact that *qibbutzim* seems to be patterned after the word for "loathsome ones," which in Hebrew read *shiqqutzim*.

Verse 15. For "who sits enthroned forever" *KJ* and *RSV* have the seemingly impressive "who inhabits eternity," which does not seem to yield a very clear thought.

Verse 16. The word "spirit" in the second half of the verse has no article. This fact makes the thought more general. We have sought to render this fact by inserting an "every" before the word. The last clause of the verse could be very properly translated: "And I myself have made life." We offer it as an alternate translation (a la *Volz*).

Verse 18. The second verb in the verse is best taken as introduced by an adversative conjunction. See *KS* 369 f.

Chapter LVIII

C. ABUSES THAT RETARDED THE RECOVERY OF POST-EXILIC ISRAEL (Chap. 58)

From this title we draw the conclusion that the chapter is predominantly a preaching of law; and so it is. It may be properly labelled an admonition (*Mahnrede*). Fitting things into a historical situation we may conclude that the fortunes of the children of Israel are at low ebb; recovery has been slow. But there are very special reasons why this is so. According to the main issues of this chapter two major abuses have been pointed out that have retarded recovery. These two are: a misdirected fasting and an inadequate Sabbath observance. Because of shortcomings in the area just indicated the people stand there as utterly undeserving of divine favors. It would then appear that the time into which this passage fits is neither the pre-exilic, nor the exilic, nor the time immediately after the Return from Exile, but perhaps the decade following the Return. Although we feel that the days of the prophet Isaiah need not be ruled out completely. The indications of a possible background are so utterly meager and consist mostly in facts like no mention of a temple — as though fasting and Sabbath observance could not be discussed without mention of the Temple — if it had already been rebuilt.

It is true that the author of this chapter speaks as a teacher and instructor, or even as a *Seelsorger* and not with the characteristic approach of a prophet. But that could happen even if the speaker had been Isaiah. For these prophets were not one-talent men; and they had many different situations to combat.

Restating the major thought of the chapter briefly, we might say: It is not externalistic piety that paves the way for Israel's restoration but true, active righteousness (*Fischer*).

1. The Wrong Kind of Fast (vv. 1-5)

58:1-5 1. Call mightily, do not let up;
lift up your voice like a trumpet
and tell my people their transgressions
and to the house of Jacob their sins.
2. Indeed, me they seek daily;
they take pleasure in the knowledge of my ways,
as if they were a nation that did what is right
and had not forsaken the law of its God.
They demand of me righteous judgments;
they find pleasure in drawing near to God.
3. "Why have we fasted and you have not taken note?
Why have we afflicted our bodies, but you are not aware of it?"
Lo, on the day when you fast, you find time for your business,
and oppress all your workers.
4. Lo, when you fast, it is for strife and squabbling,
and for hitting with a wicked fist.
When for the present you fast
it is not to make your voice heard on high.
5. Or shall it be a fast such as I approve of,
a day of mortification?
Is it to bow down one's head like a reed?
or to bed one's self in sackcloth and ashes?
Will you call this a fast,
a day acceptable to the Lord?

Verse 1. The *Jerusalem Bible* catches the spirit of this verse rather well when it renders: "Shout for all you are worth." The attitude conveyed by this word is: Speak clearly and loudly; spare no one; be sure they all hear you. Sin is to be labelled as sin. When they come with excuses, like v. 2, in answer to your charge, do not weakly capitulate. The sin is great. It is rooted strongly in the nation's life.

Verse 2. But the hearers are hurt, not wounded unto repentance. They have several excuses to offer. A certain religiousness marks their assemblies, whether they be in the synagogue, the temple, or the home. For they engage in religious subjects even so important a matter as the Lord's "ways," that is to say, the ways of proper conduct that the Lord would have them follow. On the surface they appear to be interested in godly living. But there is a fatal defect in their life and conversation: they have "forsaken the law of [their] God," and so they are not a nation that "did what is right." They have the form of godliness but they deny the power thereof. In fact, on the basis of their ungrounded assumption, they feel they have a right to "demand of [him] righteous judgments." This appears to mean they are demanding of the Lord rewards for their fidelity and punishment of their enemies, on the basis of their own religiosity. In addition to all this they behave as though they were on terms of familiarity with their God: "they find pleasure in drawing near to God." Godly exercises such as prayer, godly helps such as reading the Sacred Scriptures, seem to come easily and naturally to them. For they are sure that they are God's favored people.

Verse 3. Words such as the opening of this verse display in part where the trouble lies. They have fasted but God has not taken their fasting into account; God does not seem to notice that they have achieved a certain measure of merit by their godly exercises. When men blame God for what is befalling them there is something decidedly unwholesome about their attitude.

A brief evaluation of fasting is in order at this point. Fasting was suggested by the Mosaic law only in one instance and that was in the observance of the annual Day of Atonement (Lev. 16:29). In that connection the term used was the same as the one here used as second term: "afflict or humble the person" (*nephesh*). That meant to subdue and control the desire for food by abstaining from the use of it. Occasions where the nation Israel fasted are recorded I Sam. 7:6; Judg. 20:26; I Kings 21:12; Jer. 36:9. In all these instances the fasting seems to have been entirely wholesome and self-imposed. A special type of fast is mentioned as having been engaged in after the Fall of Jerusalem, where the outstanding days of divine judgment were commemorated by the nation, like the capture of the Temple by the Chaldeans. All instances of this sort are mentioned by Zechariah (7:3; 8:19). As Zech. 7:1-6 shows, the value of this observance had become doubtful for the people and so they inquired of the prophet whether these fasts could be abrogated. It appears, then, that fasts were chiefly regarded as "signs of sorrow." As already indicated the fasts under consideration were not wholesome for they had as their object the achievement of a measure of merit. But above all things certain flagrant abuses were tolerated and much in evidence on fast days, as the rest of v. 3 now begins to show.

The prophet follows them to their place of assembly on a fast day. There, off in a corner, two men are not evaluating their own conduct and that of their nation; they are not seeking the face of God in true repentance. They are carrying on a business transaction. Or again, while they are publicly engaged in holy exercises, at home the laborer who is working for them is slaving under heavy burdens and is being oppressed. Heavy social wrong-doings are being tolerated and practiced.

Verse 4. More than that, while they fast to obtain peace with God, as it were, their abstaining from food makes them so irritable that quarrels and squabbles are continually occurring, and that publicly; yes, even to the point of making a public spectacle of it all, by engaging in fisticuffs with their fellow men. There is something telling about the term used in this connection: they hit with "a wicked fist." No thought is given to the high and noble purpose for which the fasts were designed, the expression of sincere sorrow for manifest sins. In other words, it is not with the design of "making [their] voice heard on high."

Verse 5. Now the prophet uses a different approach (for the subject has several sides). The opening words of this verse could perhaps be given in a simpler form like this: "Or is this something you would label as a fast?" He begins to dwell particularly on the idiom of "afflicting one's body," or as some call it: "mortification." The form in which this aspect of the case also expressed itself was "to bow down one's head like a reed." This is what Jesus described in the Sermon on the Mount as making the face "look dismal." The colorful expression used here is "to bow down one's head like a reed." Is that an approach that appeases and gratifies the Almighty? Some made a special show of the physical discomfort to which they were ready to expose themselves by making a kind of "bed for themselves in sackcloth and ashes." *G. A. Smith* caught the spirit of this act when he rendered the term rather well: "they grovel in sackcloth and ashes." With intense sarcasm the prophet rightly calls out: "Will you call *this* a fast?" No one would hesitate to call all this "the Wrong Sort of Fast."

2. The Right Kind of Fast (vv. 6-7)

58:6-7 6. But rather is not this a fast such as I should choose?
Free the person unjustly bound;
loose the bonds of the yoke;
    set the oppressed free,
and rend every yoke.
7. Or is it not this?
    that you share your bread with the hungry,
that you take into your house the wretched refugees?
    When you see a man inadequately clothed,
you provide garments.
    And do not hide yourself from your own flesh?

Verse 6. The opening statement (Is not this a fast?) may be said to look both ways. What has just been described, deserves to be called a true fast. What is about to be described, likewise. In substance what now follows comes under the general classification: He who would obtain mercy from God must first show himself merciful, as *Duhm* already remarked. How very similar all this is to the words of Jesus (Matt. 25:35 ff.) is only too obvious. Jesus' words may rest on our passage. Social suffering, wherever it is found, is to be relieved as much as lies in our power. Steps are to be taken to free those unjustly imprisoned, if to do so is possible. The prophet's contemporaries, the men who were engaging in fasting, were often the ones guilty of their imprisonment. Different kinds of oppressive measures ("the yoke") were being employed. Under a pretense of justice men were being "oppressed." All these things lay in the area of judicial procedure.

Verse 7. Now comes a list of procedures that come under the head of relief of the poor and needy. The list of opportunities of helping the helpless is rather long because oppression by those in power has always been rather a common thing. Under this head comes, not only *giving* bread to the hungry, but "sharing" it. That could involve going half-hungry oneself. "Not what we give but what we share." — In the same spirit "wretched refugees" are not simply given an improvised hovel as shelter against the wind and the cold, but are, if need requires, to be taken into one's own house. Such is the nature of true mercy. Similar help is to be provided for those "inadequately clothed." In no case is a man to evade the issue involved (i.e., to "hide himself from his own flesh"). It would seem to us that this expression covers any human being who may be encountered as being in need, not only our own blood-kin. Not many in our day dare take the broad demand of this passage seriously, even as already in the prophet's day men avoided the broad scope of its demands.

3. Blessings That Will Result from a Proper Fast (vv. 8-9a)

58:8-9a   8. Then shall your light break forth like the dawn,
    and your healing shall develop speedily;
and your integrity shall go before you;
    the glory of the Lord shall be your rearguard.
9a. Then you shall call and the Lord will answer;
    you shall cry out for help and he will say: "Here am I."

Verse 8. The Lord loves to reward them that do his will. Keeping a fast in the manner just described will induce him to bestow blessings. The first of these will be that the "light" of the nation shall break forth like a brilliant dawn. This "light" would seem to be true national prosperity. In addition where the people were suffering from grievous maladies "healing shall develop speedily." Where all progress and prosperity had ground to a halt, now the nation will again begin to march forward led by a trusty guide, "integrity," that is irreproachable conduct as people. Echoes of the march of Israel through the wilderness in the days of Moses seem to ring through this description. The nation will be protected by a rearguard none less than the Lord himself (cf. 52:12). Here some claim that, since the verbs appear in the singular, the prophet is addressing himself to the individual members of the nation. That is hardly likely. The nation is merely being regarded as a unit.

Verse 9a. One further blessing is recounted as enjoyed by the nation, the fine spiritual blessings of being heard when they pray: dialog with God. Where in v. 3 God was charged with being unresponsive when his people looked up to him, now the moment they cry, he will answer them, and remind them that he delights to hear their petitions.

4. The Abuses That Are to Be Put Aside (vv. 9b-10a)

58:9b-10a 9b. If you remove from your midst the yoke,
the pointing with the finger and speaking wickedly
10a. and you offer to the hungry man the bread you crave,
and satisfy the hunger of the afflicted.

Verse 9b. The speaker is back again on the subject of righting social wrongs, of which there were many. He is making a complete appraisal of the ills that are blocking the approach of the nation to God. Every bit of oppressive treatment is to be done away with. So are unkind modes of treatment of the one by the other, like pointing with the finger in a derisive gesture with not a word spoken. Gestures can hurt. And the tongue can hurt, "speaking wickedly" by way of slander. Slander rather than curses and wicked charms appear to be under consideration. Again (v. 10a) the subject of feeding the hungry poor is mentioned by the prophet. To expect God to hear our cries when we will not let the cries of the poor reach our heart is quite unreasonable.

5. A Further Group of Resultant Blessings (vv. 10b-12)

58:10b-12 10b. Then shall your light rise in the darkness, and your gloom shall be as the noonday.
11. And the Lord will guide you continually,
    and he will satisfy your hunger in the sun-parched desert;
and he will make your bones sturdy,
    and you shall be like a well-watered garden,
like a spring whose waters fail not.
12. And your people shall build again your ancient ruins,
    the foundations of many generations shall you raise up again;
and you shall be called "Mender of the Breaches"
    "Restorer of Streets to Dwell in."

Verse 10b. The prophet is back again on the subject of blessings that will come to those who engage in a right fast. It is as though he had a kind of afterthought. He had already dealt with this subject in vv. 8-9a. This coming back and resuming a subject is called by some "palindrome" (i.e., "running over again"). Also for that matter, above (v. 8) he had used the figure of "light" breaking forth. Instead of the darkness of misery that enshrouds the nation the cheerful light of prosperity shall prevail, or, as the parallel statement puts it, there shall be a change from gloom to noonday.

Verse 11. A new series of blessings is listed. The first one is continual guidance by the Lord himself. One seems to catch echoes of Ps. 23 at this point. Besides, in an area where food is liable to fail one ("the sun-parched desert") enough food will be found to completely satisfy hunger. Besides, instead of old and brittle bones in the framework of the nation the Lord will give sturdy bones. Then too the nation shall present a flourishing appearance like a well-watered garden. Even the sources of water-supply will not fail. So by the use of a number of colorful figures the prophet shows how richly the Lord will bless those who engage in the loving service of their fellow men.

Verse 12. It is a foregone conclusion that a disaster will first strike the nation before things can get better. After the disaster, ruins will be left throughout the land. The blessings that will afterward come upon the land can be conceived of in terms of ruins rebuilt and cities and towns restored. True restoration shall finally come about. Once deserted streets shall be lined with houses for people to dwell in. Special honorable titles shall even be given the nation for this work, the first of which has been well rendered as "Breachmender" (*Jerusalem Bible*).

6. A Kindred Reform in the Matter of the Sabbath (vv. 13-14)

58:13-14 13. If you will restrain your foot from the Sabbath,
      from doing your pleasure on my holy day,
and will call the Sabbath a delight,
      and wilt call the holy one of the Lord honorable;
if you honor it so as not to go your own ways,
      so as not to find what pleases you, or to talk idly;
14. then you shall take delight in the Lord
and I will make you to ride in triumph over the
      high places of the earth,
and give you to enjoy the heritage of Jacob, your father;
      for the mouth of the Lord has spoken it.

Verse 13. Some have called the Sabbath the "grandest rite" (*grossartigste Einrichtung*) of the Old Testament religion. It had been established in Mosaic days. It served as a unique confession of the Jews during the Babylonian Captivity. Its importance was reasserted by the prophet, who in this case becomes a teacher of his people. Other prophets reasserted its importance: Jer. 12:19 ff.; Ezek. 20:12 ff.; 22:8, 26. For its proper observance could bring rich blessings upon the nation. A re-evaluation akin to that of fasting could be a very wholesome and helpful cultic rite. Above (56:7) a similar preaching of the importance of the proper observance of the Sabbath had already appeared. It is here not so much a rest-day (Exod. 20:8-11) but a day for sanctified observance. The things that are inculcated as belonging to proper observance are the avoidance of rash profanation of the day. For that is what it means to restrain one's foot from the Sabbath, an act like trampling on a pretty flower-bed. Another thing to be avoided is doing one's own pleasure, i.e., business, on that day, letting thoughts of business transaction claim attention — unholy thoughts on the holy day. This might give rise to the view that this day was one of rigid restraints, whereas quite the opposite ought to be the case — "call the Sabbath a delight." When referring to it, a man was to imply by his whole attitude that it was esteemed as an "honorable" day. In fact any kind of activity that catered to personal and selfish activity was to be shunned; not to "go one's own way," and "not to find what pleases you." In fact the tone of the activities of that day was to be kept at such a high level that all trivial and idle talk was to be avoided. The supreme honorific title applied to the Sabbath is "the holy one of the Lord."

Verse 14. Palindromically (see v. 10a) the prophet returns to the subject of blessings that the Lord will grant to those that seek to please him, whether it be in the area of fasting or Sabbath observance. The first blessing will be that they "shall take delight in the Lord." Their chief good will be to have their fellowship with the Lord a source of deepest pleasure. Practical values will result: men will surmount difficulties and obstacles, or, as is here said: they will "triumph over the high places of the earth." In addition his people shall "enjoy the heritage of Jacob." That is to say, be rewarded by God with enjoyment of peaceful possession of the Promised Land (Gen. 28:13 f.). All this concludes with a solemn promise, almost like an oath: "for the mouth of the Lord has spoken it."

Notes

Verse 2. The expression *qirebhath 'elohim* ("the drawing near of God") can in Hebrew be construed as a subjective or an objective genetive: God's drawing near to man or man's drawing near to God. In the light of the same expression in Ps. 73:28 it would appear that it means "drawing near to God."

Verse 5. The infinitive *lakhoph* ("to bow") is dependant on the verb that follows *tiqra'* ("will you call"). So the infinitive comes first and is in the absolute position (*KS* 341 k).

Verse 7. In the light of what was said above (v. 10b) on the use of the figure called "palindrome" it becomes quite unnecessary to rearrange the verses into the pattern: 9b, 10a, 8, 9a, 10b, 11, 12.

Verse 10a. A rather unusual use of the term *nephesh* appears here, the meaning "appetite." So "your appetite" comes to mean "the bread you crave."

Chapter LIX

D. THE HAND OF THE LORD IS NOT TOO SHORT TO SAVE (Chap. 59)

The material offered in this chapter is so multifarious as to make it difficult to discover a unified theme that could serve as title. However when we reflect upon the beginning of the previous chapter, recalling that the prophet was bidden to lift up his voice and to "spare not," we begin to note that in reality the prophet had not yet made a vehement proclamation in the course of Chap. 58. He first does that in Chap. 59. Then, besides, the prophets are frequently seen to observe the basic rules of good rhetoric, such as employing a meaningful topic sentence at the head of a new chapter. Then we see that the opening statement covers Chap. 59 rather adequately: "The hand of the Lord is not too short to save." Besides, the well-organized unity of the chapter is highlighted. We note at the same time that the chapter may be regarded as the continuation of the one that precedes (58). All of this need not shut our eyes to the fact that the difficulties involved are many and great. Yet on the whole a comparatively clear message emerges as we proceed.

Nor is it easy to find a convenient point in time into which this chapter may be fitted. Yet it seems safe to assume that it fits the needs of the nation as they developed a decade or two after the return from Babylonian Captivity. Does this eliminate the possibility of authorship by Isaiah? Not really. In the providence of God he may have been guided to prepare beforehand materials that stood the returned Israelites in good stead; and may even for that matter have served a purpose for Isaiah's contemporaries, where a situation may have developed much akin to that of post-exilic days. Thus the supposition that Isaiah wrote this chapter is not too far-fetched.

As to the form in which the chapter appears, it must be admitted that there are elements of a "community lament" (*Westermann*). But it must be admitted that a rather ugly description of the moral state of the nation is also drawn. There is also a free and frank confession of sins done in the community. At the same time a hopeful note is sounded of what God, for all that, still proposes to do in behalf of his people.

We doubt very much whether it will yield any profit to regard this chapter as a liturgy. It does not fit well into that category. We are equally dubious about classifying it as a sermon. Elements of a lament and a goodly amount of prophetic instruction must be conceded to make up most of the chapter. Rehabilitation seems to have taken place to quite an extent after the Return. The elements of a settled community, or commonwealth, seem to have been established. The title given by the *RSV* — "Confession of National Wickedness" — elevates one incidental factor to the level of supreme importance. So does the caption of the *Oxford Annotated Bible* with its: "Call to National Repentance."

Quite a diversity of opinion exists also with regard to the issue of the unity of the chapter. Some seem to detect verses that are later additions. We are quite content to be in the company of *Westermann* and *McKenzie* who hold to the "obvious unity" of the material included in this chapter.

One unique factor in this connection is the fact that key terms like "justice" and "righteousness" appear with varying meanings, e.g., sometimes "righteousness," sometimes "salvation," as we shall indicate in the exposition that follows.

1. The Nation's Ungrounded Complaint (vv. 1-2)

59:1-2 1. Lo, the hand of the Lord is not too short to save;
nor his ears too dull to hear;
2. but your iniquities have interposed a barrier between you and
your God,
so that he could not hear.

Verse 1. The prophets of the Lord had prophesied things
in connection with the Restoration of Israel, things which
they were wont to depict in such glowing colors. The
Restoration took place as a result of the decree of Cyrus (II
Chron. 36:22; Ezra 1:1-4). But the hoped-for glories failed
to materialize. It was an age of bitter disappointment. Israel complained. The easiest way out of the dilemma was to
blame the Almighty, charging him with inability to bring
his promises to pass. We seem to hear echoes of 50:1-3.
The first figure ("hand too short") is expressive. Israel has
fallen into deep waters. His arm cannot catch hold on
them. So impatient and short-sighted minds are inclined to
conclude. The second figure is much the same as the first.
Far from the haunts of men a traveler is in distress. He
cries out aloud for help. He cries and keeps on crying. The
Lord seems like one incapable of hearing. Fault is persis-
tently found with the divine administration of things. With
some measure of impatience the prophet rejects the charges
made, crying out "lo" — translated "no" (*Jerusalem Bible*).
The blame must be sought on the other side of the equation.
Not with God! with the *people!*

Verse 2. Putting it as bluntly and unmistakably as possible, the prophet faults Israel. It is no light offense to charge
God for things whose fault lies at our own doorstep. A
"barrier" has been interposed between the nation and God.
For "so that he could not hear" does not imply inability on
God's part but thinks in terms of a moral impossibility. From
being the accuser, the nation suddenly has the role of the
defendant thrust upon her. Sin, not repented of, becomes the
source of many evils.

2. The Unrighteousness Prevailing in Israel (vv. 3-8)

59:3-8 3. For your hands are stained with blood,
     and your fingers with iniquity;
your lips speak lies,
   and your tongues mutter injustice.

4. Nobody makes charges justly,
    no one goes to law honestly.
But each one trusts in nothingness;
    and speaks emptiness.
They conceive violence and bring forth iniquity.
5. Viper's eggs do they hatch out
    and spider's webs do they spin.
He who eats their eggs will die,
    Crush one, and out comes a viper.
6. Their webs cannot be used to make a garment;
    a man cannot wrap himself in what they make.
Their products are works of iniquity,
    and deeds of violence are in their hands.
7. Their feet run to do evil,
    they hurry their pace to shed blood.
Their thoughts are thoughts of wickedness;
    destruction and ruin are found in the roads they build.
8. The way of peace they do not know,
    and there is no justice in their paths.
Tortuous trails they make for themselves;
    he that walks in them will know no peace.

Verse 3. The prophet goes on to specify what grounds he has for the accusation he made in v. 2. His line of argument is easy to follow; he finds that hands, fingers, lips, and tongues are separately chargeable with malfeasance. He cannot be accused of implying that every member of the nation is guilty of each of the misdeeds mentioned. Still he would have us know that the nation shares in this corporate guilt.

Verse 4. At this point some believe that vv. 4-8 is a later addition; v. 3 is thought to be enough of an indictment. But one can easily see that the prophet with good reason brought the heavy hammer of the law down on the conscience of the evil-doers. Therefore vv. 4-8 are not a weak afterthought but a forceful elaboration. Verse 4 takes us into the law-courts, where justice and equity should prevail. But it soon becomes apparent that miscarriage of justice is the order of the day, a rather common subject for Biblical writers (see 1:17, 23; 3:14; 5:7, 23; 10:1, 2; — just to cite instances from the book of Isaiah). But to tell the truth, the verse begins in the courts of law and soon branches out into every walk of life. The rather general idea of "conceiving" and "bringing forth" is to be found also in Job 15:35; Ps. 7:14; Isa. 33:11.

Verse 5. From this point onward the thoughts of the writer do not move forward in a given line. Rather do we find an accumulation of separate, more or less, unrelated examples of the abundance of evil fruits that evil hearts produce. The sum total becomes appalling and overwhelming. The beginning of the verse may have been in the mind of John the Baptist (Matt. 3:7) when he uncovered the hypocrisy of the Pharisees. One item in this connection cannot be entirely cleared up — the "vipers." We seem to be unable to discover what kind of serpents are meant. There are two difficulties: Who *eats* vipers' eggs? and: Vipers *do not* lay eggs. Under the circumstances, we shall have to think in general terms of some type of poisonous serpents known well enough to the prophet's hearers. The general picture of all the mischief these evil-doers hatched out is clear enough.

Verse 6. In a sense this verse is the application of the principle: "By their fruits you shall know them." Nothing substantial comes from a life that has the marks just described. Their works have the quality of spider-webs. As little as you can weave a warm garment out of such material, so little does what these evil-doers produce have any worth or value. Worse than that: some things are produced but they are downright wickedness and deeds of violence.

Verse 7. More still must be made mention of if a complete picture is to be produced. Not only are wicked deeds the order of the day; these persons display *zeal* for the achievement of their fell plots. They approach each new wicked enterprise with zeal and alacrity. All their thoughts pivot about the center of wickedness. How could the net result be anything less than "destruction and ruin." By a clever alliteration the prophet makes this result stand out the more evidently (the Hebrew says: *shodh washebher*). If what life produces may be likened to roadbuilding, these people build elements of destruction and ruin into the very roadway.

From this point on throughout the next verse four separate terms for "road" are used, showing how much prominence the writer attaches to this figure. We all build for ourselves the roads on which we walk through life. Paul quotes this verse in Rom. 3:15-17.

Verse 8. It would seem that "peace" in this context means something like "well-being" and "prosperity." He that walks on the road with these evil-doers will be unable to find peace. For people minded, as these road-builders are, have no room for things like justice as they shape their lives. As their minds are ("tortuous") so are the roads they build for themselves — twisted. For a man living with such associates, the prophet repeats it again: they "will know no peace."

3. The Resultant Moral Confusion (vv. 9-11)

59:9-11 9. That is why justice is so far from us,
　　　　　　　and righteousness does not overtake us.
We wait for light, and lo, there is darkness,
　　and for brightness, but we walk along in gloom.
10. We grope along the wall like blind men;
　　like persons without eyes do we grope.
We stumble at noonday as if it were twilight;
　　among men of lusty strength, we are like dead men.
11. All of us growl as bears,
　　and mourn sadly as doves.
We hope for justice, but there is none,
　　for salvation, but it is far from us.

Verse 9. Given a set of conditions as such depicted in vv. 3-8, moral confusion is bound to follow, even as it is here sketched — "Justice" is far off, that means: justice in the sense of deliverance. The "righteousness" here mentioned seems to refer to the same thing: the restoration of which the prophets spoke in such glowing terms. "Light," as is so often the case in contexts such as this, refers to a bright and happy state of affairs. "Gloom" and "darkness" by way of contrast serve to describe a wretched state.

Verse 10. A few lines may yet be added to the picture of the prevailing moral confusion. Spiritual blindness has taken hold of the nation. People are groping to find a way out of their dilemma. Even in the brightness of the noon-day sun they stumble along. At this point a difficult word occurs, which has led some to assert that the text makes no sense. The word involved may, according to good lexicons (see *Koenig*, Hebr. *Woerterbuch*) be translated as "men of lusty strength." It would then refer to the oppressors of Israel, who feed themselves fat while Israel languishes. The verse as a whole seems to refer back to Deut. 28:29.

Verse 11. This verse also has its difficulties. The growling like bears seems to imply discontent. Mourning like doves seems to point to sad longing (cf. 38:14). Again the terms "justice" and "salvation" appear, pointing to blessings that are being sadly missed. Both terms seem to refer to the restoration of his people that he so often promised them. By stating that these blessings are still "far from" them, the message of the prophet harks back to the beginning of v. 9, and so rings a note of hopelessness.

4. A Frank Confession (vv. 12-15a)

59:12-15a 12. For our transgressions before thee are many; and our sins testify against us.
For our transgressions are with us,
    our iniquities — we are conscious of them;
13. Transgressing, and denying the Lord,
    and turning away from following after our God;
speaking oppression and defection,
    conceiving and uttering from the heart lying words.
14. Justice is pushed into a corner;
    righteousness must stand at a distance.
Truth is made to stumble in the market-place,
    and honesty can find no entrance.
15a. Security is missing;
    and he who avoids evil makes himself a prey.

Verse 12. At this point the sense of sinfulness on the part of the people seems to have been awakened. The dark picture that the prophet had painted seemed to be only too true. He feels that the time is ripe for a frank confession. He is merely expressing what the community feels. The confession is sincere and wholesome. There is no trace of trying to make light of a single charge that the prophet had leveled against them. The various words for sin that may be used are practically all employed. It is admitted that these sins are "many," they "testify" against the nation. They are "with them" like leeches clinging stubbornly to them. Men are "conscious" of the evil they have done.

Verse 13. With deep insight into the real truth of the situation the prophet goes on with the confession, indicating that the sins confessed are not merely a loose accumulation of deeds and practices, but going into the deeper implications of the case traces the nation's guilt and moral confusion to the fact that the proper relation to God has been disturbed ("transgressing, and denying the Lord"). Or to word it differently: "turning away from following after our God." Even the next line presents an element of this sort when it speaks of "defection" which basically means "turning aside." Note that the writer lets the first commandment dominate all the rest. Here the prophet adds a few misdeeds that play into the area of the Second Table of the Law, sins not yet mentioned ("conceiving and uttering from the heart lying words") — a thought uttered by the Savior himself: "Out of the heart proceed wicked thoughts." To claim at this point that vv. 13-15 are a later insertion into the text, fitting very poorly into this context is an approach which fails to do justice to the prophet.

Verses 14, 15a. Though this verse is still a description of a deplorable state of affairs in the land and so rings somewhat the note of lament, it is still primarily a part of a contrite confession. It takes us into the field of jurisprudence and of procedures prevailing in law-courts. In this use of terms "justice and righteousness" are legal terms. These two attributes of upright lawyers and administrators, together with the last two mentioned, "truth and honesty," are all four of them being abused and maltreated, "pushed into a corner," "stand at a distance," "stumble in the market place" and

"find no entrance." To this description of judicial malprac-
tice v. 15a quite naturally attaches itself. For while "security"
is built on the foundation of unimpeachable courts of law,
under the conditions just described, insecurity must prevail
on every hand. And should a man be conscientious about
his behavior and conduct, such a one, instead of gaining the
approval of all right-thinking persons, is instead singled out
for persecution and oppression: in other words, such a one
"makes himself a prey." With a sign the present-day reader
lays this confession aside. It rings only too modern.

5. The Lord's Intervention (vv. 15b-21)

59:15b-21   15b. And the Lord saw it and it displeased him
that there was no justice.
16. And he saw that there was no man,
    and was astounded that there was no man to intervene;
and his own arm brought him victory,
    and his righteousness supported him.
17. He put on righteousness as a breastplate,
    and a helmet of salvation on his head;
and he put on garments of vengeance for clothing;
    and wrapped himself in zeal as a garment.
18. According to men's deeds so will he repay;
    wrath to his enemies, requital to his foes.
To the coastlands he will render requital.
19. And they from the west shall fear the name of the Lord;
    and they from the rising of the sun, his glory.
And he shall come like a pent-up stream,
    which the wind of the Lord drives.
20. And he will come to Zion as Redeemer,
    and to those in Jacob who turn from transgression, says the
    Lord.
21. "And as for me, this is my covenant with them, says the Lord:
My spirit, which is upon you, and my words which I have put
in your mouth, they shall not depart out of your mouth, or out
of the mouth of your children, or out of the mouth of your children's children, says the Lord, from this time forth and even
forevermore."

Verses 15, 16. The two sections just examined — the resultant moral confusion and the frank confession — constituted an ugly enough picture in themselves for any one who

viewed the state of affairs soberly. How much more so would that have been the case if the Lord scrutinized what is going on. The situation constituted an emergency that might seem to drive any right-minded man to step forth to do what could be done to set things right. God's reaction is now described. Humanly speaking many might have been expected to intervene. But on closer inspection there is found to be such a measure of downright indifference that it was enough to astound the Almighty (v. 16a). He feels he must himself enter the arena and use his own arm. At this point "righteousness" would seem to remind us that where men have done everything wrong, He, the impeccable and entirely faultless One, appears on the scene as an adequate deliverer.

Verses 17, 18 pictures how the well-armed warrior prepares himself for the conflict. His righteousness as a breastplate renders him, so to speak, invulnerable. His whole person radiates "salvation," which is likened to his helmet. Since all who oppose his plans and purposes are his enemies and deserve to have his vengeance strike them, he is pictured as clothed in vengeance. Nor can he be thought of as engaging in his task languidly. "Zeal" envelopes him. He works his deliverance wholeheartedly. Nor will he do his work in blind zeal but whatever is inflicted on enemies will have been fully merited. It is a bit difficult in v. 18 to define clearly who are the "enemies" and who the "foes." Perhaps the two terms cover all men who oppose themselves to his laudable purposes. As the term "coastlands" comes into the picture it brings in also the far-distant areas that lie to the west — the Mediterranean shorelands. The Lord appears as *warrior* also in 42:13; 49:24 f.; 52:9.

Verse 19. But enough of that negative side of the picture! Positive results will also be attained. Men who do not wilfully oppose him, when they behold his deeds will be taught a reverent fear of God. Others will see in what he does a display of divine glory. But the Lord himself shall carry on his work like "a pent-up stream, which the wind of the Lord drives." That is to say, with irresistible power.

Verse 20. But for Zion it will appear time and again that his is the attitude of a Redeemer. And *that*, all penitent souls shall experience, i.e., those who "turn from transgression." This is a promise that has met with fulfilment for the Old Testament church many a time and for the Zion of the New Testament times without number. This theophany is reminiscent of the many theophanies recorded in the Scriptures (40:5; 60:1, 2; 66:18, 19, etc.). In Rom. 11:27 Paul gives a Messianic interpretation of the passage.

Verse 21. So vv. 15b-20 offered a description how the Lord finds that he must deal with his enemies that afflict his people. He will be stern but just. But now once again he gives a brief account of how much differently he will deal with his own people and the generations following. All his dealings are covered by the term "covenant," which embodies the mercies that he has time and again promised to them. Here the substance of the covenant is set forth in two terms, "my spirit and . . . my words." The concept spirit is practically synonymous with power, strength in the inner man. This promise met with its richest fulfilment on Pentecost. "Words" here seems to connote cheerful testimony, for it is said, "my words . . . shall not depart out of your mouth." It must be admitted that on the Old Testament level, spirit and words are an unusual combination. But both belong together and amount to spirit-filled testimony. Not only in a momentary fulfilment will this be the case, but as the generations roll on, such testimony will be characteristic of God's people "from this time forth and even forevermore."

Viewed thus v. 21 is not a loose editorial addition or a more or less vague gloss. It closes a unified chapter in an effective way.

Notes

Verse 2. The word for face, *panim*, strangely appears without the article. The versions (*LXX*, *Syriac*, *Targum*) have added a suffix (*his* face), which is probably the correct reading.

Verse 3. The form *nego'alu* is pointed both as *niph'al* and as *pu'al*, take it either way; the sense is about the same.

Verse 4. The infinitives absolute in 4b, describe what is being universally done.

Verse 7. The alliteration in *shodh washebher* is reproduced by Fisher as *Verderben und Sherben*.

Verse 11. Some suggest that the text may be improved by the following sequence: v. 11, 12, 15b, 16-20. Nothing is gained by this approach.

Verse 12. The verb *'anethah* appears in the singular with a plural subject, "sins," as is sometimes the case with feminine nouns which are plurals of abstraction. See *GK* 145 h.

Verse 13. Again the infinitives absolute are used to describe things which are universally done, as above in v. 4. The words for "conceiving and uttering" should perhaps be pointed differently, again as two infinitives absolute (*haro* and *hago*). The verb for "pushed into a corner" *hussagh* is a *hophal* from *sugh*.

Verse 19. The first word "and they shall fear" should be left as it is, coming from *yare'* (to fear). To substitute a form from *ra'ah* (to see) results in a meaningless phrase: to see the name of the Lord.

Chapter LX

E. ZION'S FUTURE GLORY (Chap. 60)

There is a world of difference between this chapter and the preceding. The mood of Chap. 59 is dull and gloomy. The situation involved is depressing. Chapter 60 breathes high hopes. It moves on a high level of poetic beauty and ardor. Great expectations are expressed, involving earthly prosperity and blessings. Or, as some have put it, economic prosperity rather than political are held up in prospect. But there is not a single note of world domination on the part of Israel.

The attitude of the foreign nations to Israel is much improved from what sometimes is sketched by the prophets. Hostility toward Israel is vanished. The nations are bringing their best treasures and are freely laying them at Israel's door. Strange as it may seem, there is no special act of deliverance expected or promised. But it might be said that such an act is presupposed. It strikes us as unnecessarily derogatory when *Duhm*, attempting to catch the spirit of this chapter, suggests that the prophet starts out on a lofty flight, then tires somewhat, and continues limping along in a prosy, repetitious style. Obviously no writer is able to move on the same high level uninterruptedly. We are safe in claiming inspired utterance for the author. The chapter is a literary unit, and bears evidence of careful composition.

No two writers arrive at the same results when they outline the chapter; but it must also be admitted that in the spirit of diversity of approach many outlines come to strikingly similar conclusions.

1. A Summons to Zion to Greet the Light that Is Dawning upon Her (vv. 1-2).

60:1-2 1. Arise, shine forth, for your light has come,
and the glory of the Lord has risen upon you.
2. For, lo, darkness covers the earth,
and a heavy cloud, the people.
But upon you the Lord rises as the sun,
and his glory is being seen upon you.

Verses 1, 2. Imagine the whole earth wrapped in total darkness. Imagine Zion, the Old Testament church, also as being overcome by this darkness of hopelessness. Then of a sudden to her, and her only, the glory of the Lord flares up. It is as though the day had dawned with the abrupt rising characteristic of the Oriental sun. This sun is God's heavenly glory, this glory of which Isaiah speaks so frequently (cf. 6:3; 24:23; 40:5; 58:8), this glory which some have called the central theme of the chapter. The vision goes on to show that the rest of the world is still shrouded in darkness (v. 2): "darkness covers the earth, and a heavy cloud the people." Zion at least can see where she is going. She can arise and be about her tasks. She is the only one to whom the light has come; the "upon you" is in emphatic position in Hebrew. Zion has been singularly favored.

Historically, what has happened? The prophet dramatically pictures the moment when Israel's liberation from Babylonian Captivity takes place, as though it had been one great burst of glory. The "light" spoken of is Israel's salvation, as is also the case in 58:8; 59:9. A salvation which took years and centuries is pictured as a sudden and instantaneous event. Viewed in spiritual perspective, all its glory is concentrated in a flash of glory: "his glory is being seen upon you."

2. What Men Are Bringing to Zion from the West and from the East (vv. 3-9)

60:3-9 3. And nations are coming to your light,
and kings to the brightness that has risen upon you.
4. Look about you on every side and see:
all these have assembled together, they come to you.
Your sons are coming from afar,
and your daughters are being borne on the hip.

5. Then you shall look and be radiant,
    and your heart shall be in awe and expand in joy;
for the wealth of the sea is being directed to you,
    and the rich resources of the Gentiles shall come to you.
6. Camels in throngs shall cover your land;
    young camels from Midian and Ephah;
all those from Sheba shall come;
    and gold and frankincense shall they bring,
and gladly declare the praises of the Lord.
7. All the flocks of Kedar shall be gathered to you,
    the rams of Nebaioth shall minister to you.
They shall come up for acceptance to your altar,
    and I will glorify my glorious house.
8. Who are these that fly like a cloud,
    as doves to their windows?
9. Indeed, the coastlands wait eagerly for me,
    and the ships of Tarshish first in order,
to bring your sons from far,
    together with their silver and gold
for the name of the Lord your God,
    and for the Holy One of Israel;
because he has glorified you.

Verse 3. The picture, or the motion-picture, expands. Zion is, as it were, rubbing her eyes and beginning to take notice. The Lord, or perhaps his prophet, is standing by her side, calling her attention to notable things that appear. People are coming, streaming in from afar, bearing gifts. The light at Zion has attracted them, the only bright spot on the whole earth's horizon. Already it is becoming apparent not only that "nations" are on the march but also "kings."

Verse 4. In fact, they are streaming in "on every side." First they congregate in groups preparatory for setting out to Zion and its holy hill. Among those that come, some are already discernible that are especially dear to her — "your sons and your daughters." By some strange magic they can be distinguished though they are still at a great distance. The little ones among her daughters that cannot travel far are being "borne on the hip," a typical Oriental mode of carrying children. These are children whose parents had apparently been led away into some Western captivity.

Verse 5. Now the prophet, who is addressing Zion, points

out to her what happy emotions are being engendered by this experience. Looking, she becomes "radiant." Her "heart," here the center of the higher emotions, is filled with the awesomeness of the experience and "expands in joy." Lesser values, but still important, are being detected as constituting a notable part of what is being transported, "the wealth of the sea and . . . rich resources of the Gentiles." The first of these may well be wealth gained by commerce, which goes largely by way of the sea. The second includes all the things that the Gentiles call precious. They are bringing their best as tribute to Zion.

Verse 6. Zion's attention is drawn to the areas that lie to the east of her. That being mostly desert land, caravans have come from there, throngs of them. First of all from Midian, where camel-Bedouins are to be found, people who had originally lived mostly to the east of the Gulf of Aqaba. Together with them are people from Ephah, an allied tribe (cf. Gen. 25:4). Now another half-turn and Zion is looking to the south, to the land of Sheba in southern Arabia. This is a land famous for its gold, which in this instance the caravans have brought, together with frankincense. All these are at the same time proclaiming the praises of the Lord, as do, for that matter, all people who have gathered in this large company; for they have all come to know the God of Israel and the knowledge of him has made them glad.

Verse 7. All this economic wealth of one kind or another that has been brought, is further increased by "flocks of Kedar" — an area that lay between Arabia Petraea and Babylonia. So Kedar gave its best. So too Nebaioth, another Arabian tribe descended from Ishmael (Gen. 25:13). This nomadic tribe was famous for its rams. The expression "rams shall minister to you" means: They shall do so by ministering to your worship needs, as it is also explained: "They shall come up for acceptance to your altar." This figure is a bit overbold, for it ascribes to the rams willing self-surrender that they might be offered in sacrifice. A slight allowance may be made for poetic exaggeration. But this much is sure, ample provision shall be made for the cultus at Zion. All these factors will contribute to a glory in worship that shall be impressive.

Verse 8. At this point Zion, now wide awake, begins to review the situation, turning back again to the West. A moving cloud seems to be sweeping toward the Holy City. In reality these are ships with their white sails swiftly moving toward Zion. In the distance they are not at once clearly discernible. The Lord has been speaking and continues to speak putting the question that is uppermost in Zion's mind: "What are these . . .?" By a somewhat attractive figure the sails of the ships give the impression of doves flying to the windows of their cotes.

Verse 9. At first glance there appears to be a sort of break in the continuity of the thought, especially as far as the first line of this verse is concerned. Having turned first to the East and then to the West, then back again to the East, it is as though the speaker (the prophet speaking in God's name) remembered that he had not yet indicated what it was that was causing such a stir among people the world over. He supplies the answer: "Indeed, the coastlands wait earnestly for me." It is the natural hunger on the part of man for contact with the living God. The "coastlands" refers to all lands adjacent to the Mediterranean. Now, on with the marvelous story of people and things streaming in toward Zion! Leading the way across the Mediterranean come the "ships of Tarshish," the technical name for the largest sea-going vessels (Tarshish is the name for smelteries in Spain). These huge vessels bring a double cargo — precious metals and a human cargo, scattered "sons" from far countries, children once dragged into captivity by some now unknown foe. At this point the author feels impelled to ascribe the whole movement in all its parts to Yahweh, the God of Israel and the only God, giving a theocentric motivation. This great stir and commotion is in the last analysis being caused "for the name of the Lord," Israel's God. It tends to the glorification of the "Holy One of Israel." Incidentally it is also tended to glorify the holy people of God.

3. The Attitude of Those Who Are Coming to Zion (vv. 10-12)

60:10-12 10. Foreigners shall build your walls,
and even kings shall minister to you.
For in my wrath I smote you,
but in my favor I have had mercy upon you.
11. And your gates shall stand open continually;
neither by day nor by night shall they be shut;
that men may bring in to you the wealth of the Gentiles,
with their kings led in procession.
12. For the nation and the kingdom that shall not serve you shall
perish,
and those nations shall be utterly destroyed.

Verse 10. According to vv. 3-9 nations with gifts were flocking in from every side. Now in vv. 10-12 the Lord probes deeper to determine the motives behind their coming. Attention first centers upon the Holy City. Building projects are under way here. On closer inspection it appears that the builders are foreigners. Traditionally foreigners were hostile to Israel; they were the ones who had destroyed the walls and the city. Now they are seen to be builders of the walls themselves. Even more than that, kings are offering their services in any need that Israel may have. 49:23 has this thought in slightly different form. If it be asked what is the moving force behind this friendly attitude on the part of so many toward Israel? the answer is, the Lord's attitude has undergone a change in reference to his people. He had been angry, and justly so, over against his ancient people. They on their part have now changed. So he can again show mercy to them (cf. 54:7). Again the Lord is the sole author of all good that may come to Israel.

Verse 11. The highly poetic and picturesque description of the nation's state and condition is again resumed. It is true, the emphasis is rather strong on material blessings. But they too come from God and are tokens of his good will.

Here the stress is on such a stream of "wealth of the Gentiles" that the caretakers do not even get an opportunity to shut the gates through which they flow in: "neither by day nor by night shall they be shut." But note! there is a break in the sequence of what enters. There appears a lone figure, a king, yea, several kings, who apparently, have willingly joined the procession to bring themselves and their goods as token of fealty to the Great King. It appears that they both come willingly and are also led with marks of great respect by those who are in charge of the proceedings.

Verse 12. Repeatedly, like in v. 10b, an effort is being made to trace some of these surprising happenings back to their ultimate cause. One principle — and to tell the truth — it is one that strikes a momentary harsh and solemn note, may profitably be regarded at this point. It is this: when God begins his dealings with the nations, trying to induce them to appropriate Israel's blessings to themselves, issues are dead in earnest. The nations that refuse to serve the King of kings "shall be utterly destroyed." This verse is not a misfit. It is not uncalled for. It does not grow out of a misunderstanding of the tone of the passage. It is a warning side-light and a wholesome one. As *von Orelli* rightly says: "A nation's welfare depends on whether it submits to Israel," or to Israel's God.

4. The Attitude toward Worship Displayed by Those Who Are Coming to Zion (vv. 13-17)

60:13-17 13. The glory of Lebanon shall come to you,
the cypress, the ash, and the fir tree;
to make the place of my sanctuary beautiful,
to glorify the place where my feet stand.
14. And the sons of those who oppressed you, shall come, bowing reverently,
and all that despised you will do worship at the soles of your feet.
And men shall call you the city of the Lord,
the Zion of the Holy One of Israel.
15. Instead of being forsaken and hated, and no one passing through,

I shall make you an eternal excellency,
a joy for generation after generation.
16. You shall suck the milk of the nations,
 even the breast of kings shall you suck.
And you shall know that I, the Lord, am your Savior,
 and that your Redeemer is the Mighty One of Jacob.
17. Instead of bronze I shall bring gold,
 and instead of iron I shall bring silver;
and instead of wood, bronze; and instead of stones, iron.
I shall make peace your government,
and righteousness your ruler.

Verse 13. Beginning with v. 13 the sanctuary at Zion becomes the center of interest. The very structure shall be glorious. The attitude of all men, natives and foreigners, shall be one of deep reverence when they think in terms of Israel's sanctuary. The most beautiful and costly building materials will not only be used for the structure, but shall even come of their own volition, to use a figure of hyperbole. "The glory of Lebanon" refers, of course, to the famous cedars. It must be conceded that when cedars are mentioned and also cypress, ash and fir trees, these could be thought of as planted in the temple area as objects of beauty. Perhaps it is best to allow for both possibilities, construction materials and ornamental trees. They all have conspired, as it were, to make a beautiful sanctuary, or "to glorify the place where [his] feet stand." For surely the Lord may be thought of as having taken his stand in his own sanctuary to be present among his people (cf. also Ezek. 43:7).

Verse 14. Now for a quick glance at an assembled worship-congregation. The strange sight presents itself that the very children of those who once were Israel's oppressors have come of their own volition, "bowing reverently," even, for that matter, the very ones that once despised lowly Israel "will do worship at the soles of [her] feet." The superior character of Israel's religion will be generally admitted. In reverent prostration in the sanctuary they will come to lie at the feet of Israelite worshippers and think it an honor to be allowed to worship there. The holy city itself shall be called by holy titles such as "the city of the Lord, the Zion of the Holy One of Israel."

Verse 15. There was a time when Zion was "forsaken and hated and no one passing through." No one sought contact with the forsaken city. That shall no longer be the case. Instead she shall be "an eternal excellency." That is to say, an object of pride, and joy for generation after generation.

Verse 16. This verse may be briefly summed up in a statement like this: In that glorious future that is to come only the best will be good enough for Israel. Zion is likened to a nursing child, who feeds on the choicest products of the nations. Only persons of highest station shall be deemed good enough for such services for Israel. Israel shall then be aware of the fact that it is the Lord who has wrought this changed attitude on the part of those who once were hostile to her. The names here given to the Lord as a result seem to stand in a sort of climax: Savior, Redeemer, Mighty One of Jacob (cf. 49:26b).

Verse 17. In the first three lines of the verse it may well be that two passages from past history are in the background of the thinking of the speaker. One, I Kings 10:14, 17, 22, 27, which reminds us of the abundance of precious metals which was available for Israel in Solomon's reign. So shall it be once again. The second, I Kings 14:26 f., telling of the humiliation that came on Rehoboam after the sack of Jerusalem by the Egyptians, how bronze shields were placed in the sanctuary as substitutes for the golden shields that had made the temple glorious in Solomon's day. Our passage indicates that the reverse of that humiliating experience shall come in the latter days. So the precious building materials shall take the place of the inferior. Of course, all this cannot take place before the glorious consummation of all things. Then in the last two lines of v. 17 the subject changes: The effective and perfect administration of government is stated in terms rich and glorious but which almost defy definition and paraphrase. "Peace" shall occupy the chief seat in government and so wars will become impossible; and in domestic rule all will be well for "righteousness" shall sit enthroned.

5. The Higher Level of Life in Evidence in the New Jerusalem (vv. 18-22)

60:18-22 18. Violence shall no more be heard of in your land, nor destruction and ruin in your borders.
You shall call your walls Salvation,
    and your gates Praise.
19. The sun shall be no more your light by day,
    neither for brightness shall the moon give light to you.
But the Lord will be your everlasting light,
    and your God your glory.
20. Your sun shall no more go down,
    neither shall your moon wane;
for the Lord will be your everlasting light
    and your days of mourning shall be ended.
21. Your people shall all be righteous;
    forever shall they possess the land,
the shoot of my planting, the work of my hands.
    that I might be glorified.
22. The least one shall become a clan,
    and the smallest one a mighty nation
I, the Lord, will hasten it in due time.

Verse 18. The drawing of the highly idealized picture of Zion is coming to a close. Every city from days of old has had its criminal element. This Holy City shall be an exception. There would usually be those who wrought "ruin and destruction" in periodic outbreaks of "violence." Not so in the Jerusalem which shall come down from heaven. Two notable component parts shall be in evidence in this city, "Salvation" and "Praise." The first of these may be thought of as a protective wall, the second, as her sturdy protective gates. Here it may be pointed out that strangely the most important factor is still missing — the Messiah. He, it may be said now already, will come to the fore prominently in the next chapter.

Verse 19. Sun and moon shall no longer function as they once did, for a higher source of better light shall replace them, a point which is taken in hand by John in Revelation

21:23 and 22:5. This first part of the verse might have been rendered: You will no longer stand in need of a sun and a moon. For the Lord will condescend to be their light and shall be dwelling perpetually in their midst. Even so wonderful a thing as physical light shall be replaced by an unspeakably more marvelous light.

Verse 20. As the chapter draws to a close, the feature that stood out prominently at the opening of it again comes to the forefront — light. Perhaps more particularly what light stands for in the Old Testament. As *McKenzie* remarks, it symbolizes two things: first the presence of God and secondly salvation. We may well think of these two at this point. This verse emphasizes that there will be no fluctuation of this true light of God's presence, and the city shall glow, as it were, with salvation. To this may be added that light frequently symbolizes joy. Therefore "your days of mourning shall be ended."

Verse 21. But a city is unthinkable without inhabitants. A weighty declaration about the inhabitants is actually given: "Your people shall all be righteous." This thought is not foreign to Isaiah (cf. 53:11). This does not so much appear as a claim of irreproachable conduct, as a declaration that a righteousness above reproach is to be imputed to them through faith, as 53:11 also signifies. In addition, long-time possession of the Land of Promise is alluded to in the words: "Forever shall they possess the land," reminding ourselves that more precisely the Hebrew word "forever" does not necessarily mean "eternity," but time long drawn out (German: *unabsehbar*). This would be in fulfillment of the promise already given to Abraham (Gen. 17:8). The two phrases "the shoot of my planting" and "the work of my hands" modify the noun "people." The people will be like a tender fruitful shoot planted with loving care by the Lord, and giving promise of much fruit. Besides they will not be people strong in self-sufficiency, but strong because the Lord gave them strength: his hands made them sturdy.

Verse 22. Wholesome growth in numbers is also promised,

unimportant individuals growing into clans and mighty nations. All these are objectives which the Lord has set for himself and will achieve in due time. Great as this promise is, it may be questioned whether this is the climax of climaxes, as had been claimed. Quite appropriately Isa. 9:7 may be compared, as another significant pronouncement, attributing all success to the Lord.

Notes

Verse 1. We have translated the verb *zarach* as a perfect in English, well aware of the fact that some commentators regard this as a prophetic perfect, i.e., a future. The issue is as long as it is broad; the event is regarded as having practically occurred.

Verse 2. We regard the article before "darkness" as a clear case of dittography. Cf. *KS* 297 b.

Verse 14. "Bowing reverently" is really an infinitive construct used as an infinitive absolute; cf. *KS* 221.

Chapter LXI

F. GOOD NEWS FOR ZION (Chap. 61)

Note the progression of thought in the last few chapters. Chapter 58, "Abuses that retarded the recovery of post-exilic Israel"; the fault of slow recovery lay at Israel's door. Chapter 59, "The hand of the Lord is not shortened to save;" his power is omnipotent. Chapter 60, "Zion's future glory"; heavy emphasis on the glories of the Messianic age. There is an obvious forward movement of thought. But Chap. 60 left one thought completely out of the picture — the Great Messianic King. Chapter 61 brings Him on the scene. He introduces himself and his work in the monologue with which this chapter opens.

But it has long been a matter of controversy whether the speaker at the beginning of Chap. 61 is the *prophet* (Isaiah — some would have it to be a so-called Deutero-Isaiah, some even a so-called Trito-Isaiah) or whether he is the *Messiah* himself, in the light of Luke 4:18, 19. We take the position that the latter is the case, the Messiah is speaking; and that for the following reasons. In describing the work that he is commissioned to perform, the speaker assigns such significant achievements to himself that one might well question whether any human being could ever venture to deal with and accomplish issues so grand and wonderful. In the mouth of the Savior the tasks he claims as assigned to him are most fitting and proper. Here the word applies: "Man never spoke like this man." If the prophet had claimed such notable achievements for himself he might well have been charged with having a most highly exaggerated opinion of himself.

Add to this the obvious fact that in the second half of his book Isaiah keeps himself modestly in the background; then this sudden outburst of self-assertion strikes us as most inappropriate.

We grant that in the position we take we are identifying the speaker with the Suffering Servant of 42:1, etc. We must also freely admit that our chapter does not mention the term "Servant," but preconceived notions on our part of the terms to be used will hardly settle the issue. Though *G. A. Smith* boldly claims that it is a minor question to whom this passage was intended to first apply, we can hardly concur. We regard the passage as directly Messianic prophecy, and must believe all other attempts to meet with fulfillment to be inadequate. So after Zion's future glory has been dealt with, the chapter following presents him who brings this glory to pass. Or to word the case somewhat differently, as some do, Chap. 60 speaks more of the outward glory of Zion, Chap. 61, of her inner glory. With equal propriety it may be claimed that the chapter is a message of joy for the grieving community of Israel (*Fischer*). Therefore it is quite uncalled for to combine Chaps. 60 and 62, and to let 61 follow. It may also be noted in passing that in Chaps. 60-62 five passages are quoted verbatim from 40-55.

1. The Messenger Who Brings the Good News (vv. 1-3)

61:1-3 1. The spirit of the Lord God is upon me,
because the Lord has anointed me to bring good tidings
to the meek,
he has sent me to bind up the brokenhearted,
 to proclaim liberty to the captives,
  and an opening to them that are bound;
2. to proclaim a year for the Lord to show favor,
 and a day of vengeance for our God;
to comfort all who mourn;
3. to appoint for them that mourn in Zion —
 to give them a headdress instead of ashes,
the oil of gladness instead of mourning,
 a mantle of praise for a spirit of despair;
and they shall be called oaks of righteousness,
 a planting of the Lord with which he may glorify himself.

Verse 1. At once one recalls that the Servant of the Lord was described (42:1) as having as characteristic mark equipment with the spirit of God for the doing of his work. For the Messiah from the line of David this also holds true (11: 2). The importance of being equipped with the spirit for doing the work of the Lord is also attested by Zech. 7:12; I Sam. 16:14-23; II Sam. 23:1-7. How proper it is to be thus equipped appears also from the fact that the spirit of the Lord and power are synonymous. Even the preposition "upon" is significant; it conveys the thought that the spirit comes down from on high. This spirit then is the strong taproot of the life and being of the one who speaks. And when was there ever a one so uniquely endowed with the spirit as to warrant his bearing the name of the "Christ" — the truly anointed one. The significant word "anointed" at once appears in the text to indicate that there was a significant act of imparting the spirit, a procedure found quite commonly when men were inducted in office. Here, since most of the activities described have to do with the *word*, it is the *prophetic* office for which the spirit is given.

In an ecstatic gush of eloquent terms the multiplicity of tasks that fall to the Messiah's lot are recited, all of them flowing from, and growing out of, the fact that a generous anointing has been bestowed upon him. Six infinitives and numerous objects of these infinitives are employed. The first gracious activity that he engages in, is really the sum of them all and in a sense the source of all that follow. It is found in the words "to bring good tidings to the meek." This stands first in emphatic position here, even as it stands last in emphatic position in Christ's statement to John (Matt. 11:5). Of all the gracious work that the Savior did, none was more important and more all-inclusive than this. The expression at the same time defines who will be the recipients of this good news — "the meek," i.e., persons whose hearts have been rendered receptive by God's prevenient grace. Such will humbly accept rebuke and gladly embrace God's gracious pardon, and so will be saved. The many forms that this grace will take are now unfolded in detail, showing how many-sided God's grace is.

There follows a list of grievous disabilities that men may become afflicted with. They fall into the categories of the physical, the mental, and the spiritual ills that afflict the children of men and from which they cannot deliver themselves. The second kind of relief listed, for which this Deliverer is sent, is "to bind up the brokenhearted." This can include all that are deeply grieved over their sins as well as those that have been all but crushed by life's adversities. To this is to be added "to proclaim liberty to the captives." In this class may be found those who are socially bound by some unhappy lot. In the background of this statement there would seem to be a reference to Lev. 25:10, in which passage the fiftieth year of jubilee was to be proclaimed throughout the land. Some render the next achievement listed as being "the opening of the prison," in which case wholesale deliverance of criminals can hardly be thought of. Our rendering, omitting the word "prison," is somewhat broader and does imply deliverance of the innocent.

Verse 2. The next two lines may be approached in two different ways: first, the contrast between "year" and "day" may be stressed as of a ratio, as it were, between 365 and 1, asserting then that "favor" will be superabundant, but "vengeance" will be exacted only as much as must be. A similar ratio to stress God's loving kindness is employed in Exod. 20:5, 6. Secondly, there is the approach which construes the term "vengeance" positively as "restoration of wholeness." Aside from the fact that there clearly are cases where the Hebrew root carries the meaning of "punitive justice" and the further fact that God's vengeance is not tainted by a spirit of unwholesome retribution, we consider the familiar meaning of the term as too well established to allow for the precarious meaning of "vengeance." These two lines then, taken together, make a strong declaration of grace abounding.

The last line asserts as one of the expressed objectives of

the Messiah's mission "to comfort all who mourn." This is a common thought in Trito-Isaiah, so called, over against Deutero-Isaiah, so called, who never expresses this thought. Using New Testament terminology, this comfort consists chiefly in the forgiveness of sins, though this message bestows other forms of comfort as well.

Verse 3. Dwelling still on what this speaker can give to mourners, the speaker asserts that his mission includes relief for those who "mourn in Zion," most welcome relief. The wholesome mourning over sins is under consideration here. Another possibility is available: the words may be translated ". . . those who mourn *over* Zion." Then the consolation available deals with the persons who grieve over the sins and shortcomings of the people of God. But that there is much need of administering comfort to men is obvious. Not only is the cause for grief overcome, but a positive ground for joy is offered — here: "a headdress in place of ashes." In place of a disconsolate mourner seated on an ash-heap, strewing ashes on his head, there is the figure of a man arranging a gaily-colored turban as his headdress for a festive occasion. The contrast tells its own story. Wholesome joy is made available. An analogous figure — instead of a mourning-robe, perhaps sackcloth, a man is given a precious and fragrant perfume to cover himself with. The same thought virtually is expressed by a new figure to which the speaker quickly turns: there is to be given "a mantle of praise for a spirit of despair." This illustration grows out of the fact that a man may, so to speak, wrap himself in his moods, like the mood of "despair." Instead, grace is given to him to be enshrouded completely in "praise." The favors bestowed by the speaker make him so joyful that his mouth overflows with vocal praise.

Summing all up, those men, to whom God's grace has been administered, now stand, to borrow a figure from the vegetable kingdom, as sturdy trees abounding in healthy foliage. These persons are "sturdy living symbols of salvation" (cf. Ps. 1:1; 92:13 f.). Carrying the figure a bit farther, they may be thought of as trees planted by the care of the Lord's hands, trees which he has set out for the glory of his name. Whether the tree-name should be translated as "oaks" or as "terebinths" is not yet determined with finality.

2. A Nation Fulfilling Its Destiny by Accepting This Good News (vv. 4-7)

61:4-7 4. Men shall build places long lying waste,
desolate spots where ancients lived of old.
They shall build anew waste cities,
　　places that had been desolate for generations.
5. Strangers shall stand alert and pasture your flocks;
　　aliens shall be your plowmen and vinedressers.
6. But you shall be called priests of the Lord,
　　and men shall refer to you as ministers of our God.
You shall consume the wealth of the nations,
　　and of their riches you shall boast.
7. Instead of your shame you shall be doubly rewarded,
　　and instead of your ignominy you shall exult
　　　　over what was their good fortune.
Therefore in their territory you shall possess a double lot.

Verse 4. The healing quality of the good news just described shall transform those who accept it. No individual, no nation can fulfill its destiny without accepting this news. That means among other things that in such a nation there will be no waste places, no desolate spots. Even areas that had once been inhabited but had long become proverbial ruins. In fact now everything flourishes. Even cities that had been so completely destroyed, so that it seemed useless to attempt to rebuild them are to be restored, no matter how long they have lain in ruins. The reference does not seem to be to the restoration from Babylonian-Captivity ruins; rather it tells how successful every national enterprise will be.

Verse 5. Going into another area of national life, the relation of the nation to those who were traditionally hostile, the acceptance of the good news will there too make all things new. Not that the former enemies will have been subdued or conquered but they shall have come in a spirit of cheerful cooperation so as to take the more menial tasks off Israel's

hands that the people whom God had once chosen as his
own might more effectively fulfill its spiritual destiny. The
strangers shall pasture Israel's flocks, as it were, and aliens
shall take care of the field work. All this is highly idealized
description which the world will not see until there be a new
heaven and a new earth, where all is right. But the gospel
carries such vast potential, if room is only made for it.

Verse 6. The spiritual aspect of the glorious state which is
here held in prospect is now detailed more fully. God had
already said to Moses that Israel was destined to be "a kingdom of priests" (cf. Exod. 19:6). What the priesthood was
for Israel, that Israel shall be to the nations. To what extent
the "spiritual Israel" of the New Testament times may be involved is almost impossible to say, but in some very positive
way Israelites will be "ministers of our God." Besides, in a
way that we can hardly conceive of, God's people will live
off the wealth of the nations, and Israel shall be able to boast
of the riches of the Gentiles as though they were their own.
The highly idealized level of thought must be maintained
and nothing cheap or mercenary dare be imputed to this description, as *Volz* does when he claims that all that is said
at this point is not exactly a "refreshing portrayal of Israel's
faith in its specific election."

Verse 7. The somewhat exuberant tone of the description
of the nation fulfilling its destiny continues. Whereas in
times past Israel was often but lightly esteemed among the
nations, her good name is to be fully restored. Israel shall
reap where others have sowed.

3. God's Hand in Evidence (vv. 8-9)

61:8-9   8. For I the Lord love righteousness,
                I hate robbery with transgression;
and I will faithfully give them their recompense,
    and an everlasting covenant will I make with them.
9. Their descendants shall be known among the nations,
    and their offspring in the midst of the peoples;
All who see them shall acknowledge them,
    for they are descendants whom the Lord has blessed.

Verse 8. The Lord now speaks. The marvelous transformation of the nation is traced back to him and particularly to the fact that he loves and upholds fair play, here referred to as "righteousness." When Israel was led away into Captivity by the Babylonians there was many a deed of wanton cruelty laid upon them. They were deprived of their rights as normal human beings. This is here called "robbery with transgression." And this the Lord who watches over, and rules, all nations, hates and is now in the present restoration and in the coming future perfect restoration going to uphold righteousness and vindicate his people. In this sense he will "faithfully give them their recompense." So he will vindicate his "covenant" which he made with his people at Mt. Sinai (cf. 59:21).

Verse 9. Since one aspect of a thriving and successful people is numerous population the prophet develops this aspect of the case, tracing the development of this blessing to the Lord. The descendants of Israel instead of being ill-spoken of among the nations, shall "be known," i.e., "famous" (*Jerusalem Bible*). Men will "acknowledge," not slight them. Men will recognize that the blessing of the Lord is upon them. In the light of the rest of the Scriptures, this cannot be thought of apart from their acceptance of the Christ and his salvation.

4. The Nation's Joy at the Lord's Blessing (vv. 10-11)

61:10-11 10. I will greatly rejoice in the Lord,
  my soul shall be glad in my God;
for he has clad me with garments of salvation,
  he has covered me with the robe of righteousness,
as a bridegroom decks himself with the fine care of a priest,
  as a bride decks herself for her wedding.
11. For as the earth puts forth its sprouts,
  and as a garden makes the things sown in it to shoot forth,
so the Lord God will make salvation and praise
  to sprout before all the nations.

Verse 10. After describing a choice number of great blessings that the Lord will bestow upon his penitent people, the text breaks forth into an exclamation of joy over the rich grace of God — which is most appropriate and fits most aptly into the text at this point. The speaker is the nation, or Zion. Summing up all the great things promised and using a new figure, the nation describes itself as having been clad by God in spendid robes ("garments of salvation, robe of righteousness") using terms that are reserved in the New Testament for gifts like justification through faith. A very choice figure to cover the case is used by reference to how bridegroom and bride adorn themselves for their wedding day. This, on the part of the bridegroom, is likened to the meticulous care employed by the priest as he equips himself for the performance of his sacred duties (cf. Exod. 29:5-9; Zech. 3: 4 f.). For the high point of joy marked by the wedding day, see Ps. 19:5; Jer. 33:11; Rev. 21:2; Matt. 22:2.

Verse 11. Since the Lord often seems to accomplish work in a tardy fashion, the prophet indicates that a powerful drive and forward surge marks the Lord's carrying out of his purposes. It is like the thrust in the realm of nature when in spring vegetation bursts into bud and flower. Just as certainly as spring brings the impulse for growth and sprouting, just so surely will the Lord's plans for Israel eventuate. In other words "salvation" and "praise" for this salvation will burst into evidence in the sight of all the nations.

Notes

Verse 1. "Lord God" is slightly inaccurate as translation, since *Yahweh* is regularly translated as Lord and so is *'adhonay*. But "Lord Lord" is most objectionable. Therefore "Lord God."

Verse 2. To gain the thought "*a* year" the Hebrew inserts a *le* — sign of the dative. Cf. *KS* 280 n. The last three words of the verse could be prefixed to v. 3, chiefly for the sake of a better Hebrew verse, as the *Kittel* text has it.

Verse 3. Having said "appoint," after a pause the writer resumes with "to give" as a more appropriate verb. In the expressions "oil of gladness" and "mantle of praise" we have two genetives of apposition (oil which *is* gladness, etc.). Cf. *KS* 337 l.

Verse 8. The expression "robbery with transgression" constitutes a sort of superlative, and is more easily understood than "robbery for burnt offering" (KJ). The *Septuagint* also reads "with transgression" a reading for which the text allows.

Verse 10. The verb "decks himself with the fine care of a priest" is a rare and colorful one, and should be retained, although *yakhin* for *yekhahhen* would be permissible.

Chapter LXII

G. THE IMPENDING SALVATION (Chap. 62)

No two writers come up with the same theme and parts on these chapters. Still a measure of unity prevails. An undertone runs through these chapters — God has great things in store for his people; of that he assures and reassures Israel unwaveringly. We might say that in this chapter in particular God testifies to Israel that her salvation is near at hand, long as he may have waited and seemingly delayed.

It does not matter too much into whose mouth the words of this chapter are laid. In days of old they were ascribed to the Lord. Most more recent writers claim that the Prophet is speaking. Even so they attribute the message to the Lord. Ascribing this message directly to the Lord appeals to us most, especially from v. 6 onward. If then at times the Lord would be speaking of himself in the third person, that is a rather common feature in Old Testament prophecy.

If some writers fail to find the deeper things of the prophetic message, things like forgiveness; that is not a serious defect, if a defect at all. Discourse, also prophetic discourse, may with full propriety touch upon the Lord's gifts at their various levels. Pardon and forgiveness are implied even if not expressly treated. To make it obvious that rich prophetic words cannot soon be caught in their richness of meaning by way of outlines, we mention a few titles chosen for this chapter more or less at random. "The Prophet Cries Out for Zion's Salvation" (*Fischer*). "The Messianic People" (*Muilenburg*). "The Progressive Achievement of Jerusalem's Salvation (*Delitzsch*).

1. The Lord's Objectives for His People (vv. 1-5)

62:1-5 1. For Zion's sake I dare not remain inactive,
and for Jerusalem's sake I dare not merely look on;

until her vindication comes forth as a light,
  and her salvation as a torch that burns.
2. And nations shall see your vindication,
  and all kings your glory;
and you shall be called by a new name,
  which the mouth of the Lord shall designate.
3. And you shall be a glorious crown in the Lord's hand,
  and a royal diadem on the palm of your God's hand.
4. You shall not any more be called Forsaken [Hebrew: *Azubah*]
  and your land shall not any more be referred to as Desolate
    [Hebrew: *Shemamah*]
But you shall be called My Delight is in her [Hebrew: *Hephzibah*]
  and your land shall be termed Married [Hebrew: *Beulah*]
For the Lord delights in you,
  and your land shall be [so to speak] married.
5. For as a young man marries [i.e., takes possession of] a virgin,
  so shall your children take possession of you.
and as a bridegroom rejoices over a bride
  so shall your God rejoice over you.

Verse 1. We seem to catch the spirit of the passage better
by translating the verb in the imperfect by the use of the
auxiliary "dare." The Lord, for reasons of his own, has apparently been doing nothing by way of furthering Israel's
interests. He dare not continue thus any longer without
creating the impression among the neighboring nations that
he has lost interest in his people. Zion and Jerusalem represent a major investment of his. It is true that God often is
deliberate in his actions. His "mills grind slowly" as the
proverb has it. In his own wise providence the time has come
for her vindication (Hebrew: "righteousness") to be made
manifest. The Lord must furnish visible proof that Israel's
interests are a matter of deep concern. As the Oriental dawn
flashes across the skies suddenly so must Israel's vindication.
Or it must shine forth "as a torch that burns." Isaiah foresaw
a time when Israel's situation would demand divine interfer-
ence. Such periods, demanding intervention come repeatedly, even down to the very end when the consummation of
all things comes to pass.

Verse 2. Such vindication, whether it pertains to Israel of
old, the Old Testament community, or whether it is done in

behalf of the spiritual Israel, will often be done in a most manifest fashion, demonstrating that the Lord has not forgotten his people. "Nations shall see it," "kings shall behold [Israel's] glory." The new situation that shall therefore develop will be so radically different that the old vocabulary will no longer be adequate. A new name must be employed to cover the new situation. That name is not given at this point. It is merely indicated that it will be a matter of divine choice. There are other passages in Scripture in which the new-name concept appears (1:26; Jer. 3:17; 33:16; Ezek. 48:35). These various new names do not rule out one another. They merely supplement each other. Each new name expresses some valid aspect of God's dealings with his people. Even the New Testament deals with this concept (cf. Rev. 2:17; 3:12).

Verse 3. How utterly glorious the people of God shall be when God remakes them is indicated by another attractive illustration: Israel shall be "a glorious crown." This illustration locates the crown in this case, not upon the King's *head*, but in his hand. The Lord is inspecting it, looking at it from different angles. The work of his hands contributes to his glory. The parallel statement says the same thing in other words, but it still has the "diadem" in the Lord's hands.

Verse 4. A few samplings are given of such new names of the Lord's choice. Two negatives are rejected as no longer appropriate. Two positives are added by way of showing how many possibilities are involved. The negatives are "Forsaken" and "Desolate." These two names could once have been aptly applied to her in the days of her Captivity. God abandoned his people and they became desolate. Here he asserts that this shall no more be the case. The word speaks in terms of the ultimate achievement, and is conditioned by Israel's attitude, whether she remains humble and penitent, and continues to hold her faith in the Lord. This verse thinks in terms of an ideal situation.

Two positive names follow. "My Delight is in her" and "Married." God's people shall adopt such an attitude that it provokes his strong delight. He cannot cast her off but will remain married to her. Her infidelity in that case shall not be in evidence: the Lord will not cast her off. That these names are not fantastic or unnatural appears from the fact that the mother of Jehoshaphat bore the name Azubah, i.e., For- saken (I Kings 22:42), and Manasseh's mother bore the name Hephzibah, i.e., My Delight is in her (II Kings 21:1). All this is reminiscent of 54:1-8 and deals with the same general picture largely taken from married life. In the last line we have inserted the brackets "so to speak," because strictly speaking one cannot be married to a *land*. Still the figure conveys the thought of being strongly attached, and loyal to the people and their land.

Verse 5. To ward off the inferior approach that attributes the Lord's kindly dealings with Israel to a sense merely of obligation, this verse shows the deeper and kindly feelings that are involved. The analogy used as illustration is the warm love displayed by a young man to a virgin. A use of words comes into the picture at this point, because of the double meaning of the Hebrew *ba'al*, which means "marry" and also "take possession of" or "become master of." So the incongruous picture of sons marrying a mother does not ap- pear in the original, but rather the children will fulfill their obligation in the family. To this the second half of the verse adds the note of joy and warm satisfaction that marks the new relation to the Lord, as deep and true as that of a faithful bridegroom. This is the brief sketch of the objectives which God has in store for his own.

2. God to Be Implored to Carry Out His Objectives (vv. 6-7)

62:6-7 6. Upon your walls, O Jerusalem,
                I have appointed watchmen.
All the day and all the night
   they shall never keep silence.
They are the ones that keep reminding the Lord:
   Take no rest.

7. Do not grant him any rest,
   until he establishes Jerusalem
   and makes it famous in the earth.

Verse 6. A new theme is introduced, Watchmen on the walls continually at prayer. Ordinarily watchmen were a safety-device, appointed to guard a city from a surprise attack. Here that feature does not appear. The sole duty of these watchers is "to continue instant in prayer" that Jerusalem be established inwardly and outwardly. It is somewhat difficult to determine the identity of these watchers. Looking at Dan. 4:18 and I Kings 22:19 we might incline to the opinion that they are angels. Since intercessory prayer is not elsewhere noted as a particular function of angels we may prefer to think that the watchmen are faithful prophets of the Lord. Perhaps since nothing definite is asserted on the subject we may hold the opinion that they are merely a means for having faithful and earnest prayer to be made. For "day and night they shall never keep silence." There is something anthropomorphic about it all: if enough persistent prayer is offered God will yield and finally see to it that Jerusalem is re-established. 49:16 presents an analogous point of view from the divine angle. They go too far who deduce from this verse that at the time these words were spoken the walls of Jerusalem had already been rebuilt. Watchmen could stand and offer prayer on ruins of walls. One thing certainly is not intended by these words, that is to create the impression that man could be more concerned about the welfare of the people of God than he himself.

Verse 7. God honors believing prayer and heeds the intercession of his children. The objective of the prayer in this case is twofold: first to "establish Jerusalem," that is to give her inner strength and stability; secondly, "to make her famous in the earth." That means to give her rank and standing in the world, that is commensurate with her spiritual importance. The watchmen are not to rest till both are achieved.

3. Successful Achievement Guaranteed on God's Part (vv. 8-9)

62:8-9 8. The Lord has sworn by his right hand,
and by his powerful arm:
"I will not again give your grain
to be food for your enemies,
and foreigners shall not drink your wine
for which you have toiled.
9. For they who have gathered your grain shall eat it,
and shall praise the Lord.
and they who have gathered your vintage shall drink it,
in my holy courts."

Verse 8. And they that prayed faithfully will not have prayed in vain. The Lord assures them of this by an oath. The oath is not required to make the Lord's word valid, but it is added by the Lord because of the frailty of man's faith (cf. also 45:23; 54:9). The "right" and "powerful arm" are mentioned as the customary gesture accompanying the oath. Surprisingly that which is guaranteed by the oath is more economic in character than spiritual — grain guaranteed and wine. But this must be understood in the light of Deut. 28:30-33, where one of the most striking marks of divine displeasure is the disappointing experience of having one man sow the field and have the enemy come along and reap it. So this word does nothing more than to guaranty tokens of divine approval. These blessings are not exhaustively listed, but are mentioned by way of significant examples. The "foreigners" could be the Persian officials, or even the Samaritans and Edomites.

Verse 9. The success that the Lord will achieve is recounted in some measure of detail. In the second half of the verse the "gathering" of the vintage obviously includes the treading out of the same. Onc last touch reminds Israel of her high festivals where food and drink were partaken of in the "holy courts" of the Lord, a memorable and happy custom.

4. Israel Invited to Make God's Salvation Her Own (vv. 10-12)

62:10-12 10. Go out, go out through the gates;
prepare the way for the people.
Grade up, grade up the highway;
  clear it of stones;
lift high an ensign over the people.
11. Behold, the Lord has made a proclamation
  to the ends of the earth:
"Tell the inhabitants of Zion:
  'Lo, your salvation is coming
lo, his reward is with him
  and his recompence before him.' "
12. And men shall call them The Holy People,
  the Redeemed of the Lord.
And you shall be called "Sought Out" [Hebrew: *derushah*]
  a city not forsaken.

Verse 10. Repeated imperatives are common to our prophet — "Go out, go out" (see 40:11; 51:9, 17; 52:1; 57: 14; 65:1). It would seem that this word addresses itself to those who have stayed behind in some of the cities of the Captivity. Here the theme of the wonderful road comes into the picture again (cf. 35:8-10). Add the figure of the ensign, as a sign of invitation for people to congregate. Echoes of Chap. 40 are beginning to be heard.

Verse 11. To make the invitation to join the assembly and go up to the holy city more attractive this verse points to a proclamation emanating from the Lord to the effect that he himself is coming along this road accompanied by those who have heeded his call. They are his "reward" and "his recompense," whom he has won for himself in bitter conflict (cf. 40:10 again).

Verse 12. Another look is cast in the direction of these people who are coming along this road. They are called by an old name, the "holy people" or also "the redeemed of the Lord." They would seem to indicate that more than *Zion's* children are involved, or even the Jews of the Dispersion; but all the children of God. All the saints of God down to the day of the final judgment are envisioned in this scene. Here comes one last backward glance: She who was forsaken and abandoned (the ideal Holy City) will be an object of interest and concern. She shall no longer be forsaken.

Notes

Verse 1. An attractive suggestion has been offered inasmuch as this verse speaks of the "coming forth of the *light*," the suggestion that this chapter was spoken originally on the occasion of the festival of booths (cf. John 7:2 and 8:12), where Jesus referred to himself as "the light of the world." The only difficulty is that the abundant use of lights, which was actually associated with this festival at Christ's time hardly seems to have been in use at as early a date as this.

The difficulty of v. 5, where "children take possession" of their parents, which we have interpreted to mean that they fulfill their obligation to their parents, may be met in another way. Many take the consonants *bnykh* and by inserting a new set of vowels arrive at the meaning "thy builders" or singular "thy builder." Especially the singular would in this case refer to the Lord, who, as the builder of Israel takes charge of her.

Verse 6. *Hammazkirim* presents an interesting case of how a participle takes up the line of thought. Cf. *KS* 411 e.

Verse 7. *RSV* makes a rather genial move, quite in keeping with the thought, when it takes the object "Jerusalem" and moves it up into the preceding clause.

Verse 10. The *min* before *'ebhen* conveys the idea that not a single stone remains. *KS* 406 p.

Chapter LXIII

H. ESCHATOLOGICAL UNDERTONES (Chaps. 63—65)

Things are rather loosely woven together in these last chapters of Isaiah. Strict logic does not control the situation. It is difficult to find a unit title for our chapter. Therefore we have chosen the one we have, which could serve as title for the rest of the book. Then we can observe, too, how v. 1-6 may be worked into the picture: they offer a part and aspect of eschatological truth that belongs to a well-rounded treatment of the subject — judgment on God's unrelenting foes. This is an aspect of divine righteousness. For righteousness is a two-sided attribute of God. It deals with blessings and rewards for the faithful servants of the Lord, as well as with stern judgment of the ungodly. These verses (1-6) have been much misunderstood, as though they savored of a spirit of hatred and revenge. Fact of the matter is that the Edomites, wherever they appear on the scene in Scripture are cruelly spiteful and vindictive. Edom's hatred of Israel is proverbial (cf. 34:5-15; Obad. 20 ff.; Ezek. 35:1-15, to list but a few). Therefore we even hesitate to use captions like "The Terrible Treader of the Winepress" (*Volz*), for it could imply that the Almighty had lost control of his anger. These verses involve a stern truth but a wholesome one. Besides, too much stress should not be put on an incidental feature of the passage. It may be said that it speaks not in terms of punishment so much as in terms, seemingly, of destruction. What the passage wants to assert is that God has his foes totally under control, even when they are doing their worst. So *Muilenburg* has spoken well when he classifies the passage as "belonging to the literature of eschatological judgment." He also speaks well when he says that the characteristic style and terminology of the *lament* prevails, although it might be safer to say that some undertones of lament appear in vv. 1-6.

Duhm and those of his class speak in a derogatory fashion of the chapter, insisting that it begins on a high level, but gradually subsides and drops into a weak repetitiousness or even a repulsive overornamentation (*unangenehm wirkender Redeputz*).

Care also should be taken in regard to the Messianic interpretations of vv. 1-6. They look upon the passage as a description of the blood-stained Messiah in his great passion. But the blood is that of his enemies. Furthermore it is a punitive task that is here ascribed to the figure appearing on the scene. There is nothing redemptive about it.

This passage furthermore is very difficult to pin-point as to time and circumstances under which it was first spoken or written. 64:10-12 would seem to point to a date after the fall of Jerusalem and the destruction of the Temple. In that case, according to our conviction that one Isaiah wrote the whole book, Isaiah, the son of Amoz, these chapters would involve prophetic prediction, divinely inspired, revealing what would come to pass and preparing Israel for it.

1. God's Program Includes Vengeance on Edom and on All Like Her (vv. 1-6)

63:1-6 1. Who is this that comes from Edom
in crimson garments from Bozrah,
he is glorious in his apparel,
   striding along erect in the abundance of his strength?
"It is I who dictate righteousness,
   who abound in ability to help."
2. Why this redness on your garments,
   why are your garments like those of one
      who treads in the wine-press?
3. "I have trodden the wine-press alone
   and no one of the nations was with me.
And I trod them down in my anger
   and stamped them down in my wrath;
and their life-blood spurted on my garments;
   and my whole garment became sullied.

4. For a day of vengeance is in my heart,
   and my year of redemption has come.
5. And I looked out,
   but there was no one who could assist;
   and I was amazed,
   but there was no one to stand by me.
So my own arm gave me help,
   and my wrath supported me.
6. And I stamped on nations in my anger,
   and I made them drunk in my wrath,
and let their lifeblood run down to the ground."

Verse 1. The prophet suddenly beholds a majestic figure striding toward him, coming from the direction of the people of Edom. He cannot identify the person approaching. It seems significant that he is definitely coming from the neighboring nation to the south, as though he had had dealings with them. The prophet seems to have suspicions that the one approaching did some punitive work on this southern brother-nation. Another notable feature about this figure, a feature that at first glance stands out, is his blood-bespattered appearance. The garments, though rich and costly, may almost be said to have been dipped in blood — a scene bound to startle any beholder. So the prophet utters a rhetorical question, which expresses his eagerness to identify the one coming on. A third striking thing about the on-coming one is that he strides along like one who has achieved a notable bit of success. His whole bearing emanates success and victory. We must fall back on the totality of Scripture to determine why Edom (also often called the land of Seir) and its one-time capital Bozrah, should be singled out as apparently deserving of exceptional punitive treatment. Then it appears that whenever Edom appears over against Israel, Edom's attitude is one of unyielding, never changing hostility. So Edom is guilty in itself and at the same time a symbol of unreasonable hostility on the part of surrounding nations.

Though the one who answers the question put in v. 1 is not formally introduced as speaking, it is immediately obvious that the one about whom the question was raised is the one who himself supplies the answer. As the chapter progresses it becomes increasingly clear that the one who gives the answer is the Lord. For the present one particular attribute of the Lord is to be stressed. He is the one who "dictates righteousness," that is, speaks with authority, that righteousness may be upheld and prevail throughout the world, an assignment that includes that they who have been wronged are assured of their rights. In this respect he "abounds in ability to help." So this particular function of his might be stated thus: I direct the affairs of history.

As to the *form* in which this section (vv. 1-6) appears, there is hardly enough evidence to arrive at the conclusion that these verses fall into the category of "the sentry's question." The following passages, though they employ the rhetorical question form, may hardly be used as evidence to the contrary (cf. Song of Sol. 3:6; 6:10; 8:5; also Ps. 24:8 and 10).

Verse 2. One item still intrigues the prophet, though he may have been able to form a shrewd guess as to source of the blood that so abundantly stains the garments of the victor, yet to make sure that he is construing rightly what he sees, he addresses him in a clear question: "Why this redness on your garments?" The only one to whom he can liken the man in stained garments is the man who treads the wine-press, an occupation which invariably caused spattering with the blood of the grape. So he puts a direct question: "Why this redness . . . ?" At least twice in the Old Testament, the same figure is employed (Joel 3:13; Lam. 1:15).

Verse 3. The One in the wine-press was the Lord — he accepts the figure as quite proper, but adds a second feature that should be noted: He was "alone." In times past when judgment-work was to be done, especially on Israel, the Lord used other nations (e.g., Egypt, I Kings 14:25 or Assyria, Isa. 10:5 f.). In this case none appear to have been available. So he stresses that works of judgment are, in the last analysis, *his own*. He is the only one qualified for such acts of supreme importance. God's "anger" is a wholesome indignation. It was the motivating force behind his actions. If the account given and the figures used are a bit on the gruesome side, they are no doubt meant to be, for judgment is gruesome business. In reference to Israel the same figure was employed in 59:16.

Verse 4. In the nature of the case, times for such action on God's part are so essential that one may very properly assert that the Lord has a "day of vengeance." These days are in his heart, that is to say, are part and parcel of his plans. But never are features like this stressed unduly. God's vengeance may be said to be held in balance by his "redemption," which also will have its day, and, in fact, in a ratio of 365 to 1 over against vengeance. For where sin abounds, grace does the more abound. This aspect of the case keeps everything wholesome.

Verse 5. This verse describes the Lord very anthropomorphically. He may be likened to a man who is confronted by a tremendous task. In such a situation one almost instinctively looks for men to stand by him. It would seem that his is so clearcut a case of being in the right that there would be many who would flock to his banner to help support a just cause. But there is no volunteer. The Lord must fall back on his own resources exclusively, and these resources are entirely adequate: "(his) arm gave him help and (his) wrath supported him."

Verse 6. In keeping with the approach of the beginning of the chapter a type of description is used that strikes the present-day reader of Scripture as unnecessarily gory and cruel: "nations" thrown into a vat, nations made drunk with the wine of God's wrath, blood running to the ground in streams from the veins of the guilty nations. Not that Hebrew writers, in a spirit of revenge, gloated over the disastrous fate of their adversaries. But judgment is grim business. "Be not deceived, God is not mocked." So ends the description of the Lord's Judgment on Edom. But the words may not be limited to Edom. For all that display the spirit of Edom will suffer the vengeance that befalls Edom.

2. A Comprehensive Prayer for Those Days in the Spirit of 62:6 (63:7-64:11)

It is impossible to tell whether this prayer stems from Jerusalem or Babylon. Consequently the dating of it is fraught with difficulties. From our point of view it was divinely provided for evil days which are ominously beginning to threaten on the horizon. As prayer it has a character all its own. It has a heaven-storming aspect. It is impetuous. It devises motive after motive why God should hear and come to the redemption of his people. It also has a generous element of the lament in it.

a. Recalling a Glorious Past (vv. 7-9)

63:7-9 7. I will call to mind the deeds of loving kindness of the Lord;
the praiseworthy acts of the Lord;
according to all that the Lord has done for us,
and the great goodness to the house of Israel,
which he granted to them according to his mercy
and according to the multitude of his lovingkindnesses.
8. For he said: "Surely they are my people;
they are children who will not prove faithless,"
and he became their Deliverer.
9. In all their affliction he was afflicted,
and the angel of his presence helped them.
In his love and in his pity he delivered them;
he took them up and carried them
all the days of old.

Verse 7. Looking at the contents of 63:7–64:11 *Delitzsch* says rather aptly that it is "a prayer of thanksgiving, penitence, and petition." Looking more at the outward form, *Westermann* calls it "a community lament." It has much of the flavor of Pss. 77, 78, 105, 135, and 136. Some things are reminiscent of Deut. 32. First the whole of the history of the people of God is reviewed (vv. 7-10), then the history of patriarchal times (vv. 11-14). Verses 7-10 carries echoes

of 1:2-3. The beginning of v. 7 is translated literally by
KJ: "I will mention the lovingkindnesses of the Lord."
Clearly we would say "deeds of lovingkindness" ("steadfast love" here fails to catch the intimacy of the expression).
In recalling God's deeds of mercy the writer's heart grows
warm and his tongue eloquent; thoughts gush forth. For certainly Israel's history was a catalogue of merciful dealings
on God's part. Seldom has the pen of man captured this
truth more fittingly. Especially the deep taproot of his dealings is detected: goodness, mercy and lovingkindnesses.

Verse 8. This verse seems to clash with reality. For Israel
was most stubborn and continually going counter to the revealed will of the Lord. None knew that better than the
Lord himself. Surely, the Lord was not blindly deceiving
himself. Again we have a striking instance of anthropomorphic speech. Love might induce a man to put the better construction on all that the nation does. Strict reasoning is not
going to fathom the depth of divine love. This verse surely
says with emphasis that the Lord's favors toward the nation
were utterly undeserved. The last statement of the verse
may be a reference to what God did in Egypt and the wilderness.

Verse 9. There is something touching about the manner
in which the Lord identified himself with his people's sufferings. This is divine empathy at its best. This empathy led
him to delegate a notable messenger of his to appear on the
scene again and again, "the angel of his presence," about
whom the generation of the Exodus seems to have had an
understanding which went farther than our speculations can
reach. God appears to have manifested his presence through
this uncreated angel in a kind of incarnation before the
Great Incarnation. He was the nation's best gift from God.
His mere presence was a deliverance (Exod. 33:15). Where
the prophet might have dwelled on the Lord's *obligation*
toward the people whom he has chosen for his own, he goes
deeper into the warm and affectionate heart of God and ascribes all "to his love and pity." He concludes this approach

by likening God to a compassionate father who "took them up" when they fell down and "carried them" till they forgot their hurt. Here we find ourselves almost at the point of the New Testament approach of "our Father." The prophet, and the nation speaking after him, ascribe this attitude not merely to a few exceptional cases but to "all the days of old." What a delightful way of recalling the past!

b. Why Divine Mercies Then and Not Now (vv. 10-14)

63:10-14 10. But they on their part rebelled,
and grieved his holy Spirit.
So he turned to be their enemy;
he even fought against them.
11. Then his people remembered the ancient days [Moses]
Where is he that brought us from the sea
the shepherd of his flock?
Where is he that put in the midst of them
his holy Spirit?
12. causing his glorious arm to go
at the right hand of Moses;
dividing the waters before them,
to make for himself an eternal name;
13. leading them through the depths?
As the horse in the plain, they did not stumble.
14. As the cattle go down into the broad valley
so the Spirit of the Lord always gave them rest.
Thus didst thou lead thy people.

Verse 10. Now comes the stern reality: Israel did not measure up to specifications. Stubborn-hearted and stiff-necked, they manifestly and again and again rebelled. To this stubborn rebellion the divine reaction was that he "was grieved." Divine love was wounded. The Holy Spirit enters into the picture unexpectedly. He does not often appear in the Old Testament. He is more than a potency; more than an attribute. For he can be grieved, which is a purely personal reaction. His reaction was more than a mood of temporary displeasure. When Israel rebels something of extreme value and importance has been despised and rejected, causing a powerful and stern reaction: "he turned to be their enemy; he even fought against them." This is strong reaction. When he fought against them that was apparently done through the world powers: God gave Israel over into the hands of nations greater and mightier than themselves and let them be subjugated. It is an evil thing to have God go on record as hostile to a nation, Egypt and Assyria being their lords. All this is recorded against a background of sincere repentance.

Verse 11. The several textual problems involved in this verse will be discussed at the end of the chapter in the *Notes*. — Affliction set Israel thinking time and again. In the good sense of the word they remembered "the good old times." This was wholesome because it was done penitently. The Mosaic Age in particular seemed to be rich in comfort and instruction. Here is the essence of this section, Israel crying out: Why help *then* and not *now?* The figure used to exemplify this is that of a shepherd (Moses) leading his flock (Israel) into a situation of grave peril but coming out — (shepherd and flock) unscathed. The reference to God's "putting in the midst of them his holy Spirit" would seem to be an allusion to the incident in Num. 11:24-30. For though it was not the whole nation which at the time was indued with the gift, still it was a rare token of good will designed to help a nation get its bearings. A further overall description of the deliverance at the Red Sea follows in v. 12.

Verse 12. The figure employed is unusual but clear. As Moses, the shepherd, strode along, there was, visible to the eye of those who believed in the Lord, the "glorious arm [51:9; 52:10; 62:8] [going] at the right hand of Moses." God's arm is here personified. Without the use of a rhetorical figure, it might be said that God's omnipotent power at every point sustained and upheld Moses, enabling him to do the impossible, like dividing the waters (Exod. 14-16) before the nation and removing an insuperable barrier to their escape This act enhanced the "name," i.e., the renown and reputation of the Lord (cf. 55:13; 56:5; 64:2) with an undying lustre.

Verse 13. Moses led Israel; God's right arm led Moses; God directed his arm. Under this effective triple leadership the nation passed safely through "the depths." Though the waters of the Red Sea, as far as we know were comparatively shallow, in the situation immediately confronting Israel these waters constituted an insurmountable obstacle. Two rather effective illustrations help the reader to catch the point. The first — the "horse in the plain." A level plain, encumbered by no obstacle, makes the passage of the horse swift and safe. Such was the nature of the passage of the sea by the nation. To sum it up, the words are added: "they did not stumble." In other words, an insuperable obstacle becomes not even the least bit of an obstacle.

Verse 14. Abandoning the illustration of smooth passage, a pastoral figure is now employed. Cattle having grazed on a hillside drift down easily into the valley, where water may be found and thirst slaked. But the chief point at issue is that time and again, where there might have been distress and trouble, God's Spirit "gave them rest." Many are the instances where God thus helped his people in what might have been grievous trouble. "Thus didst thou lead thy people." A kind of nostalgia pervades the account. But the point as a whole still is: Why *then* and not now?

c. Bitter Lament over Present Misfortunes (vv. 15-19a)

63:15-19a 15. Look down from heaven and see,
          from thy holy and glorious habitation.
Where is thy zeal and thy might?
   The yearning of thy heart and thy compassion
      toward me are withheld.
16. For thou art our father —
   for Abraham does not know us
and Israel does not recognize us.
   But thou, O Lord, art our father,
      Our Redeemer from of old is thy name.
17. Why then didst thou make us stray from thy ways?

> Why didst thou harden our heart,
> so that we no longer fear thee?
> Return for the sake of thy servants, the tribes of thy inheritance.
> 18. Thy holy people possessed thy sanctuary
> but a little while.
> Our enemies had trodden it under foot.
> 19. We have become like those over whom
> thou hadst never ruled,
> like those over whom thy name was not called.

Verse 15. The lament proper does not commence before v. 17. Verse 15 is a plea to be heard by the Almighty. Heaven apparently is far removed and the Lord seems to have withdrawn himself into his glorious habitation. He appears indeed to have become, in the language of *Luther*, a *"deus absconditus"* (a hidden God). He appears to take no note of what is going on against his children. This criticism is implied, not spoken. Another failing on God's part would seem to be that where once he manifested "zeal" in the interest of his people, this all seems to have vanished. "Zeal" coupled with "might" made an invincible combination. But both are not in evidence. The change might be said to have taken place deep in the heart of God. Compassion for Israel once dwelt there. Now all this seems to be cancelled out. The whole verse constitutes a restrained and reverent complaint.

Verse 16. The Jews felt that the patriarchs were interested in the welfare of their descendants, as Luke 16:22 would seem to indicate. Yet that interest would have its limitations and be inadequate for an emergency like that of the present. Now nothing less than the paternal concern of the Lord himself could cope with the present. That this was not a meaningless concept appears from the words, "thou art our father." But that again seems to avail little. Somehow the blessing of this truth has become momentarily submerged. For reasons not specifically known, the Lord has cancelled out the "yearning of [his] heart and [his] compassion" as the close of v. 15 states the case. But here is a truth that the prophet and the nation will not let go, "thou, O Lord, art our father." And for emergencies this means "our Redeemer." There is no doubt about it; *that* prayer reached its mark.

Verse 17. The commentator's last word on this verse has not yet been spoken. It is doubly difficult if the first verb is taken as a straight causative, which it actually is, and then translated: "thou didst make us stray" rather than to soften it a bit: "thou didst let us stray." The first of these two seems to agree best with the Hebrew idiom. Then the blame for present misfortunes is squarely laid at God's door, both the straying from his ways and the hardening of the nation's heart. If God is sole ruler of the lives of men then some conclusion such as this could be reached. But that involves God in the sin of man, in fact, makes God a sinner. Men no longer fear God, but God made their hearts hard so that they could no longer fear him. A nation in distress, trying to solve the problem of sin and evil in this world has recourse to such logic but sin is illogical. So we consider this as an example of how man can get entangled in his thoughts, especially on the question, How does, or did, sin and evil originate? As for the rest of this verse, we believe that its difficulties are best solved by a translation like this: "Be kind again for the sake of thy servants, the tribes of thy inheritance." It is in this way that God is to "return" or turn back, or, become as he once was. As basis for this attitude the prophet in this lament adduces the fact that there still are some within the "tribes of [God's] inheritance" who are "servants" of the Lord. He is urged to take these into consideration.

For a fuller treatment of this involved subject the reader may consult our *Exposition of Isaiah*, *Vol. 1*, Excursus, p. 142 f.

Verse 18. Another motive is set forth why God should hear and help his people. The destruction of the temple is reckoned with as an inevitable consequence and is stated, as in the whole of the second half of the book, as having practically happened. The specific point that is involved is that the temple of Solomon functioned as national shrine but a "little while." Then the enemy took and destroyed the city and "trod it under foot." This is a unique plea for being heard. It practically amounts to this: the Lord appears as unable to maintain himself for any length of time. The Lord's honor is at stake.

Verse 19a. From the point of view of looking into the future and seeing the great calamity that is inevitably to come, still another motive is provided, to press home upon the Lord. The space of time where the Lord effectively upheld his people was comparatively so short that is hardly seemed worth considering. It is as though he "had never ruled" over his people. It was so short a space of time that it was as though God's ownership of his people had never actually been realized. For to call one's name over a people is a way of pronouncing that he is their lord, and is strongly committed to see to their welfare. If God does not help, he will appear remiss in looking after the welfare of his people.

Note: we are taking v. 19b together with Chap. 64.

Notes

Verse 1. "In crimson garments" in Hebrew reads: "crimson of garments," the latter word being an accusative of specification — "crimson in respect to garments." *KS* 336 h.

Verse 3. We have translated *darakhti* as a perfect: "I have trodden." The possibility of translating it as a prophetic perfect, that is, as a future, must be allowed for. In that case the time of the whole section (vv. 1-6) would point to the future.

The difficult form *'egh'aleti* points to either a piel or a hiphil. One seems to fit as well as the other. See *GK* 53 p.

Verse 6. *'ashakkerim* ("I have made them drunk") appears to some to be overbold language to use in reference to the Lord. Quite a few manuscripts read *b* instead of *k*, arriving at the meaning: "I have broken them." The burden of evidence appears to be on the form: "I have made them drunk."

Verse 7. *RSV* has also at this point translated *chesedh* as "steadfast love." We believe "loving kindness" in this case deserves the preference.

Verse 9. We prefer to follow the ancient Hebrew tradition where the Masoretes read *lo* ("to him") rather than *lo'* ("not"), although both were pronounced the same. Much further evidence points in the same direction.

Verse 11. Everything falls into place in the first line of this verse if the last word (*'ammo*) is regarded as subject "his people remembered. . . ." The word "Moses" is inserted parenthetically indicating what area of history it was that the people remembered. That approach eliminates the need of changing the noun *'ammo* to *'abhdo* ("his servant"). The second line of this verse may be treated as follows: strike the final *m* of the second word (a clear case of dittography). Then the object of this participle is the word "shepherd" which is not plural construct ("shepherds of") but a singular construct to be written with a final *h*. This makes Moses the one whom the Lord brought up from the sea, and the one in whose midst he put his holy Spirit. This entire approach eliminates the need of many changes of the text.

Verse 14. The verb "he gave them rest" (*tenichennu*) is apparently a frequentative imperfect and therefore suggests the insertion of "always" in the translation (*KS* 157).

Verse 15. The word "might" in Hebrew appears as a plural of potency (*KS* 262 b) and amounts to a kind of superlative.

Verse 18. To try to make this verse interrogative, as *Koenig* does in his Kommentar, results in a very artificial construction.

Chapter LXIV

d. Prayer for Divine Intervention (63:19b—64:11)

This prayer began at 63:15. It has rightly been termed one of the prayer-gems of the Old Testament. With Chap. 64 it begins to narrow down to a prayer for divine intervention, or that the Lord might display his might and power in behalf of his people to the world. *Fischer* has rather aptly called this chapter a cry to Yahweh that he might bestir himself.

It has long been a question whether 63:19 should be included with Chap. 64 as its beginning or as the conclusion (according to the Hebrew notation of verses) of Chap. 63. Following the lead of the *Septuagint* and the *Vulgate* it seems best to let the verse constitute the beginning of a new chapter (64).

They who see a third major author of the book in Chaps. 56-66, find some difficulty in dating the chapter, but advance the suggestion that it may be assigned to some date between 538-520 B.C.

(1) The Prayer in Brief (vv. 1-3)

64:1-3 1. O that thou wouldest rend the heavens and come down,
O that the mountains might sway at thy presence —
2. as fire ignites brushwood,
as fire makes water to seethe —
to make thy name known to thy adversaries,
and that the nations might tremble at thy presence;
3. when thou dost work awe-inspiring deeds,
which we had not anticipated;
O that thou mightest come down,
and that the mountains might sway at thy presence.

Verse 1. It appears in the time set for this prayer as though the Lord had withdrawn himself from men, had spread out an impenetrable garment across the heavens and hidden himself from his children. This prayer makes bold to beseech God to tear this covering wide open and appear in the rift of the clouds. The Sinai event (Exod. 19), as the first major appearance of this sort of which we have record, is thought of as basic for future interventions. One outstanding element in all passages where the same thought occurs is "fire" (cf. Ps. 144:5; Deut. 32:22; Judg. 5:4-5; Mic. 1:3-4; Hab. 1:4-6; 3:3-15; Ps. 18:8-16. So much so is this the case that the New Testament has summed it up effectively in the statement (Heb. 12:29): "Our God is a consuming fire." As remarked above, God is asked to appear in the clouds, then to go one step further, and "come down." A notable side-effect, visible to all eyes when the theophany occurs will be that the mountains would sway at his presence. A huge created object, like a mountain trembles, so to speak, with awe and reverence in the awesome presence of its Creator.

Verse 2. The first two lines of this verse are parenthetical. They indicate that something must happen to the earthly, material object when brought into the presence of the Holy God. Fire kindled near dry brushwood ignites and consumes quickly. Hot fire brought into touch with water makes it to seethe. As natural as these results are, so it is the normal thing for mountains to "quake" (*KJV*). But far more striking is the effect of the divine theophany on those who thought they might confront the Almighty without fear. Were they to be confronted by the Lord, they would come to know the "name" of the Lord, that is, become aware of his superlative majesty. But if such awareness did not result they still would be strongly affected, overcome by fear and trembling. That the prayer is not dealing with things purely imaginary and fantastic is made plain by the fact that at the close of each of these first three verses appears the phrase "at thy presence." God can and will intervene in a drastic, visible appearance.

Verse 3. This is the continuation of one long sentence of

prayer. The theophany of God is now thought of as part of a general plan, namely the doing of "awe-inspiring deeds," which the nation had not thought possible ("awe-inspiring" is better than "terrible.") For such an event as God appearing on the scene is too overwhelming for words. Since the essence of what is asked for in this prayer is that God might actually intervene in person, this item is repeated at this point. The last two lines are therefore not an idle repetition, or a copyist's mistake.

(2) God, the Sole Author of Effective Intervention (vv. 4-5a)

64:4-5a 4. From of old, men have not heard,
     nor has the ear perceived,
nor has the eye seen a God besides thee,
  who does deeds for those who wait for him.
5a. O that thou wouldest come to meet him,
  who rejoices to work righteousness,
those who remember thee in thy ways.

Verse 4. The uniqueness of the God of Israel is under consideration. He alone has been known to appear unto the help of his people. Go back as far as the annals of history or the memory of man can carry you, there is nothing on record like deeds which the Lord has done. There are involved here not idle appearances to no effect or purpose. The Lord has "[done] deeds for those who wait for him." That is the uniqueness of Israel's tradition that their God has manifested himself in visible and audible fashion. His people did not call upon him in vain. Therefore they make bold to call upon him again.

Verse 5a. It fits better with the spirit of this word to take it to be a direct prayer and petition: the wish introduced, v. 1, by "O that" is still going on, only now God's appearance is thought of as encounter with man rather than as simple manifestation to the eye and the ear. However man must also meet certain conditions if the appearance of God is to become a reality. God's favors are not bestowed according to deserts but man must be receptive for what God has to give.

Such receptivity is measured by the attitude that a man "rejoices to work righteousness," that is to say, he remembers what God has taught his people to do and delights in doing it. But always God is in the background of such a man's thinking, or man remembers him in his ways. He cannot forget how God has helped and is sure that he will help again.

(3) Renewed Misgivings and Hopelessness (vv. 5b-7)

64:5b-7 5b. Lo, thou wast angry and we kept on sinning;
in our sins we have been a long while,
and shall we be saved?
6. And we have all of us become like an unclean person,
and all our righteous deeds like filthy rags.
We all fade like a leaf;
and our iniquities bear us away like the wind.
7. And there is not a one that calls upon thy name,
bestirring himself to take hold of thee.
For thou hast hid thy face from us,
and thou hast delivered us into the power of our sins.

Verse 5b. Prayer has its moods. It may fluctuate. In the preceding words a fact was firmly established: God is well able at any time to take things in hand for his people. But this note of confidence is now lost for the moment. Misgivings assail the individual and the nation. A touch of hopelessness takes hold. Where the speaker had come to some measure of assurance about pardon for his sins, he now feels that there may be some doubt about forgiveness. He feels that he and the nation are still under God's anger (cf. Ps. 90: 9). In spite of the fact that the nation knew that God was displeased, they had to admit "we kept on sinning." Sin had become a strongly ingrained habit. They had been so long in this unhappy state that it had become second nature. They even felt for that matter, that they were perhaps beyond the point of recovery: "shall we be saved?" (cf. Ezek. 33:18). A series of comparisons, describing Israel's miserable state now follow. In a sense they have become untouchable like a leper (Lev. 13:45), ceremonially unclean, but still unclean. They are not in a state of worthiness to approach God and his sanctuary. Or they may be likened to a woman, ceremonially unclean because of her monthly period. This may be an unusual comparison, it may offend the fastidious taste of our day, but it does convey a feeling of deep sinfulness. The ethical and the ceremonial aspect of things blend here somewhat uniquely. No matter how you construe it, it speaks of a deep awareness of sin, and is a powerful word: "All our righteous deeds are as filthy rags." The next comparison illustrates the blighting effect of sin: "We all fade like a leaf," for sin separates man from the source of life, and so he withers away. The last comparison stresses the total instability of the life of sin: "Our iniquities bear us away like the wind." The disruptive effects of sin are under consideration.

Verse 7. The note of hopelessness becomes stronger. No encouraging signs may be detected. No one recalls that God is a God who forgives. So no one dares venture to approach the Lord to take him by the hand and claim mercy from the all-gracious Lord. Whatever of repentance there is, it has not dared to claim any of God's gracious promises as including him, the poor sinner. All they can sense is the negative side of God's attitude: "Thou hast hid thy face from us." That things then must go from bad to worse is all that seems to be left under the circumstances, as the concluding word of this section indicates: "Thou hast delivered us into the power of our sins." Similar is the case of the Gentiles (Rom. 1:28).

(4) Various Reasons for Divine Intervention (vv. 8-12)

64:8-12 8. And yet, O Lord, thou art our father;
  we are the clay and thou art our potter;
and we all of us are the work of thy hand.
9. Be not angry, O Lord, over us;
  do not remember iniquity forever.
Behold and see, we are all of us thy people.
10. Thy holy cities have become a wilderness;
  Zion has become a wilderness, Jerusalem a desolation.
11. Our holy and glorious house, where our fathers praised thee,
  has been burned by fire;
    all our treasure has become a desolation.

12. In the face of all these things,
    canst thou stand aloof?
    canst thou keep silence,
        and afflict us still more?

Verse 8. The mood changes in this prayer. Recalling
God's deeds in the past, all of them a matter of record among
God's people, the writer displays a certain inventiveness for
finding motives why God should intervene in behalf of his
people. The first of the motives mentioned is the fact that
the nation is made up of children of his. They are "the work
of [his] hands." This is merely a variation of the theme that
they are children. The potter/clay figure indicates that they
owe their very existence to him. The Lord will not abandon
that upon which he has bestowed infinite pains and care.
Here the potter-figure and the children-figure blend into one,
also the potter-figure and the father-figure. It may be questioned whether in this passage the heavier emphasis lies on
God's being the father and in 63:16 Israel's being the children
(*Westermann*).

Verse 9. Another reason why the Lord should show consideration under the circumstances is brought forth — Israel
are "[his] people." The election of Israel by God is being recalled. If being God's people means anything it implies that
God will be ready to forgive after his justifiable anger has
flared up. In fact he cannot "remember iniquity forever"
(cf. Ps. 79:8).

Verse 10. The writer now goes on to reflect upon the
desolate sight presented by all the cities, by Zion and by the
city of Jerusalem. This does not necessarily mean that this
part must have been written after the fall of Jerusalem (586
B.C.). Prophetically he may be foreseeing a situation that
will ultimately arise if Israel persists in her sins. But such a
scene of utter ruin should stir the Lord's compassions. The
cities are called "holy" because they lie in the Holy Land.

Verse 11. In a sense the chain of thought that is being developed rises to higher values. Now comes the Temple, the
Lord's "glorious house," which is thought of as lying in

356 *Exposition of Isaiah*

ruins, as it needs must ultimately be if the nation continues to go on in its present sinful ways. One major purpose that was served by the Temple was this that it furnished a place for the true fathers of Israel to praise the Lord. Those were deeply satisfying experiences. Many holy aspirations were associated with this national shrine; here they are called Israel's "treasure." This even may include such items as the altar of burnt offering, the sea of bronze, the beautifully ornamented buildings, and the like.

Verse 12. So now this verse appropriately sums up and presses home its point: "canst thou stand aloof? canst thou keep silence, and afflict us still more?" It takes boldness and the courage of faith to pray thus. The intense earnestness of this prayer is touching.

Notes

Verse 1. The *Jerusalem Bible* renders the first verb quite effectively in the idiom of our day: "tear the heavens open." The two effective comparisons how fire operates, may not be quite the same as some that *we* might have used, but that does not yet warrant the criticism that they are "lame" and "do not fit the situation" (*Duhm*). In the second of these two, the verb goes over from the infinitive construction to the finite verb.

Verse 3. "Terrible things" (*KJ, RSV*) could carry wrong connotations in our day. Therefore we have rendered "awe-inspiring deeds."

Verse 4. When Paul cites this verse (I Cor. 2:9) he seems to be quoting freely from memory. He sees new possibilities in this verse.

Verse 5. It seems better to take the verb "and we sinned" as a durative, "we kept on sinning." So the logical sequence of things is preserved; or perhaps with *Delitzsch*: "We stood there as sinners." *Bahem* (lit. "in them"), can well, according to the context, refer to sins. Therefore *RSV* did well to translate "in our sins," injecting the word "sins." To take the last verb of the verse as a plain indicative produces a strange effect (*KJ*). To construe it as interrogative seems much more to the point.

Verse 9. The *Jerusalem Bible* goes too far when it translates the opening words: "Do not let your anger go too far," as though God needed the supervision of man.

Chapter LXV

3. God's Answer to Israel's Prayer (Chap. 65)

The caption for this chapter looks back to Chap. 64, which we had labelled "Prayer for Divine Intervention." However two major approaches to the subject treated in the present chapter are to be noted. Some go so far as to claim that such a title fits the chapter so poorly as to make it impossible. On their part they who take this position maintain that the subject under consideration is "the Faithless and the Obedient" (*Westermann*). This conclusion is arrived at as a result of a slightly dubious observation, namely, that in this chapter for the first time in prophecy in the pronouncement of doom, this doom is not any longer regarded as befalling the entire mass of Israel but the nation is approached from the angle of being a divided group — some guilty and deserving of punishment, others faithful and to be spared when the punishment is meted out. We believe that the division of the nation into faithful and faithless was implied by the prophets who seemed to be pronouncing doom on the nation *en masse*. It would appear then that at this point that which was previously *implied* now is expressly *stated*. Chapter 65 is therefore closely bound to Chap. 64. Prayer and answer to prayer go hand in hand.

It should however be noted that an unusual omission seems to be characteristic of this chapter. The outstanding sins of the nation are spelled out. Nothing however is said of the forgiveness which God's grace grants to the sinner when he is penitent. On the other hand, when the salvation is depicted, which God has prepared for his people, the emphasis lies largely on the external things involved. This is unusual but is not to be regarded as a shortcoming of the state described. Oftentimes, especially in the Old Testament, the external, visible blessings bestowed by God's grace are rated as obvious manifestations of God's benevolent goodness.

Then it should be observed, as *Fischer* remarks: In the sequence of things as portrayed in this chapter, first comes a judgment which separates the godly from the ungodly; then salvation itself is to be bestowed.

As to details — this chapter may fit the needs of the returned exiles, of the date of about 538-521 B.C. From our point of view of the composition of the entire book by Isaiah, that would mean: God allowed the prophet to anticipate that a state of affairs would develop after the Return of the exiles, where they would need to be taught why God delayed answering their prayer, and furthermore a division of the people into the faithful and the renegades would take place.

The meter is somewhat difficult — sometimes 3 and 3; sometimes 3 and 2. *Westermann* prints the whole chapter as poetry. Most writers agree that vv. 8-16 may be more readily scanned.

a. His Answer Is Delayed because of the Unwholesome Attitude of Many of His People (vv. 1-7)

65:1-7 1. I made myself available to those who did not ask for me;
I was ready to be found by those who do not seek me out.
I said, "Here am I; here am I"
    to a nation that was not called by my name.
2. I spread out my hands all the day
    to a stubborn nation,
that walked in a way that was not good
    after their own devices;
3. a people who continually provoke me brazenly,
    who sacrifice in gardens,
and burn incense on bricks;
4. who sit about in tombs,
    and spend the night in secret places;
who eat the flesh of swine,
    while the broth of repulsive meat is in their vessels;
5. who say, "Stay by yourself;
    do not come near me,
lest I make you taboo."
These persons are a smoke in my nostrils,

a fire which burns all day long.
6. Lo, it stands recorded before me;
  I shall not keep silence until I have repaid them,
and I will repay them in their bosom.
7. Your iniquities and those of your fathers
  (saith the Lord)
  which you sacrificed upon the mountains,
and by which you reviled me upon the hills;
  now I shall first measure out to them
their recompense in their bosom.

Verse 1. It should be borne in mind that this chapter shows how God is minded toward his people and their prayers. God was willing enough to be approached by his people; he had done enough to make himself available. The first approach did not begin with Israel. They were a people who did not seek *him* out. He was hoping that he might be found by them. But they were a people who did not make advances. His friendly attitude was manifest by his invitation: he represents himself as continually saying: "Here am I; here am I." The last line of this verse seems to invite a textual change: they were a people who were not calling upon his name. But the passive, a people "called" may well be retained. For that unique expression signifies to be regarded as the Lord's own special property. But they were not behaving as God has a right to expect that they would. So the point made by the verse is: Israel was calling upon the Lord; that action seemed good; but it was disappointing because there was no outreach on the nation's part to the Lord.

It is obvious according to our translation and interpretation that we regard v. 1 as describing *Israel's* attitude toward God, just as v. 2 clearly refers to Israel. Isaiah is making it clear why even Israel's prayers had to be rejected. Strangely Paul (Rom. 10:20 f.) quotes these first two verses, applying v. 1 to the *Gentiles* and v. 2 to Israel. According to the text and context Paul does not abide by the letter of the passage. It would appear that, according to the Greek translation, the words lent themselves to a fresh application of the words used. Paul is not employing strict scientific exegesis, but with great freedom is readapting the original as an effective statement of his case.

Verse 2. How eager this outreach on *God's* part was is indicated by the gesture accompanying his call — "[he] spread forth [his] hands all the day" — a pleading gesture of tender invitation. Whatever religious practices they, as nation, may have engaged in, they were still "a stubborn nation," and "[walking] in a way that was not good," as the prophet is about to explain. They were walking "after their own devices."

Verses 3, 4. The indictment grows sharper. In the Lord's sight, Israel, after its Return from Captivity, was far from being a dedicated people. There was an element among them that continually provoked God brazenly, an offensive form of conduct which is charged against the nation continually, especially in the historical books. Now follows a list of specifications — instances of offensive conduct that prevailed within the nation, although they are misdemeanors which hid their face and were often done in secret. The sins that had done particular damage to the nation and were the distinct vices prevalent among the renegades, were mostly in the area of cultic practices, as the next six lines clearly indicate. All manner of strange and even repulsive procedures are mentioned. Detailed explanations are not offered, but, no doubt, the nation understood the references made. First of all sacrificing in gardens seemed to have achieved popularity (cf. 1:29; 66:17). No doubt the cult involved planting delightful gardens in honor of certain deities that were reputed to love such homage. Then there was the burning of incense on bricks, which is usually explained as involving the use of incense jars. Incense figures in many religious practices. Then sitting about in tombs was involved in certain other rites. That would seem to have involved expecting messages from the dead. It could have involved contact with demons which were somehow associated with tombs (cf. Matt. 8:28; Mark 5:3-5). For messages from the dead cf. 8:19; 29:4. When it is charged that men spend the night in secret places that could have involved the same irregularities, though "secret places" means places difficult to access. Secrecy lends some kind of attraction to forbidden practices: "stolen waters are sweet" (Prov. 9:17). Besides they did eat the flesh of swine, a practice forbidden (Lev. 11:7). Swine were sacrificed among many nations; Israel frowned upon offering a creature of unclean habits. Exactly what is meant by "the broth of repulsive meat is in their vessels" is hard to determine, but it may be in line with the eating of pork. *JB* translates: "using unclean foods in their kitchens."

Verse 5. What now follows may well exemplify the "conceit of the cultist." Because of their exotic practices they believe that they have achieved a superior grade of holiness, which might be contaminated by contact with those who have not engaged in these unusual rites, or may even prove harmful to the unsanctified, if they but touched these high ranking religionists. "Stay by yourself" means: Do not touch me, as the next line suggests: Do not even come near me. Some of the "taboo" might rub off on the outsider. In a strongly anthropomorphic expression, the degree of vexation that these super-saints convey to the Almighty are said to be "smoke in [his] nostrils," or "a fire which burns all day long." So irritating to the Lord are those that employ rites that stem from idolatrous usages. Yet these persons esteem themselves to be persons of superior sanctity.

Verse 6. The remaining two verses of the section develop the thought that God will not remain passive in the face of prevailing irregularities that stain his people. He has recorded their misdeeds as something that calls for action. They are scheduled for attention. Punishment is announced with a certain solemnity. To declare that God will not remain inactive, the writer used a special expression: "I shall not keep silence" (cf. 62:1; 64:12). He further represents himself as coming to the renegades in person to mete out just punishment, we might say, "upon the head" of the guilty. The Hebrew idiom has it that evil will "repay them in their bosom," for which again we might say: "into their very lap" the entire unholy mess is to be deposited.

Verse 7. This verse indicates that there is such a thing as "mass guilt," where the sins of generation after generation are not completely broken with and the amount grows higher and higher. Ultimately, or time and again, it then happens that God visits the "sins of the fathers upon the children." The fathers had sacrificed upon the mountains; the children had continued the pernicious usage. God had warned; prophets had expostulated; the renegades had continued after as before. Israel prided itself upon such irregularities, which really amounted to a "reviling" of God upon the hills. The "first" issue noted down by God as the order of the day was to measure out to them their recompence in their bosom. All this must have made it abundantly clear to Israel why her cries for help were not meeting with a divine response.

b. The Wholesome Element to Be Spared, the Renegades to Be Punished (vv. 8-16)

65:8-16 8. Thus says the Lord:
"Just as men find new juice in a cluster,
　　and they say, 'Don't destroy it
　　　for there is a blessing in it,'
so shall I proceed for my servants' sake,
　　so as not to destroy everything.
9. And I shall bring forth descendants from Jacob
　　and from Judah inheritors of my mountain;
and my chosen ones shall inherit it,
　　and my servants shall dwell there.
10. And Sharon shall become pasturage for flocks,
　　and the valley of Achor shall be for cattle to lie down in.
for my people who have sought me.
11. But as for you who forsake the Lord,
　　who forget my holy mountain,
　　　who prepare a table for Fortune [Gad],
　　who fill up a drink offering for Destiny [Mani],
12. Lo, I will destine you to the sword,
　　and all of you shall bow down to the slaughter;
because I called and you did not answer,
　　I spoke and you would not listen;

but you did what was evil in my sight,
   and you preferred what I did not delight in."
13. Therefore, thus says the Lord, Yahweh:
   "Lo, my servants shall have food, but you shall be hungry;
      lo, my servants shall have drink, but you shall be thirsty;
   lo, my servants shall be happy, but you shall be put to shame;
14. lo, you shall be exultant for joy of heart,
   but you shall howl for pain of heart;
      and shall wail for anguish of spirit.
15. And you shall leave your name behind
   for a curse to my chosen ones;
      and the Lord Yahweh shall slay you
   and to his servants he shall give a different name.
16. So that he who blesses himself in the land
   will bless himself by the God of truth [Amen]
and he that swears in the land
   will swear by the God of truth.
Because the former troubles are forgotten,
   and are hid from my eyes.

Verse 8. At this point a distinction sets in: punishment is not pronounced indiscriminately on good and wicked members of his people but what was often implied before is now plainly stated: the wicked shall meet with just punishment. An excerpt is quoted perhaps from an old vintage song. A cluster of grapes is picked up with quite a few bad grapes in it. Shall it be thrown aside, good and bad grapes together? The verdict will be: "Don't destroy it." The reason? "There is a blessing in it": the juice of the good grapes is worth the saving. So shall the Lord proceed for "his servants' sake, and not destroy everything." What happens to the evil-doer need not be spelled out. It was already stated above in v. 7. As "servants" the faithful have a claim upon their Lord. He honors their claim. This is the doctrine of the remnant cast in a new and different form.

Verse 9. In particular in this verse the achievement of one blessing is stressed: the possession of the land by the generations to come. The land is described as "my mountain" because almost all of the Promised Land was mountainous territory.

Verse 10. Just a casual glance at the land already presents

a picture of idyllic peace and security throughout its entire breadth, from the plain of Sharon to the west to the valley of Achor to the east (cf. Josh. 7:24). For wherever one looks in the land there is an abundance of cattle with an abundance of pasturage. Against such a background of prosperity those loyal to the covenant spend their days.

Verse 11. In sharp contrast to the ones just referred to, stand the unfaithful. Their behavior betrays how they are minded toward him who should be their Lord. One overall descriptive phrase covers their case; they "forsake the Lord." Hand in hand with their infidelity goes neglect of the holy temple-mountain, i.e., true worship is not maintained as the seed-bed for faith. Rites honoring other foreign deities are resorted to, honoring, for example, the god of good luck (Hebrew: *Gad*); honoring him by preparing a counterpart to the table of shew-bread (cf. Exod. 25:23-30) that symbolically represented a fellowship meal with the Lord. Or they honored the less-known God of Destiny (Hebrew: *Mani*) who may have been resorted to to ward off all evil destinies that might befall. In any case, by honoring these Israel pushed the Lord aside.

Verse 12. God actually destines men as justice demands. Note the play on words (God destines [*manithi*] rather than destiny [*mani*]). His destinies are stern — "to the sword" and "to the slaughter." Personal infidelity brought this doom down on their heads: for he called but they did not even deign to answer. He spoke and they would not listen. They went farther than that. They added to do evil in his sight and preferred what he did not delight in.

Verses 13-14. Two lines of destiny run parallel to one another, according as men have chosen for themselves. For though in a sense they are parallel they are also opposites at the same time. Two great chapters of old furnish the material for these two verses, Lev. 26 and Deut. 28: having food versus going hungry; having to drink versus being thirsty; being happy versus being put to shame; being exultant versus howling for pain.

Verse 15. For a moment the prophet looks at the final outcome when the congregation of evil-doers will have perished from the land. Only one thing will they leave behind — their name to furnish a new curse for the chosen ones to refer to as a horrible example. In contrast to this he will give a new name to his servants that in its meaning will cover how richly God has blessed them.

Verse 16. The phrase "in the land" seems to indicate that the people may have been out of the land for a time. When they come back they will wish blessings on themselves and on others by the name of the Most Holy One, "the God of truth," which may be translated "the God of Amen." Oaths generally will be made in the name of this God whose utterly truthful word will have taken on a new meaning. The truth of the matter is that the new state of affairs that the Lord will create will be so completely blessed that it will blot out completely "the former troubles" (cf. 43:18 f.). A higher state of perfection cannot be conceived.

c. God's New Creation in All Its Splendor Is Portrayed (vv. 17-25)

65:17-25 17. For, lo, I shall create new heavens and a new earth,
and the former state of affairs shall not be remembered,
nor shall they even come to mind.
18. But rejoice and be glad forever,
over that which I shall create.
For, lo, I shall create Jerusalem a rejoicing,
and her people a joy.
19. For I shall be glad over Jerusalem
and rejoice over my people;
nor shall be heard in her anymore the sound of weeping
nor the sound of an outcry.
20. Nor shall there spring up from there a child
living but a limited number of days;
nor an old man
who shall not get his full measure of days
For a lad of a hundred years may die,
and he who falls short of a hundred years
shall be reckoned accursed.
21. And men shall build houses and inhabit them,

and they shall plant vineyards and eat the fruit of them.
22. They shall not build and another inhabit;
they shall not plow and another eat their fruit,
for like the days of a tree shall be the days of my people,
and my chosen ones shall use to the full
the work of their hands.
23. They shall not toil in vain,
nor shall they bring forth children for terror
for they are a race of the Lord's blessed ones;
and so are their offspring;
24. and it shall come to pass
that before they call I will answer
and while they are still speaking I will hear.
25. The wolf and the lamb shall be in the same pasture,
and the lion shall eat straw like the ox,
and dust shall be the serpent's food.
They shall not hurt nor harm in all my holy mountain,
says the Lord."

Verse 17. From this point to the end of the chapter the New Age is being depicted. Faith here rises to new levels; nowhere in the Old Testament is a more glorious picture of the future kingdom drawn. There will be a new heaven and a new earth. Both together spell a new universe. According to analogous Scriptures, transformation of the old is involved, not destruction of the old followed by a new creation. Yet the transformation will be so complete that the former state of affairs on this old sin-ridden earth shall not even be remembered or come to mind (cf. also 51:6).

Verse 18. The point now is that not only is there ample occasion for joy, but it is a joy that will last forever. Strangely at this point Jerusalem, the newly created Jerusalem, enters the picture as the center about which everything in the new creation rotates. To create "Jerusalem a rejoicing," of course, means an object of rejoicing. Note the emphasis that all this is work of God, the Creator. Even the people shall be transformed so as not to be a cause of vexation, but also an object of rejoicing.

Verse 19. The Lord reiterates the thought just expressed that he will have ample occasion for joy over his people. The negative aspect of the situation is now spelled in fresh

colors: the sound of weeping and of an outcry shall no longer
dull the picture (cf. 25:18; 35:10).

Verse 20 is concerned with another blessing that shall
stand forth prominently — longevity on this new earth. This
passage as such does not rise to the level of maintaining that
there will be an eternal life, but merely a long continuation
of life on this earth enabling man to taste to the full this
pleasant existence. Therefore the level of 25:8 is not
achieved here. The truth concerning the eternal blessedness
of God's children was, in the providence of God but slowly
revealed through the centuries. Approaching the issue from
this angle it is asserted that the dying of children will be out
of the question, in other words a child "living but a limited
number of days." Then there is the additional claim that old
men shall not die prematurely; each man will "get his full
measure of days." With the light on this whole issue glowing
but dimly, a new measure of long life is promised. At least
this much is granted that, should a man die in youth at least
he would not die at less than a hundred years, for less than
that would mark a man as accursed.

Verse 21. One unique reward, so to speak, of the Old
Testament saints was the fulfillment of the hope of not being
subject to frustration, such as building a house and not getting to live in it, or, planting a vineyard and not getting to
eat the fruit of it. Such disappointment would have been
caused perhaps by war or other calamities.

Verse 22. Repeatedly in the Old Testament the long life
of a man is compared with the long life of a tree (see Ps.
1:3; Jer. 17:8; Ezek. 19:10). No disappointing defeats will
be encountered in this New Age. What a man achieves will
be enjoyed by him who achieved it. Such is an effective way
of saying: a man will get full satisfaction from life (cf. Ps.
92:12-14).

Verse 23. This verse continues on the note that the new
earth shall not be marked by disappointments and frustra-
tions. Common, everyday toil shall not be marked by futility, and be done "in vain." One striking example of major

disappointments in life could be to have children, whose life would be shortened by accident and disaster, that is, not realizing the promise "that it may be well with thee and thou mayest live long on earth." The expression "to bring forth children for terrors," might be another way of saying "for death," for according to Job 18:14, death is "the king of terrors." This would then be the very opposite of the ghastly scene mentioned in Ps. 137:9. Instead, God's faithful, here called "the race of the Lord," shall be manifestly blessed, they and "their offspring." God's enduring blessings shall extend over generations.

Verse 24. A new aspect of God's blessing bestowed upon his children will be experienced in the field of prayer, where before they have uttered their prayer God will already be answering them; while they are still speaking, he will hear them.

Verse 25. Suddenly the thought veers over into the area of nature, characterized by peaceful coexistence of, and with, what were wild beasts. Instead of regarding this as a valuable supplement to what has already been described as a new creation, this verse is treated by some as suspect, as an unfortunate addition. This is an example of the type of criticism which we rightly deplore. For this addition beautifully illustrates how far-reaching the blessings of this new creation will be. True, the passage may be a take-off on 11:6-9, but even our Lord sometimes repeated himself in his discourses spoken here on earth. At least the critic would have us consider the line "and dust shall be the serpent's food" as a gloss. But even this is a colorful item. It indicates with a kind of half-sigh that the fallen state of man will not be entirely forgotten. As a reminder from Gen. 3:14, it indicates that the propensity of the serpent to attack man will be a thing of the past. It shall indeed "eat dust," i.e., taste defeat, but its presence in the picture shall not mar the perfection of God's new creation. In fact (and now quite naturally comes the crowning touch), nothing shall savor of imperfection and harm: "They shall not hurt nor harm in all my holy mountain" says the Lord. As in 10:9 we must allow for the possibility of the "holy mountain" being a reference to the entire land.

Notes

Verse 1. The first word of the verse could be translated as a passive — witness *KJ* and *Luther*. But to take the *Niphal* as a *Niphal tolerativum* — witness *RSV* — is much to be preferred. Cf. *GK* 51 c. To add a pronominal suffix object ("ask of *me, as Septuagint* and *Targum*, do) brings the construction in line with the other verbs of the verse.

Verse 2. "Not good" — a case of litotes. Cf. *KS* 385 d.

Verse 7. "Your iniquities" (Hebrew text) is changed to "their iniquities" (*RSV*). Yet the Hebrew makes good sense, and, being the more difficult, should be retained, though most versions make the change.

Verse 10. The words "and Sharon shall become pasturage," seeing that Sharon was rich grainland, could be construed as involving a demotion. But as we have construed it above, it shows the thought involved is rich pasturage for cattle.

Verse 14. The unusual form which we have translated "howl," is explained *GK* 70 d.

Verse 15. "Your name" (*RSV*) for "their name" is an obvious improvement.

Verse 20. *RSV* translates the latter part of the verse "the sinner a hundred years old," which makes a very difficult translation. The word rendered "sinner" (Hebrew "*chote*") comes from a basic root which means "come short" or "miss the mark." So we have translated: "he who falls short of a hundred years" — a translation which makes good sense.

Chapter LXVI

I. ISRAEL'S HOPE (Chap. 66)

The prophet's book has built up to a climax by way of a well-ordered progression. Though apparently written long in advance by a prophet living in the seventh century, yet it builds up to a logical conclusion. A good number of the people is to return from the Babylonian Captivity, and will be faced with the problem of setting up a state, and a temple for purposes of worship. The main altar for burnt offerings was functioning daily; the temple may have been restored, but unfortunately it was not the scene of a truly spiritual worship. Only the externals of worship were at hand. No concept of the greatness of the God of Israel was in evidence. At least the unspiritual worship could be corrected by ousting those who held only to routine procedures. Just who it was whom the Lord was to repel and remove is difficult to determine. But from the last two chapters of this book it appears that the prophets, and the men of deeper spiritual insight began to regard these as unworthy and as a blemish upon the fair name of the nation. Our chapter takes direct issue with such.

Time and place, where and when, these words were spoken, are difficult to determine. To think that the opening verses are directed at the Samaritans is a case of judgment on the basis of insufficient evidence. The same holds true in the case of classifying vv. 17-24 as a later addition by some unknown editor.

1. Corrupt Worship (vv. 1-4)

66:1-4 1. Thus says the Lord
The heavens are my throne
   and the earth my footstool,
What manner of house is it that you would build for me?

And what sort of place would be the place of my rest.
2. All these things my hand has made,
  and so these things have come into being,
    says the Lord.
Yet to this man will I look, namely to the man
  that is humble and of a contrite spirit
and trembles with awe at my word.
3. He that slaughters an ox is as if he slew a man;
  He that sacrifices a lamb is as if he broke a dog's neck.
He that offers a cereal offering
  is as if he offered swine's blood.
He who makes a memorial offering of incense
  is as if he blessed an idol.
These have chosen their own way;
  It is their abomination that their soul delights in.
4. So I too will choose their calamity
  and bring their fears upon them;
because when I called no one answered
  I spoke and they would not hear.
But they did what was evil in my sight;
  they chose that in which I took no delight.

Verse 1. This first verse is much like Ps. 113:5 f. Besides, I Kings 8:26; Ps. 50:9-12; Amos 5:21-25 may be compared. This verse shows what great and mighty issues are involved when an individual or a group assembles for worship. He, before whom they come, has a throne that is indeed nothing less than the heavens. He has a footstool — the earth in all its vastness. It is, so to speak, almost presumptuous for earth-dwellers to erect a structure to serve as, and to be called, the Lord's habitation. Or what could serve as the place where he takes up residence. These things being so, there will always be a wholesome awe when men, as they worship, come to what is known to be a temple for the Almighty.

Verse 2. To expand the thought a bit more — all things that are within the compass of heaven and earth still in spite of their vast number are things that came into being as the work of his hands. They are his creatures. Some of mankind, in the nature of the case, are people in whom he takes pleasure; some he cannot delight in. Who are they that stand in the shade of his pleasure? The answer that comes from the lips of the Lord is one that man could hardly have thought possible. It is the man "that is humble and of a contrite spirit." This implies that the person in question has some awareness of the sins he has done and sincerely regrets that by his misdeeds he has incurred the displeasure of his Creator. None are good enough of themselves. Sinless persons cannot be found. The Lord can make something of those who sincerely repent of what they have done. And somehow, since they have heard of the mercy of the Lord, they have a deep respect for every word that falls from his lips: "they tremble with awe at [his] word."

Verses 3, 4. This difficult verse shows how the lack of penitence mars every act they may engage in, in the practice of worship. Suppose a man goes to some expense in connection with an act of devotion: he offers an ox. In the eyes of God, that which he performed counts as nothing better than if he had slain a man and had blood dripping from his hands as he stands before the Lord on trial. Or, another example — in the course of his worship he might bring a lamb as an offering to the Lord's temple. If such a one steps forth not actually penitent, he gains no more favor by his offering than if he had broken a dog's neck. A third example: suppose an impenitent person offers a comparatively unimpressive offering, through the agency of his sacrifice he has achieved no more than if he had offered swine's blood. Or suppose that which was presented was a memorial offering, the fact that it was not prompted by a contrite spirit would make what he did drop to the level of praise spoken in honor of a pagan god. Apparently some of these whom the prophet was rebuking were attempting to carry the Lord's worship on one shoulder, and idolatry on the other. They certainly were not choosing to walk in the ways of the Lord. As a result, all acts of piety and worship amounted to no more than "abomination" before the holy God.

2. The Lord Stands by His Faithful Ones (v. 5)

66:5 5. Hear the word of the Lord, you that tremble at his Word;

Your brethren, who hate you
  and thrust you out for my name's sake, say:
"Let the Lord step forth in his glory
  that we may see your joy."
But it is they who shall come to grief.

Verse 5. A deep line of cleavage runs through the congregation of Israel. There are unworthy ones who actually hate and despise the meek souls among God's people. They regard themselves as the elite and have already thrust out from the community these whom they despise. They are so sure of themselves that they are ready to take their case up to the court of heaven. In their presumption they venture to challenge the Lord and vindicate themselves before their very eyes. They speak sarcastically, as much as to say, You are claiming the Lord as standing on your side, or yourselves as having special relations with the Lord. Bold as they may be, they will find that their presumption is ill-founded. The opposite is the case: "It is *they* who shall come to grief."

3. Sending Recompense on the Ungodly (v. 6)

66:6 6. "Hark, an outcry from the city
        and uproar from the city,
  Hark, the Lord will render recompense
    to his enemies.

Verse 6. Suddenly and without warning the enemy strikes. All over in the city shouts of men engaged in conflict! They are even battering away at the temple gates. In its deeper aspects the Lord is at work in the conflict which is developing. But we seem to be totally at a loss as to the historical incident that the prophet has in mind.

4. Miraculously Rapid Birth of the New Nation (vv. 7-9)

66:7-9 7. Before she [the city] was in labor she gave birth,
        before her pains came upon her,
  she was delivered of a son.
8. Who has heard of such a thing,

who has seen things like these?
Shall a nation be born in one day?
  Shall a nation be brought forth at once?
For as soon as Zion was in labor
  she brought forth children.
9. Shall I bring to the birth and not cause to bring forth?
  says the Lord.
Shall I who cause to bring forth, shut the womb?
  says the Lord.

Verse 7-9. It may well have puzzled even the faithful in Israel when the new and prosperous ones in Israel pondered how things would go with God's people. For though God's promises were known it seemed too much as if even the strength of the Almighty was insufficient to accomplish the things promised. So the Lord speaks in terms of the birth of a nation. Who the mother is that is to bring forth, not children but an entire nation, we are not told. But speaking in eschatological language the prophet insists that the miracle will be accomplished. It is now as though the labor pains were about to begin, and already the birth has taken place. The hyperbole employed is bold and speaks in terms of the seemingly impossible. Dropping the figure used, we could regard those experiences like Pentecost where as a result of one sermon three thousand were added to the church.

The section just covered begins to take on eschatological coloring. Commentators list the following as items that are typical of the treatment of the "last things": many people, Zion's happy state; judgment on the Lord's enemies; revelation of God's glory in the sight of his enemies. Yet one could hardly expect a strict logical arrangement of the items listed.

5. An Exhortation to Rejoice over the New Nation (vv. 10-11)

66:10-11 10. Rejoice with Jerusalem and be jubilant over her
             all of those who love her
Rejoice greatly with her
  all you who mourn for her;
11. that you may suck and be satisfied

with her consolotary breasts,
in order that you may drink deeply and enjoy it,
   from her bountiful bosom.

Verse 10. Such good things are in store for Jerusalem,
that is, in the last analysis, inclusive of the church of the New
Testament, that when they who wish her well consider the
situation, they will be moved to rejoice and be jubilant. This
includes those who mourned over her when her lot was a
less happy one.

Verse 11. Here is the spot where true satisfaction is to be
found. To drive this thought home, the prophet uses an
analogy which is very meaningful, though it might draw an
indulgent smile to the lips of a modern reader. The true
satisfaction that a healthy and normal child enjoys at its
mother's breast may be somewhat naive for the sophisticate
of our times but it is still very meaningful and instructive.

6. The Lord Is with His People and against His Enemies (vv. 12-14)

66:12-14 12. For thus says the Lord:
        "Lo, I am offering prosperity like a river.
and the wealth of the Gentiles, like an overflowing stream;
   and you shall be nursed, and carried on the hip,
      and dandled on the knee.
13. As one whom his mother comforts, so shall I comfort you;
   even in Jerusalem shall you be comforted.
14. You shall see and your heart be glad;
   your bones shall flourish as the grass.
And it shall be known that the hand of the Lord
      is with his servants,
and his indignation is with his enemies,

Verses 12-13. God is speaking through his prophet. The
sum of all blessings is here contained in one word, "peace."
We translated this by "prosperity," of which an abundance
will be available, as is indicated by the words used: "river,"
"overflowing." Then comparisons are borrowed from the
intimacies of the care of young children. Another area of
life is drawn on to describe how precious God's resources

are. He comforts men (v. 13) as only a mother can. To make this comfort more precious, the prophet lets it be given against the rich prospects of the Holy City — even Jerusalem.

Verse 14. All these good things will not only be idle dreams: Israel shall see them with her own eyes. The happiness caused by the experience shall go deep, that is, down to the very marrow of her bones. It shall be obvious to all who share in the event that God has once again had a hand in the course that things took, that the hand of the Lord has been at work, in behalf of his servants. But for his enemies indignation lies in store.

7. The Lord Coming for Judgment on His Opponents (vv. 15-19)

66:15-19 15. For lo, the Lord will come in fire,
and his chariots like the storm wind
to render his anger in fury
and his rebuke with flames of fire.
16. For the Lord will hold judgment by fire
and by his sword upon all flesh;
and the slain of the Lord shall be many.
17. They that sanctify and purify themselves to go into the gardens,
following one in their midst.
eating swine's flesh and the abomination and mice
shall come to an end together, says the Lord.
18. But as for me, their deeds and their thoughts have come to my attention.
to gather all Gentiles and tongues;
and they shall come and behold my glory.
19. And I will set up a sign of remembrance among them. And from them I will send survivors to the nations, to Tarshish, and Pul and Lod, who draw the bow; to Tubal and Javan, and to the far-off coastlands, who have not heard about me; and have not seen my glory, or made known my glory among the Gentiles.

Verse 15. Evidently, ever since especially Exod. 19:18, fire in one form or another was an index of the Lord's coming to judgment. Two things blend into one another. Either fire is the element which God uses for inflicting punishment upon the guilty, or else fire is the agency in which he envelopes himself for purposes of the theophany. The overtones of this chapter seem to emphasize the second aspect of the case. His purposes are indicated in this as being "to render his anger in fury." His anger is a very real and stern thing.

Verse 16. Aside from the fire-aspect of his theophany this verse shows the warrior-aspect of his nature. He has a sword, the use of which will make the slain of the Lord to be many.

Verse 17. Certain sins have in a special way roused his indignation. These cult-gardens are briefly described. They required a functionary who led the way in the performance of certain rites. Certain repulsive things were eaten, swine's flesh; then something called "the abomination," and lastly mice. Of all the rites and foods involved, none shall be left; they "shall come to an end together." They thought they had kept these repulsive things secret. But they have come to the Lord's attention. It seems that the prophet pictures the scene as involving "all Gentiles and tongues" so as to have them witness the scene where the Lord let his fury burn upon his people. For such a scene could involve a stern beauty and a certain beauty of holiness. — On the whole issue cf. also Ezek. 8.

Verse 18. The Lord has been aware of what his people are doing, though they thought that it had been kept from him. The Lord speaks anthropomorphically, as though he had just become aware of it all. But this verse actually thinks in terms of beholding God's glory in the sense that God's just judgment both on Israel and upon the Gentiles is also a glorious thing.

Verse 19. That is what v. 19 has in mind when it speaks of "a sign of remembrance." That which these spectators will behold is the judgment, dead bodies of those who opposed the Lord. A certain ironic tone falls on the beholding of the dead. This is also considered as beholding the Lord's glory in Joel 3:2; and Zeph. 3:8. At least they who did not appear to witness this display of glory are sent out as ambassadors of the Lord to the far corners of the earth, to Tarshish, far to the East in Spain; Put, in East Africa; Lud, also in Africa; Tubal, in the Caucasus, and Javan, in Greece; also the coastlands of the Mediterranean. All that did not perish in the first onslaught, are the survivors who are thought of as agents, to make known abroad the glory of his name. So there is one positive factor in the whole transaction.

8. New People for a New Earth (vv. 20-23)

66:20-23 20. And they shall bring all your brothers from all the Gentiles as an offering to the Lord on horses and wagons, and in litters, on mules and on dromedaries to my holy mountain at Jerusalem, says the Lord, as the children of Israel are wont to bring offerings in clean vessels to the house of the Lord. 21. And some of them I will also take for priests and Levites, says the Lord.
22. For just as the new heavens and the new earth
shall continue before me, says the Lord,
so shall your descendants and your name continue.
23. And from new moon to new moon
and from Sabbath to Sabbath
all flesh shall come to worship before me,
says the Lord.

Verse 20. The turn of thought that comes as a glorious climax grows out of the thought with which the chapter opened — new heavens and a new earth. That calls for a new people deeply consecrated to the Lord. This group shall be made up of Israelites and of Gentiles. As an index of the wholesome feelings that shall prevail when the endpoint shall be reached, all the so-called "survivors" shall deem it an honor to bring their scattered brethren, especially from the Gentiles on all manner of vehicles and conveyances. As Israel brought offerings to the sanctuary so shall these new ministers bring people as an offerings to the Lord. Of these Gentiles in particular the Lord will select certain ones to serve as legitimate priests and Levites. All this is, of course, New Testament thought cast in Old Testament language.

Verse 22. All the things promised will not soon pass off the scene but shall be as stable and fixed as the heavens and the earth themselves, for, in the last analysis, God builds for eternity. When it is said that these, worshippers and ministering personnel, shall "continue," that does not imply merely long continued existence, but involves being deeply in the Lord's service and in the joy of that service.

Verse 23. Festivals in particular shall mark high days in this new people that resort to this sanctuary, as God's new people. The particularism of the Old Testament is brushed aside and "all flesh shall come to worship before the Lord in spirit and in truth."

9. The Sad Fate of the Impenitent (v. 24)

66:24 24. And they shall go forth and shall look upon the dead bodies of the men who have rebelled against me; for their worm shall not die and their fire shall not be quenched. But they shall be an abhorrence to all flesh.

Verse 24. The enduring nature of the lot of those on whom the sentence of eternal death shall be visited is here unequivacally set forth, so much so that in certain editions of the Old Testament a notation appears to the effect that v. 23, with its more ironic tone is a more apt conclusion.

Peace eternal and death eternal! On this note the book of Isaiah comes to a close.

Notes

Verse 15. The Hebrew preposition *b* may be translated "in" or "b" fire. See *G.K.* 1191.